Experienced Life and Narrated Life Story

Gabriele Rosenthal is a sociologist and Professor (Emerita) of Qualitative Methodology at the Institute of Methods and Methodological Principles in the Social Sciences, University of Göttingen in Germany.

Gabriele Rosenthal

Experienced Life and Narrated Life Story

Gestalt and Structure of
Biographical Self-Presentations

Translated by Ruth Schubert

Revised and enlarged edition

Campus Verlag
Frankfurt/New York

ISBN 978-3-593-51886-2 Print
ISBN 978-3-593-45748-2 E-Book (PDF)
ISBN 978-3-593-45747-5 E-Book (EPUB)

Revised and enlarged edition 2024

All rights reserved. No part of this book may be reproduced or transmitted in any form or by any means, electronic or mechanical, including photocopying, recording, or by any information storage and retrieval system, without permission in writing from the publishers.
Copyright © 1995 Campus Verlag GmbH, Frankfurt-on-Main
Cover design: Campus Verlag GmbH, Frankfurt-on-Main
Typesetting: le-tex xerif
Typesettig font: Alegreya
Printed in the United States of America

www.campus.de
www.press.uchicago.edu

Contents

Preface to the new edition 7

Preliminary note 17

1. Introduction 19
   1.1 Problem 19
   1.2 What is the "benefit" of applying Gestalt theory to life stories
      and life histories? 28

2. On the Gestalt nature of experience 33
   2.1 That which is presented to the observer 33
   2.2 The intention of the agent 44
   2.3 The formal organization of what is presented 46

3. On the Gestalt nature of memory and narrative 73
   3.1 Experience – Memory 73
   3.2 Memory – Narration 88

4. On the Gestalt of narrated life stories 99
   4.1 Biographical preconditions for shaping a life narrative
      as a Gestalt 99
   4.2 The simple grasping of orderedness 127
   4.3 Orderedness after biographical turning points 130
   4.4 Formal factors for Gestalt connection 140

5. The healing effect of biographical narration 161

   5.1 The ambiguous Gestalt of the experienced life history 161

   5.2 The healing effect of life narratives for survivors of the Shoah .. 166

6. Methodological implications 179

   6.1 Principles of interviewing to obtain a biographical narrative .. 179

   6.2 Principles of a reconstructive case analysis 198

7. Biographies – Discourses – Figurations: Social-constructivist and figurational biographical research
Artur Bogner & Gabriele Rosenthal 217

   7.1 Introduction 218

   7.2 Commonalities and differences between biographical research and figurational sociology 220

   7.3 Discourses as an intermediary element? 230

   7.4 Voices of established and outsiders in Palestine and Uganda .. 242

   7.5 Conclusion: methodological consequences 250

Appendix 253

   Transcription symbols 253

   Criteria to define the sequences 254

References 257

Preface to the new edition

The present volume is an extended new edition of my habilitation thesis from 1993, published by Campus Verlag in 1995. This thesis and my writings relating to biographical research based on it, some of which have been published in several languages, are recognized as important contributions to sociological biographical research both in the German-speaking world and internationally. A new German edition of this book[1], and also an English edition, have been a concern of mine for some time. This concern is justified by its continuing importance both for my own work – empirical research projects, which I have always carried out together with colleagues – and for many of the research projects I have supervised, mostly in the context of doctoral or other theses. This research continues to be based on the conception presented at that time of a dialectical relationship between experiencing, remembering, and narrating or, more generally, speaking about the experienced and handed-down past. The investigation of this relationship, combined with an increasing focus on the interactions between it and the collective memories of diverse groupings in respect of events and activities in different historical phases, as well as their effects in the present, runs as a central theme through my later work (Rosenthal 2016a). For example, I am currently co-leading a research project with Maria Pohn-Lauggas on slavery and the slave trade in individual and collective memories in Brazil and Ghana.[2] An essential concern of this research, in addition to reconstructing

---

1 A translation in Brazilian Portuguese was published in 2017.

2 This project, funded by the German Research Foundation (DFG) from 2022–2025, is being carried out in cooperation with Steve Tonah (University of Ghana, Legon/Accra) and Hermílio Santos (Pontifical Catholic University of Rio Grande do Sul, Porto Alegre). The team in Germany includes Eva Bahl, Artur Bogner and Lucas Cé Sangalli. See: https://www.uni-goettingen.de/en/650363.html.

current patterns of action and interpretation or discourses, is to investigate their genesis. This means that we always have to ask to what extent speaking about the past is based on memories of what has been experienced (which also includes the experience of transmitting the past by the older generations), and to what extent this gives us clues to what was experienced at the time. While this question is at the forefront in this book, the later methodological modifications – that is, the increasing use of other methods of data collection – are due to an effort to reconstruct, to a greater extent than before, discourses that prevailed at different times and present patterns of activity. I will return to this later.

Until 1995, my empirical and theoretical research was focused on the social and individual consequences of the collective crimes committed during National Socialism. Even after that, it has been largely focused on the thematic field of collective violence and its consequences (see Bogner 2021). With Artur Bogner, I conducted research on extremely traumatized "child soldiers" of the so-called Lord's Resistance Army (LRA) in Northern Uganda who had returned to civilian life (Bogner/Rosenthal 2020).[3] Thus, I was still confronted with the question of the extent to which narrated life stories are determined by the components of a memory damaged by traumatization in the context of macro-violence (see chapter 4.1.4), by the discourses prevailing at different times, which often deny violence, and by the frequent outsider position of victims of collective violence. When interviewing victims of collective violence, we social scientists are particularly challenged to support the interviewees in the process of remembering and narrating. In addition, it is necessary to decipher the differences between the present perspective and the perspectives of the interviewees at different times in the past when analyzing or evaluating the interviews. This is a challenge that is all the more important in biographical interviews with (former) participants in violent crime, who often try hard to deny their involvement or to omit this topic and the corresponding phases of their life as far as possible, or even try to invent a different biography (cf. Rosenthal 2001, 2002).

However, when we conduct interviews with people, or use their written biographical self-testimonies, regardless of which groupings they belong to,

---

3 This project "Child Soldiers in Context. Biographies, family and collective histories in Northern Uganda" was funded by the DFG (2014–2017). Principal investigators: Dieter Neubert & Gabriele Rosenthal; researcher: Artur Bogner; research assistants: Josephine Schmiereck, Katharina Teutenberg. See: https://www.uni-goettingen.de/en/153963.html

we are always confronted with the problem that we cannot draw direct conclusions from texts about the behavior and action patterns of the speakers or writers, let alone about what they experienced in the past.

The methodological implications of the basic conception of mutual interaction between remembering, experiencing, and the presentation of experiences, as discussed in this volume, as well as the method of biographical case reconstruction which I propose (see chapter 6.2), continue to inform my conception of a fruitful research design. This is primarily due to the need for historically grounded social research that seeks to understand and explain social phenomena in their processes of emergence, reproduction, and change. This involves reconstructing the collective and biographical trajectories that led to particular behavior or actions, to particular ways of remembering, and to the establishment of particular discourses. For about twenty years now, especially as a result of my collaboration with Artur Bogner, I have integrated into my work theoretical and methodological approaches from figurational sociology, partly because of my increasing interest in the methods of historical sociology, but mainly because of my growing awareness of the constantly changing balances and inequalities of power that are operative in all human relationships. The assumption of the constant presence of power balances and power inequalities presupposes an at least partially "structural" concept of power, as discussed by Norbert Elias, but also, for example, by Max Weber or Richard M. Emerson (cf. Bogner 1989: 36–41; 1986; 1992). In Weber, power is the "chance" one has for a certain form of action, and thus does not *per se* imply the corresponding form of intention or its active realization or passive perception.

With a greater interest in the perspective of figurational sociology, the focus on individual interviewees which the present volume might suggest – although this was by no means intended at the time – shifted to a more strongly applied focus on we-groups, and other, less clearly networked or integrated groupings of people, which is more clearly laid down in the research design. I began to focus increasingly on reconstructing the interconnectedness of individual cases, the figurations between different groupings, we-groups, and organizations, and, concomitantly, the changing power balances and power inequalities between the various groupings over the course of history.[4] Many

---

4 Roswitha Breckner und Monica Massari conducted an interview with me on the theoretical, methodological, and above all content-related development of my work, which has been published (2019).

of the research projects I have supervised take into account the additional perspective of figurational sociology. To explain this development toward a synthesis of social-constructivist and figurational biographical research, the present edition concludes with a chapter co-authored with Artur Bogner (see also Bogner/Rosenthal 2022).

Parallel to developing a more figurational perspective, my methodological approach changed significantly as a result of my field experiences in the "Global South". These taught me to combine biographical case reconstruction – which always remained at the center of my work – even more strongly with other interpretive or reconstructive methods. I began to follow more consistently the principle of openness (cf. Rosenthal 2018: chapter 2), not only in terms of modifying the original research question or sample, but above all in terms of increased flexibility in the planned use and combination of methods of data collection. It should not go unmentioned here that my own research planning, the use of certain methods, and the resulting experiences have also been shaped by quite a few of the dissertations I have supervised. It will not be possible for me to go into all these research projects in this context, but I can say that they have all been based on the method of biographical case reconstruction presented in this volume. However, at least some of them should be mentioned. An explicit combination of social-constructivist biographical research with discourse analysis in the tradition of Michel Foucault and of the sociology of knowledge was first carried out by Bettina Völter (2000; 2003; Schäfer/Völter 2005) in the research project "The Holocaust in the Lives of Three Generations", described below.[5] As in the other works cited, Völter's case analyses, which refer to the case level of both the individual biography and the family, are characterized by a careful reconstruction of family history and family dynamics.

This combination of methods was also used by Maria Pohn-Lauggas (2014; 2017; 2021[6]), first in her study of so-called *Trümmerfrauen* in Austria, and later (together with image analysis[7]) of resistance fighters under Na-

---

5 This DFG-funded project, "The Holocaust in the Lives of Three Generations. Family Biographies in Germany and in Israel" was conducted from 1992–1996 in cooperation with Dan Bar-On (Beer Sheva, Israel). The principal investigators were Fritz Schütze & Regina Gildemeister. The interviews with most of the members of the grandparents' generation of Jewish families in Israel had been conducted by me in the period 1989–1991.

6 Published up to 2014 under the author's former name, Pohn-Weidinger.

7 See Pohn-Lauggas (2016). An elaborated, differentiated conception of combining biographical case analyses with image analyses has been presented by Roswitha Breckner (2010; 2021).

tional Socialism. Other dissertations based on a reasoned combination of biographical analysis and discourse analysis in the tradition of the sociology of knowledge include that by Ina Alber (2016a; 2016b) on civic engagement in Poland, and that by Rixta Wundrak (2009; 2010; 2018) on the Chinese community in Bucharest. In addition to the reconstruction of collective discourses, it very often makes sense to include participant observations in the analysis of case reconstructions, whether of individuals, families, social groupings or local settings (cf. Bahl/Worm 2018; Becker/Rosenthal 2022). This makes it possible to contrast what is said in the interviews with behavioral patterns and concrete interactions in the interviewees' everyday life. A consistent and not simply incidental inclusion of participant observation in the case analyses was first practiced by Michaela Köttig (2004; 2005) in her work on right-wing extremist young women and girls. This research was done at a time when, in contrast to the beginnings of sociological biographical research in the USA or Poland, biographical research in German-speaking countries was based primarily on autobiographical material (including, for instance, letters or diaries, in addition to interviews). Michaela Köttig was one of the first biographical researchers to present a methodologically justified proposal for combining biographical case reconstruction and the analysis of interactions documented in observation situations. By the time Rosa María Brandhorst (2015; 2023) presented her analysis of migration and transnational Cuban families, this combination had become established in sociological biographical research. With her field research in Cuba and in Germany, this author demonstrated the advantages of a "multi-sited" approach (in the sense of a "multi-sited ethnography"), which is unfortunately not yet common in sociology.[8] The empirical study of structures and contradictions of police work by Miriam Schäfer (2021), in which conducting biographical interviews was made possible by her previous participant observations in the field during patrol service, showed very clearly the potential of linking observation and analysis of professional practice with an investigation of the biographical experiences of those acting in this professional field. The combination of interviews, group discussions, and participant observations also had a significant impact on the dissertations that emerged from the research projects I describe in more detail below.

---

8 In fact, sociological biographical research had been characterized from the very beginning by a procedure that is comparable to the demands of "multi-sited ethnography". See Apitzsch/Siouti 2014 and Ruokonen-Engler/Siouti 2014.

While Johannes Becker (2013; 2017) and Eva Bahl (2017; 2021) placed more emphasis on an ethnographic approach, Hendrik Hinrichsen (2020, 2021) and Arne Worm (2017; 2019) combined individual with group interviews. Here, too, however, biographical case reconstructions were at the center of the analysis.

So, what does this multi-method research, and especially this flexibility in methods of data collection, mean in detail? In our research project on three-generation families of Shoah survivors and Nazi perpetrators (Rosenthal 1998/2010), my collaborators and I used a combination of individual interviews and family discussions. This research constituted an important empirical basis for the methodology explicated in the present volume, both with regard to the effects of trauma on memory and narrative processes, and in respect of a trauma-sensitive but memory-supportive interviewing approach (see chapters 5 and 6.1.). Due to the often extremely difficult family dynamics caused by the distressing family past, whether in families of Nazi survivors or perpetrators, it was only after analyzing the individual interviews that we were able to decide which combination of family members we could propose to the interviewees for a family interview.

This kind of advance planning changed in the following projects with an increased awareness of the need to react spontaneously to conditions and events in the field. This meant that both the choice of methods and the order in which they were used depended on the particular situation, including unexpected means of access to the field, on the problems that arose, and what was found to work well or less well. In other words, whether we started our research with group discussions, family interviews, individual interviews or participant observation depended on what emerged in the research field. In a study on *established* and *outsiders* in Israel and the West Bank[9] (Rosenthal 2016b), it was often the case in the Palestinian groupings that peers or family members showed up for what was initially intended to be an interview with only one individual, or visitors arrived unexpectedly and joined the family members. This requires the competence to decide in each situation whether

---

9 This comparative project "Belonging to the Outsider and Established Groupings: Palestinians and Israelis in Various Figurations" was funded by the German Research Foundation (DFG) and located within the Program for Trilateral German-Israeli-Palestinian Cooperation. Duration: 2010 – 2015. Besides the author further principal investigators were Shifra Sagy (Ben-Gurion University of the Negev, Beer Sheva, Israel) and Mohammed S. Dajani Daoudi (Al Quds University, Al-Bireh, Palestine). See: https://www.uni-goettingen.de/de/77993.html

PREFACE TO THE NEW EDITION   13

to continue a one-on-one interview with the person initially contacted, or whether to gradually switch the mode of interviewing to a family interview or group interview. Many other aspects of our planning were also changed according to our experiences in the field. It happened repeatedly that we conducted interviews (sometimes through online media) with members of groupings or families who were not in the geographical area where we intended to collect data, or in the focus of our research. This led to an expansion of the geographical and national context. This process became very clear in the context of a project on figurations of refugees and long-established residents in Jordan.[10] Here we were able to empirically reconstruct a number of distinct groupings, both among the old-established residents and among refugees or families of former refugees, that are not normally considered in the research literature (Hinrichsen/Becker 2022). Expanding the sample also affects whether we decide to expand or narrow down the geographical space of observation, how long we decide to stay in the field, and whether we need to change or limit our research questions. All of this may require us to change the case level; that is, rather than the "biography" of an individual, we may choose the case level of a "clique of friends", or a "family", or that of a neighborhood or district.

For a project on the construction of border zones[11], in which we interviewed refugees in Israel and North Africa, for example, we had not planned to remain in contact with the interviewees. Initially, we maintained contact via online media in certain cases only, because we cared about these interviewees, wanted to give them emotional support, or simply to keep in touch in case of unanticipated questions or problems. However, it became increasingly clear to us that the stations of their continued migration and their different experiences of national and other collective borders could be important for our analyses. Also, new questions kept emerging during our background research on the collective histories of the people we had interviewed. This then led to further online interviews, or an exchange of written messages, or follow-up interviews in the usual face-to-face format (see Rosenthal et al. 2017). We needed to broaden our ideas of the geographic or national

---

10 This project: "Dynamic Figurations of Refugees, Migrants and Old Residents in Jordan since 1946" was also funded by the DFG (2017–2022). See: https://www.uni-goettingen.de/en/555157.html.

11 In this comparative DFG research project (2010–2015), led by myself, the German researchers Eva Bahl and Arne Worm focused their research on the Morocco-Spain border zone, and the Israeli colleagues, who were our cooperation partners, Efrat Ben-Ze'ev and Nir Gazit on the Israel-Egypt border zone. See: https://www.uni-goettingen.de/en/477891.html

context in which the interviewees lived, and do further research on the legal conditions under which they had lived, or were still living, in the different countries they had passed through.

The method of online interviews, which has become increasingly established in our research practice, was extremely useful during the Covid-19 pandemic for two research projects that were ongoing at the time, when it became impossible to carry out the planned field trips to Jordan and Brazil (cf. Bahl/Rosenthal 2021).[12] The experience that even biographical-narrative interviews with people with whom there had previously been no contact could be carried out online was also beneficial for doctoral dissertations currently in progress. For the thesis by Lucas Cé Sangalli (forthcoming), a comparison of Sudanese migrants living in Germany and Jordan, only a sample of online interviews with those living in Jordan was available. He also conducted online interviews with experts in Sudan. Victoria Taboada Gómez (2021), who is writing her PhD on the life histories of indigenous women in Paraguay and who was not able to carry out the second field trip planned for this purpose until much later, due to the Covid-19 restrictions, has the advantage of being able to examine the differences between online interviews and face-to-face interviews.

Such a comparison of face-to-face and online interviews, or a comparison of several interviews conducted by different interviewers with the same person, makes it possible to analyze more specifically the effect of different framings on biographical self-presentations, on the rejection or allowing of memories and narrative processes. Thus, I have been able to further empirically substantiate the theoretical conception of a processual dialectic between experiencing, remembering, and narrating presented in this volume (cf. chapter 3). According to this conception, memory processes are determined both by past experience and by the constantly changing present perspective, as well as by the concrete narrative situation. To illustrate this, Ahmed Albaba, Lucas Cé Sangalli, and myself (Rosenthal et. al. 2022) have used the example of a man who fled from Mauritania to France via Spain and was interviewed several times in very different settings by different interviewers between 2014 and 2021. We investigated how the framing of the interviews, and the collective history and biography presented with regard

---

12 The field work in Brazil which was planned for 2020 was part of the project "Biographies of Migrants from Syria and West Africa in Brazil and in Germany" and funded by the German Research Foundation (2019 – 2023). See: https://www.uni-goettingen.de/de/586186.html

to the experience of enslavement and, more generally, the continued existence of slavery in Mauritania, depended on the ethnic, religious, social, cultural and national affiliation of the interviewers. The presentations were also clearly determined by the respective contexts of the man's life, the milieus in which he moved, and the discourses that prevailed there, and thus differed considerably.

Up to the time of the first edition of the present book, my work had been based already for a long time on a combination of biographical case reconstruction and discourse analysis. However, since then I have devoted myself increasingly to reflection on, and consistent implementation of this combination of methods (cf. chapter 8 in this volume). Chapters 1–7 correspond to the text of the first edition, apart from updating some references. Regarding citations from literature in German, I have referred to English translations if available and if I deemed the translation as consistent with my reading of the German text. In other cases, the quotations are my translation from the German.

Finally, I would like to express my sincere thanks to Lukas Hofmann, who has supported me with great dedication in producing this new edition. I am also very grateful to Ruth Schubert for her careful correction of the English text.

Gabriele Rosenthal

Berlin, September 2023

Preliminary note

The willingness and openness of all my interviewees enabled me to gain insight into a wide variety of life worlds. My special thanks go to all of them.

The closeness and gratitude I feel towards my interviewees in Israel, who supported me as a non-Jewish German in my research, can hardly be expressed in words. Over the years, many of them have repeatedly motivated me to continue and publish my analyses through their sympathy for my work and their detailed feedback, especially after my lectures in Israel. My friend, Dr. Viola Torok, who herself survived the Auschwitz extermination camp, has supported me quite substantially in my less sentimental and more objectifying form of scientific presentation of the subject of "survivors of the Shoah". I thank her above all for her trust.

Without Prof. Dan Bar-On Ph.D. from Ben-Gurion University of the Negev this part of the study would not have come about. Not only that he invited me to Israel and enabled me to have so many contacts there, but with his supervision of my interviews and with his empathy he has played an essential part in my scientific but also personal life journey. I would like to take this opportunity to thank him and all the members of the Department of Behavioral Sciences for their warm welcome.

The ease with which I was able to write this thesis, in which I freed myself from disciplinary constraints and got involved with Gestalt theorists, who for some seem slightly dusty, is primarily due to Prof. Dr. Fritz Schütze. His liberality and his confidence in my abilities were a very important support for me. Many thanks to him as well as to the other colleagues involved in the habilitation process.

Furthermore, I would like to thank Roswitha Breckner (Berlin), Christiane Grote (Essen), Dr. Lena Inowlocki (Rotterdam) and Yael Moore (Tel Aviv) for their many suggestions. They have helped me again and again to overcome depths and to not let attacks against my work have a blocking effect.

Wolfram Fischer put me on the track of Aron Gurwitsch as early as 1985. At that time I would not have thought it possible how much reading this much too little respected phenomenologist could give me. I thank him above all for always encouraging me on days when I doubted my ideas.

Gabriele Rosenthal

Berlin, September 1994

1. Introduction

1.1 Problem

The boom in biographical research that began in the 1970s continues; in a wide variety of disciplines, narrated and written life stories are used as a data basis.[1] Sociologists and psychologists, for example, hope that biographical material (interviews, diaries, essays, letters) will give them insight into certain milieus and into the perspective of the actors; anthropologists approach foreign cultures with this method of data collection, and scholars of Oral History use biographical interviews as a further source for their analysis of historical epochs. The biographical method is also increasingly used in various fields of practice, such as social work or job interviews.

Is biographical research just a fashionable trend that will soon fizzle out, contributing little to social science research and hardly anything to theory building? In my estimation, biographical research in recent years has gone far beyond what could be called a fashionable trend. It is also becoming increasingly clear that, due to the changes of the modern world, biographies are becoming established as a means of social structuring and that biographical analyses are becoming more and more compelling. Especially in the Federal Republic of Germany, well-founded conceptions and programmatic outlines for the advancement of the theory of biographical research in sociology, developed by authors such as Peter Alheit, Wolfram Fischer-Rosenthal, Martin Kohli and Fritz Schütze[2] – to name but a few – have been brought into

---

1 Cf. the bibliographies in Ohly 1984; Ohly and Legnaro 1987; Heinritz 1988; and the survey by Alheit et al. 1990 made for the Biographical Research section of the German Sociological Association (DGS).

2 Cf. Alheit 1990a, 1990b; Fischer-Rosenthal 1989, 1990a, 1991b, 1995; Kohli 1983, 1985, 1988; Schütze 1981, 1983, 1984, 1992.

the discussion. Also, the methodologies and methods for reconstructing life histories that emerged from these conceptions have been continuously developed in recent years, and the narrative method presented by Fritz Schütze (1977; 1983) has become established in sociology beyond this circle[3]. Furthermore, it has been convincingly shown to what extent the concept of "biography" is a way out of the dualistic impasse of subject and society (cf. Fischer-Rosenthal 1990b). The phase in which biographical sources were used only instrumentally as a source of information is gradually being replaced – especially in sociology – by a phase in which biography as a social construct or as a social reality of its own kind (Kohli 1983) is itself becoming the object of social science analysis[4]. The "study of the biographical as a social quantity" is concerned with both the question of the social function of biographies and the social processes of their constitution (Fischer-Rosenthal 1991b: 253). Fischer-Rosenthal further breaks down the socio-biographical guiding question: "What *meaning* and significance has biography acquired for members of society in the course of socializing and socio-historical developments? Which *functions* does it assume on the lifeworld level of social action, and which on the level of society as a whole? How are biographical *structures* generated, maintained, and liquefied?" (ibid.).

The conception of biography as a social entity that constitutes both social reality and the worlds of experience of the subjects, and that constantly affirms and transforms itself in the dialectical relationship between biographical experiences and patterns offered by society, offers a chance to come closer to answering one of the fundamental questions of sociology, the relationship between the individual and society. Through "biographical self-presentation"[5] we gain access not only to the biographical process of internalizing the social world in the course of socialization, but also to the integration of biographical experiences in the stock of knowledge, and thus to the constitution of patterns of experience that give present and future orientation in the social world.

---

3 Cf. the studies by Heinemeier et al. 1981; Hermanns et al. 1984; Inowlocki 1990, 2000; Riemann 1987.

4 In addition to the authors already mentioned, see the anthologies by Brose/Hildenbrand 1988; Kohli/Robert 1984; Matthes, J. et al. 1981; and the compendium by Fuchs 1984.

5 Since life histories are not only presented through narratives, but also through descriptions of past or present lives, through argumentations about the past, present, and future, or with the help of self-testimonies from the past – such as photographs, letters, or documents – I use the term "biographical self-presentation" as being more accurate than "narrated life story".

This integration, which constitutes the experiences as meaningful and generates the *biographical overall view* and the biographical designs of the subject connected with it, can by no means be understood as an accidental, individual achievement. Rather, it too is socially constituted. It takes place in the interaction with others and follows social guidelines, "recipes" for "how what is to be classified where" (Schütz/Luckmann 1979: 172 ff.). However, it is not identical with the intentions of the individual, nor with social prescriptions. Biographical research that analyzes only the patterns offered, and not their spelling out by the biographers in the biographical practice of action, as well as their linkage with the respective biographical experiences, remains with a conception of the subject as a passive projection surface of social processes.

The central concern of this study is how to analyze the constitution of the biographical overall view, which is relatively stable but changes in the course of a person's life as a result of experiences. In contrast to *biographical global evaluations*, which represent the biographer's consciously presented and intentionally directed assessment of his past and future life in the present, the biographical global view is a latently acting mechanism that controls both the retrospective view of the past and present actions and plans for the future. Global evaluations which are expressed in comments such as: "I have had a fulfilling life so far", sometimes deviate considerably from the biographical overall view, which is constituted by the person's biographical experiences (cf. chapter 4.1.3).

The biographical overall view is not an intentional achievement of the individual, but the latent ordering structure of the organization of experience and action. Even if social researchers grant biographical self-testimonies the same status as other sources, or even place them at the center of their analyses, they usually strive nevertheless to use methodological testing procedures that are intended to help them distinguish between the true and the untrue – in the sense of what actually took place and what is invented. Such efforts are usually based on a dualistic conception of the experienced *life history* and narrated *life story*. This dualism is often preceded by that of event and experience. The experienced life history breaks down into what objectively took place and what is subjectively interpreted, what was experienced at the time and what has been subjectively falsified in the process of remembering. This means considering not only what was really experienced, but also the events themselves, which, freed of the subjective, receive sanctification as objectivity. What happened then is to be investigated here and now. Those who only search for what actually happened at that time, just like those who only want to grasp what was experienced at that time, fail to recognize the constitutive part of the currently *narrated* life story. Life and text are seen as two things that can be separated from each other, where the function of the text is seen as providing information about what it refers to: about the reality outside the text. Here the text interferes, so to speak, with the search for objective reality. The dualistic conception of experienced life history and narrated life story mostly follows from the basic conceptual dualism between what is presented to the subject's perception, i.e., an object or an event, and its perception. Thus, the first "sources of error" are to be found in the experience itself. Furthermore, there can be corrections in the memory process, the autobiographer may not have "stored" some things, or may have forgotten them in the course of the years. The third "source of error" lies in the narrative situation, in which the autobiographer turns to what has been stored in his memory and – depending on his attitude towards this constant object – reproduces it in the narrative in a colored or falsified way. Both in the experience and in the narrative situation, according to this conception, the autobiographer is offered something constant, something endowed with a hard and unchangeable core, which is then seen and represented in a different, more or less adequate light, depending on the perspective.

If one understands the experienced life history as something constant, as something that has taken place and is fixed in memory, this means that it presents itself to the autobiographer in a particular way because that is the way it is. The Gestalt theorist Kurt Koffka (1935/1963: 75) describes this position as follows: "things look as they look because they are what they are". If one then notices again and again that the biographer does not perceive his life as it was, one must look for the reasons why his perception is wrong. Thus, it is not the perceived that is subject to modifications, that is constituted in the act of perception – it always remains the same – but the attention paid to it, its observation is modified, or lets it appear in a different light. The "distortion" or one-sided observation may be due to the specific situation during the production of the text – like the influence of the interviewer, the internal condition of the perceiver – like the need to see life in a rosy light, or by a deficient memory. Accordingly, this position assumes that the perception of the event when it occurred was affected by external influences: "things look as they do because the proximal stimuli are what they are" (Koffka 1963: 80). Applied to the consideration of biographical events, this means that they appear as they do because situational stimuli external to the organism shaped the way they were experienced at that time. They have already been stored in "distorted" way because of these stimuli. What is decisive about this conception is that it assumes a constancy of what is to be perceived, of the objective events. To this constant objective, something subjective is then added, a) in the situation of the experience, and b) in retrospect, in each case by the act of perception and memory. If social researchers succeed in subtracting this unwanted added something, then they come to the events as they really were. The experienced events play the role of an objective stimulus, which would be experienced in the same way by all people. Although this is by no means in accordance with empirical experience, the assumption of constancy is not abandoned, but the differences between event and experience are explained by additional factors added to the stimulus.

Even among those social scientists who give an important place to the subjective, to the interpretations of the autobiographers, or who consider its analysis necessary for understanding social action, there is still a certain belief in the "objective world" independent of subjective experiences and interpretations. Early biographical research in the social sciences, which began during World War I with the study of migration by William Isaac Thomas and Florian Znaniecki (1918–1920) at the University of Chicago, and then blossomed in the 1920s at the sociology department there through the initiative of Ernest W. Burgess and Robert E. Park[6], was motivated by insight into the need for "getting inside the actor's perspective". The advantages of the biographical case study for capturing subjective perspectives of members of different milieus were recognized. However, even these so meritorious works contain traits of dualism between the subjective and the objective, although this is in contrast to the theoretical and methodological positions of the pragmatists or interactionist action theorists. These tendencies are not overcome even in later studies, but rather maintained or strengthened by understanding the perspective of the agent as subjective and internal, and observable behavior as objective and external[7].

The distinction introduced by Thomas and Znaniecki between attitudes as individual dispositions of action, as a "process of individual consciousness", on the one hand, and social values as "givens with an empirical content accessible to the members of a social group and with a meaning in

---

6 Chicago School works include, for example, Wirth's study of the ghetto, Zorbaugh's of slums, and Trasher's of gangs. For a discussion of the Chicago School and Symbolic Interactionism, see Schütze 1987b.

7 Herbert Blumer (1973) in particular contributed to this reading of Symbolic Interactionism.

terms of which this givenness can be an object of action", on the other (ibid. 1918–1920/1965: 75), which they discussed in their methodological preface to the "Polish Peasant", can certainly be interpreted as, for example, Sigrid Paul (1987: 27) does, as an individual disposition to act, on the one hand, and objectively given social facts, on the other. If one considers the narrated life story as the individual sense-making of an objective course of events, one can deny its value as a reliable source for capturing the "factual course of life" and consider it, like Martin Osterland (1983), as a "retrospective illusion"[8] – a position that was also supported a few years later by Pierre Bourdieu (1986/1990) in complete ignorance of sociological biographical research.[9] Osterland draws from his view the consequence that the narrated life story can only serve to capture current patterns of interpretation. Is the narrated life story then only an "invention", as formulated by Max Frisch (1968: 9): "Every man invents a story for himself, which he then holds, at enormous sacrifice, to be his life". If we do not understand this invention as one that is based on what is experienced and is by no means arbitrary[10], we only go to the other side of dualism with a position such as that advocated by Osterland. While some are in search of the "outer world" and thus let all inwardness of experience be absorbed in the outer behavior triggered by stimuli, others are on a one-sided search for inwardness. Those who intend to reconstruct patterns of interpretation without reconstructing their biographical genesis, and thus the biographical constellations of action, assume that it is possible to interpret interpretations of the past independently of the past. Thus, some search one-sidedly for the events to which the narrated life story refers, while others search one-sidedly for patterns of interpretation in the present of the narrators. In both, though from opposite poles, the interaction of past, present, and future is missed. It is not seen that the past is constituted by the present and the anticipated future, and the present is constituted by the past and the future. The extent to which the biographical past manifests itself in the present of the narrative has been elaborated in particular by Fritz Schütze (1981; 1984) in his empirical work. Schütze's analyses show how narrative structures correspond to the structures of experience, and how

---

8 Cf. the critique by Harry Hermanns (1985).

9 Bourdieu (1990: 80) insinuates that researchers working with biographies are "complicit" "in the construction of the perfect social artifact … called 'life history'" and ignores the achievement of biographical research in reconstructing the social processes of construction. For a rejection of Bourdieu's critique, see Lutz Niethammer 1990.

10 Cf. Henningsen (1971: 75), who discusses the "pre-formedness" of stories.

the accumulated layers of experience correspond to the way the narrative is structured, which by no means implies homology of the narrated and the experienced.

Rejection of these dualistic positions, however, does not mean that we can claim to have found a better way. How can we find our way out of dualism at all – for are we not always faced with the dual? According to Waldenfels (1980), certainly not by thinking that inside and outside, objective and subjective simply coincide. Nor is it enough to insist on a dialectical conception, and to hide behind this or other conceptualizations that may evoke respect but not understanding. What does a mutual interpenetration of what happened, what was experienced and what was narrated mean? What does the narrated life story tell us? Which methodological procedures can help us to understand and explain this social phenomenon? Building on a phenomenological interpretation of Gestalt theory, as done by Aron Gurwitsch (1929; 1964/2010), and the consequent rejection of the assumption of constancy, I would like to pursue these questions here, based on my empirical analyses of narrated life stories. About 110 biographical narrative interviews conducted in different research contexts by myself or by students taking part in the teaching projects I have led serve as the empirical basis. For the "Hitler Youth Project" (Rosenthal 1986; 1987) at the Free University of Berlin, members of the Hitler Youth were asked to tell their life histories, focusing on the Nazi and postwar periods. For the project "Living with the Nazi Past" (Rosenthal 1990) at the University of Bielefeld, we interviewed members of three generations (born 1899–1929) with the same focus. For the project "Biography" (Rosenthal 1989) at the University of Bielefeld, as in all following projects, we asked relatives of different ages, occupational groups and milieus to tell their entire life history. In the state of Hesse (West Germany) I spoke with veterans of the First World War, born between 1888 and 1900 (Rosenthal 1991/2019). As a visiting lecturer in Israel, I interviewed European Jews whose lives were affected by National Socialism, i.e., both those who fled Europe and survivors of the Shoah (Rosenthal 1995a). In addition, I had at my disposal interviews carried out by the graduate students I supervised and from a project led by Dan Bar-On in Beer Sheva, Israel, in which I was a methodological adviser. The life stories of survivors of the Shoah stand in this study next to biographies of people with completely different backgrounds, along with autobiographies of fellow travellers and perpetrators of National Socialism. For me as a non-Jewish interviewer, and for me as interpreter of these life stories, this entails very different experiences, feelings, and also political and moral responsibilities. In the presentation of my analyses, on the other hand, I address the common constitutive mechanisms of the biographical constructions. Can this be seen as a "violation of the First Commandment of Holocaust scholarship – "Thou shalt not compare", as sarcastically formulated by Henryk M. Broder (1993: 8)? Without comparisons, the extreme experiences of survivors would sink into the realm of the unmentionable and the unspoken. Even if, contrary to my intention, we tended to develop special conceptions of biography for severely traumatized people, this would not be possible without reference to other biographies. Nevertheless, in order to prevent misunderstandings, I would like to emphasize at this point: comparing does not mean equating. Rather, comparing means reconstructing the structural differences and similarities. If, on the other hand, we persist in discrepancy and in viewing Auschwitz as another planet whose survivors no longer belong to this world, we contribute to the further isolation of the victims. By assuming an insurmountable discrepancy between us and the survivors of the Shoah, we prevent any empathic interpersonal encounter. Ruth Klüger (1992: 109 f.) writes as a survivor of Auschwitz about the silence imposed on her by Germans: "You may and can speak about your war experiences, dear friends, but I cannot speak about mine. My childhood falls into the black hole of this discrepancy. ... And I remain silent and am only allowed to listen and not to speak. We were people of the same generation, well-meaning and able to speak the language, but the old war has blown up the bridges between us, and we are squatting on the pillars jutting into our new houses. But if there is no bridge at all from my memories to yours, why am I writing this at all?" (1992: 109 f., translated from the German). As already mentioned, in this study I will turn to the question of the interrelation between experienced life history and narrated life story in a phenomenological interpretation of Gestalt theory. I will concentrate on this theoretical approach and draw on discussions from other theoretical traditions only for additional explanation and substantiation. On the one hand, this limitation is due to a desire to make Gestalt theory fruitful for biographical theory building and research. On the other hand, I consider the newer discussions that have taken place since the 1980s, for instance in the fields of narrative psychology[11] or psychoanalysis[12] about the

---

11 Cf. Bruner (1987), McAdams/Ochberg (1983), Rosenwald/Ochberg (1992), Ochberg (1994).

12 Here, the discussion was triggered primarily by the work of Donald Spence (1982) and Roy Schafer (1983). For a critical discussion of Spence and Schafer, see Kerz-Rühling (1984) and Leary/Arbor (1989).

relationship between life and text, to be new editions and rediscoveries of a longstanding and, in my opinion, theoretically more sophisticated sociological discourse. Furthermore, using Gestalt theory to consider the question of the relationship between life and text offers us more insights into the dialectical relationship between the presentation of a life (noema) and the meaning given to this life (noesis). By contrast, Donald Spence (1982), who rejects the archaeological reading of psychoanalysis which assumes that "historical truths" or past realities can be excavated, comes down squarely on the side of "narrative truth". By arguing that "historical truth" is unknowable to the analyst because he lacks the tools to do so, Spence moves to the other side of dualism with his constructivist approach, which lacks a methodology. As important as his study may be for psychoanalytic practice and critical discourse within the psychoanalytic community, theoretically it is far from a dialectical conception of life history and life story, as also called for by the philosopher Widdershoven (1993), among others, who draws on the analyses of Husserl and Merleau-Ponty. The experienced life history can neither be understood as presenting itself as a constant, unchanging object which is remembered and presented differently by the autobiographer depending on perspective and mood, nor as an object that can be constructed arbitrarily each time it is considered. Rather, I argue that the narrated life story is mutually constituted by what is presented to the consciousness in the situation of experience (perception noema) and the act of perceiving (noesis), by experiences that are presented by memory and sedimented in Gestalt-like form (memory noemata) and the act of considering the experience in the present of the narration. Experienced life history and narrated life story are bound up in a mutually constituting relationship.

I will discuss this basic assumption in chapters 2–4 on the different levels of experiencing, remembering and telling. The discussion is based on the following additional assumptions:

On the level of *events and experiences* (cf. chapter 2):

1. Events are not perceptible as they are, but only in the how of their presentation.
2. Not only does the act of perception produce the organization of what is presented, but also what is presented to perception gives structuredness.
3. Event and experience are mutually constituted.

On the level of *memories and narration* (cf. chapter 3):

4. Experiences cannot present themselves to the biographer in the present of the narrative as they were experienced, but only in the how of their presentation, i.e., only in the interrelation between what is presented in the present of the narrative and what is intended.
5. Not only does the narration produce the orderedness of the story, but also the memory noema that is presented by the memory gives structuredness.

On the level of *experienced life history and narrated life story* (cf. chapter 4):

6. Not only does the presentation of the life story produce orderedness, but also the experienced life history gives structuredness.
7. The sequences – whether narratives, argumentations or descriptions – of a biographical self-presentation are part of a Gestalt.

After this, I will discuss the *healing effect of biographical narration* (chapter 5), which in my opinion is based on the Gestalt ambiguity of the experienced life history and the related possibility of restructuring in the narrative process. The *methodological implications* of a phenomenological conception based on Gestalt theory (chapter 6) can be summed up in the principles: "space to develop a Gestalt" and "reconstruction of the Gestalt of experienced life history and narrated life story".

1.2 What is the "benefit" of applying Gestalt theory to life stories and life histories?

Before entering into the theoretical discussion of a phenomenological interpretation of Gestalt theory and its applicability to narrated life stories, we will present an empirical example to give a preliminary idea of the methodological consequences of this approach and its advantages in the analysis of life stories. If we assume that the individual parts of the narrated life story are all part of a Gestalt, this implies further assumptions, each of which has far-reaching consequences in terms of research practice.

1. individual parts or segments of a biographical self-presentation do not possess properties independent of their integration into an overall context. Parts of Gestalts exist only by virtue of their functional significance for the Gestalt. Each part contains references to the whole. This assumption implies

that the interview must be conducted in such a way that the autobiographer is given "space to develop a Gestalt" and the process of formation is not interrupted by questions (cf. chapter 6.1). During the analysis of the interview text, the individual sequences of the biographical self-presentation must be reconstructed consistently in the overall context of their occurrence and in their organization. The interpretation of a part requires in each case the formation of hypotheses about its functional significance for the overall Gestalt.

The decontextualization of sequences and their embedding in thought-experiment contexts, following the principles of structural hermeneutics, is very helpful for the reconstruction of the context of origin, provided that these sequences are then replaced in the overall Gestalt – or let us call it overall configuration – of the biographical self-presentation. If, on the other hand, we assume that we can interpret parts detached from the overall context of their occurrence, we are subject to the illusion of parts with an unchangeable core, but since parts can always only be interpreted as parts of a whole, we are nevertheless compelled to place them in a whole designed by us. This whole designed by us according to our everyday or scientific concepts can then be structurally completely incompatible with the Gestalt in the context of origin.

2. The biographical self-presentation is not constituted by the sum of its parts, but by their organizedness. If we interpret parts of an interview in the context of their use with the best hermeneutic intention and sum up the interpretations of these parts in the overall interpretation of the case, we miss the original Gestalt. In the reconstruction of narrated life stories we thus need an analysis procedure in which the design process in the presentation and the design of the temporal and thematic connections of experiences are reconstructed (cf. chapter 2.3.5; chapter 6.2).

3. Similar Gestalts are possible, even if they do not agree in any of their parts. And vice versa: Gestalts can be very different, even if they agree in many of their parts. Which life stories are structurally similar or which ones belong to the same type can therefore not be determined on the basis of their parts. Type formation in this Gestalt theory and structuralist understanding means reconstructing the Gestalt of the life narrative and the underlying rules of its constitution, and not just summing up individual features as in a descriptive formation of types. Only then can the contrastive comparison succeed in the sense of comparing structurally similar with structurally different life

stories, which serves to further verify the typification already undertaken in the individual case analysis.

In order to illustrate how Gestalt theory can be applied to a part of a biographical self-presentation, an example from a case interpretation (cf. chapter 4.4.4) will be presented here. It concerns the ending of an interview by an autobiographer, which came unexpectedly for the interviewer. The use of the term "unexpected" means that the interviewer had fixed ideas about the overall shape of a biographical narrative that the autobiographer, who presented his life history only up to the year 1944, did not live up to. In seeking to understand why the interviewee ended his self-presentation so abruptly, perhaps because he thought he had exceeded the allowed time, we need to embed it in the context of the interview. But how far do we have to go in reconstructing the context? First, some information about the interview. The autobiographer is a Jewish Israeli who was forced to emigrate from Germany to Palestine in 1938. I had asked Mr. Jarok, as I will call him, to tell me his life history. After he had spoken for about an hour, he broke off the interview rather abruptly, slightly aggressively and unexpectedly, with the words: "I can't go on. I have told you enough now. Turn off the tape" (translated from the German). He offered me another cup of coffee and then complimented me out of his apartment without arranging another meeting. It was only after a few weeks that he resumed contact with me and agreed to another interview, in which he then continued to tell me the history of his life after 1944 in chronological order. Confused and worried by what I saw as the initially unsuccessful course of the interview, I searched for an explanation. Regardless of the context of the interview, some hypotheses can be quickly formulated, such as: Mr. Jarok is one of those people who do not talk for hours, or: he had not prepared himself for such a long interview. If we take into account the "external context" of the interview independently of the meaning of its abrupt termination, we could further assume that this man had no trust in a non-Jewish German interviewer. But let us consider the "internal context" of his refusal to continue: in the presentation of his life history, Mr. Jarok had arrived at the situation in which, in 1944, when he had been living in Palestine for six years, he realized that his parents and his younger brother had probably been murdered by the Nazis in Europe. A Jewish woman who had escaped from Treblinka had come to his kibbutz and spent an entire night talking about the genocide in Poland, where Mr. Jarok's family had been deported. Here, among other things, the hypothesis can be formulated that this memory of the "most terrible situation in my life" actualized his grief and the associated feelings of guilt, which then turned into aggression against the Germans and the interviewer. Grief and guilt led to the statement, "*I can't go on*" and the aggression was directed against the German non-Jew present, with whom he refused further cooperation.

In methodological terms, one might think we have correctly followed the rules of hermeneutic analysis. We have considered this part of the interview, its abrupt termination, in the context of its occurrence, and we have considered the external contextual data of the interview. But we have not considered the termination in the overall context of either the narrated life story or the experienced life history. If, on the other hand, we look for its functional significance for this biographical self-presentation in terms of Gestalt theory, a much more far-reaching meaning is revealed that goes beyond the situation of the interview: we see a biographical narrative up to the point when the autobiographer realized the death of his parents and his brother, then a few weeks intermission or pause, and then a continuation of the narrative of his life without his parents in Israel. Considered as a Gestalt, we can now formulate the following hypothesis about the connection of these parts: Mr. Jarok has to put a lot of effort into splitting his life into two parts that do not touch. He does not do this argumentatively, as we know it from other life stories, such as narratives of conversion, but tries to draw two independent figures. Several weeks between the interviews enable him to prevent too many points of contact between these two figures. The plausibility of this assumption is reinforced, among other things, by what he said at the beginning of the first interview, the meaning of which I did not understand at the time: "I can offer you different things: my life in Germany, my life in Israel. Choose". I then asked him to tell me his entire life. He responded, "Oh that will hardly be possible". I ignored this hint, since it did not fit into my conception of the overall shape of a biographical self-presentation, and said, "Why don't you start with your childhood?" Thus, I did not take him seriously with his need to prevent the two halves of his life from coming close to each other, and perhaps aroused his aggression against me at this point.

By considering his "termination of the interview" in the overall context of his life story, we now have hypotheses not only concerning why this autobiographer ended the interview and only continued after a few weeks, but also concerning the overall Gestalt of his narrated life story and experienced life history. For our further case analysis, this means we first need to reconstruct which parts of his biographical self-presentation belong to which figure and how they are organized within the two figures. We also need to consider the functional significance of what happened in 1944 for Mr. Jarok's life history. This event represents a break in his life and the following questions need to be asked in the case analysis: Why did Mr. Jarok not realize before 1944 that genocide was being committed in Europe, and why did this realization come so abruptly? How did he, and how does he deal with this break, and how does his attempt to avoid contact between the two phases of his life manifest itself in the practice of his everyday life?

Our analysis of Mr. Jarok's life history and life story then shows that his entire biographical self-presentation is an attempt to keep his past in Germany, the leaving behind of his family and their murder, separate from his life in Israel. In terms of Gestalt theory: the determination not to touch the biographically existing lines of connection between these two figures under any circumstances. He not only sticks to this separation in his biographical self-presentation, he also tries to avoid any mention of the German past in his life in Israel. This separation is also connected to the interaction dynamic with me as a German working through the past. On the one hand, Mr. Jarok does not want contact with me, and on the other hand he seeks it. Among other things, this dynamic also makes him aggressive. If we had stopped at the level where the memory of that experience actualized Mr. Jarok's feelings of guilt and that he channeled them into aggressive feelings against the German non-Jewish woman, we would have grasped an important component of his problem with past persecution, which became apparent at many other points in the interview. But it would have remained hidden to us how he deals with this problem, or how he tries to avoid it. Only further use of Gestalt theory can help us to decipher the interplay between the way he deals with the past and his problem with the past. If we now wish to compare this biographical self-presentation with a structurally similar one, we can base our selection of the life story to be analyzed next on individual constitutive components such as "loss of family in the Holocaust and associated survivor guilt", but these factors will not necessarily lead to a similar Gestalt formation in which the autobiographer tries to keep two figures separate. Rather, embedded in a different biographical self-presentation, they can take on a completely different functional significance, just as the splitting of the narrated life story into two figures can serve a different function. In other words, whether the comparison of two life stories is a comparison within one type, or a comparison of cases belonging to two different types, can only be determined after both case analyses have been completed.

2. On the Gestalt nature of experience

2.1 That which is presented to the observer

2.1.1 The presentation of the world of things

If one rejects the assumption of the constancy of what is perceived, and thus the conception of "objective" stimuli, which was convincingly questioned at the beginning of this century by the Gestalt theorists Max Wertheimer, Wolfgang Köhler and Kurt Koffka, on the basis of a wealth of empirical investigations in the field of perception, one no longer moves in the world of things, but in the world of the noematic. Instead of following the idea of "constant" and incomprehensible things, one then considers what can be grasped, what is experienced: "Objects in the normal sense of the word fall away, and noemata alone are left over; the *world* as *it really is* is bracketed, the *world* as *it looks remains*" (Gurwitsch 1929/1966: 194). Edmund Husserl's philosophical and theoretical program of bracketing the belief in being means taking things as they present themselves to our consciousness. A search for things as they really are is unsuccessful, since every object can only be given as an "object for consciousness". That which presents itself to our consciousness – whether in immediate perception, in memory or in imagination – is called by Husserl noema:

"Perception, for example, has its noema, most basically its perceptual sense, i.e., the *perceived as perceived*. Similarly, the current case of remembering has its *remembered as remembered*, just as its 'remembered', precisely as it is 'meant', 'intended to' in the 'remembering'; again, the judging has the *judged as judged*, liking has the liked as liked, and so forth. In every case the noematic correlate, which is called 'sense' her (in a very extended signification) is to be taken precisely as it inheres 'immanently' in the mental process of perceiving, of judging, of liking; and so forth; that is, just as it is offered to us when *we inquire purely into this mental process itself*" (Husserl, Ideas I: p. 214).

Aron Gurwitsch clarifies Husserl's understanding of noema very succinctly: "By *noema* Husserl understands not the object *simpliciter*, as it is in itself, per se, but *the object as it is meant*, the object just – precisely just, but also only just– as it appears through the act of consciousness in question, as it is apprehended and intended through this act, the object in the perspective, orientation, illumination, and role in which it presents itself" (Gurwitsch 1943a/1966: 339).

The act of turning to the noema, which Husserl calls noesis, does not depend on the object, but on the noema, on how it presents itself to the perceiver or the rememberer. Let us first take an example chosen by Gurwitsch (1943a/1966; 1964) from the world of things, which he took from Husserl. Let us imagine that we are standing in front of a house and see what is presented to us as a facade. In our immediate perception, we see the house only from one side. If we walk around the house, we can only directly perceive its rear side; the front side is only available to us in our memory of it. If we enter the house, its outside is no longer perceptible to us. Direct perception of the house as a whole is thus never possible. Nevertheless, the perception of a part like the facade always requires a preliminary conception of the whole in order to perceive it as a house at all. Thus, the house as a whole can only be perceived as a constructive act of consciousness. Consequently, we can never see things as they really are. That which we perceive appears only as the facade or the back of a house, as it is in the light of that which we do not see. Thus, in every present sense-experience, "other aspects at the moment not given in the sense-experience must somehow be present in the perception under consideration so as to contribute towards shaping that perception into what is actually experienced" (Gurwitsch 1964/2010: 187). A conception, a knowledge – however indeterminate – is necessary. In looking at the house, "the side that is seen is aside only insofar as it has sides which are not seen, which are anticipated and as such determine the sense" (Husserl EJ: p. 35). We can hypothetically infer the whole from the part perceived as the front, only because it presents itself to us as part of a whole, that is, because it indicates that there must be other sides and an interior. The sides and the inside which are not present in the immediate perception exist in our imagination; only by this can the house be recognized as a house. Thus, every noema necessarily always refers to other noemata of the same noematic system. The facade we see is a part of the whole noematic system or – in the terminology of Gurwitsch – of the theme: house. Only in this relation between part and whole, between noema and noematic system, is the relation between noema and object specified.

Aron Gurwitsch's (1929; 1964) Gestalt analysis of the noematic side of perception, which in Husserl's analyses was neglected in contrast to the noetic side, and still bears features of the assumption of constancy (see below), gives us information about the organized nature of noema and system, of part and whole. An interpretation of Husserl's analyses based on Gestalt theory, in which not only the intentional acts are ascribed the organizing activity, but a given organizedness of the noema is assumed, makes it possible to overcome a dualistic conception of noema and noesis. Between the parts of the noematic system, in this view, there is the special relation of Gestalt coherence; all parts are in a continuous interdependence with each other: "*In thoroughgoing reciprocity, the constituents assign to, and derive from, one another functional significance* which gives to each one its qualification in a concrete case" (Gurwitsch 1964/2010: 131)[1]. The noematic system, in which each noema belonging to it presents itself as part of a whole, thus possesses unity through Gestalt coherence. Gestalts are, whether as static wholes or holistic processes, more or less structured wholes with inner laws of their structuredness (Wertheimer 1922: 52). Thus, they are not "piecemeal summative givens" (ibid.) in which individual pieces atomistically coexist simultaneously or follow one another. Rather, "by 'Gestalt' is meant a unitary whole of varying degrees of richness of detail, which, by virtue of its intrinsic articulation and structure, possesses coherence and consolidation and, thus, detaches itself as an organized and closed unit from the surrounding field" (Gurwitsch 1964/2010: 112). To remain with the example of the house and thus in the world of things, we can only perceive this thing, seen from the facade, as a house, because we grasp this part in its functional significance in relation to the overall architectural form (Gurwitsch 1943a/1966: 347).

By starting from a part, we imagine a whole, and can make conclusions regarding this single part, and vice versa, from the perception of the single part we can make conclusions regarding the whole. With the conception of the whole, the seen part is qualified as what it appears to us, and the whole

---

1 It should be noted that it is Gurwitsch's achievement to move from the empirical work of the Gestalt theorists to the level of theoretical concepts. In letters to Alfred Schütz (Grathoff 1985: 231) he writes that the studies presented by the Gestalt theorists served him only as illustrative material: "I had to create the whole conceptual apparatus myself". For example, the concepts of Gestalt coherence or functional significance are formulated by Gurwitsch.

is qualified through the conception of the part. Parts and whole thus qualify each other reciprocally. It is essential for a Gestalt approach that the qualification of a single part – like the facade of a house – is not to be understood as if there were a constantly presenting part to which something else is added due to the idea of the whole – like the house. Rather, the part is constituted solely by its function for other parts and by its arrangement within the whole, i.e., by the configuration of the parts within a whole that stands out from a background. The extent to which parts of figures receive their meaning exclusively through the configuration of the whole, i.e., have no identity independent of the respective figures, has been convincingly shown by the Gestalt theorists with a wealth of empirical perceptual experiments. When geometric figures are changed by adding or omitting parts which are functional for the figure (cf. Köhler 1947: 115 ff.; Wertheimer 1933), not only the total appearance of the figure, i.e., the figure as a whole, changes, but also the meaning of the parts. Formerly perceptible parts are hardly recognizable when, for example, further parts are added. Here is an example from Köhler (1947: 115):

Chart 1 Figure 1 and Figure 2
Source: Köhler (1947: 115)

Figure 1, the letter E, disappears completely in figure 2, since the lines forming the E are also related in their functional significance to other lines that play no role whatsoever in the configuration of the letter E (Gurwitsch 1964/2010: 130). Conversely, completely different figures can be created by taking away parts (cf. Wertheimer 1923). This does not mean, however, that the figure changes whenever something is added or taken away. If we take something away from a figure, it will remain recognizable provided the structure of the whole remains perceptible in the rest.

The figure is also preserved if we add something that does not enter into a Gestalt relationship with it, i.e., if the parts of the figure continue to have their functional significance only in relation to one another. Thus, the house as a noematic system continues to exist, regardless of whether the sky surrounding it darkens or not. If, on the other hand, we change a part within the house as a system, the noema becomes reorganized. Parts of figures do not have properties or attributes independently of the whole; they are not elements that possess something like core properties, "those which it displays regardless of its integration into a contexture and which therefore may best be ascertained when this constituent is as isolated as possible ..." (Gurwitsch 1964/2010: 113). We can speak of a house facade only because we perceive this part not only as belonging to the whole house, but also in its arrangement with other parts and in its function for the overall configuration. Thus, a facade can only appear as such in relation to the other sides of the house. If, when walking around the object imagined as a house, it turns out to be a theater backdrop without side walls, and thus without an interior, not only the idea of the whole changes, but the previously perceived part, "facade of a house", now turns out to be something completely different, for instance the "front of a backdrop". Thus, this perceived part is no longer seen as part of the previous noematic system house; rather, it is now incorporated into a new system: theatrical dummy. Thus, there is a change from one noematic system to another, and a completely new Gestalt emerges. It would be different if, while walking around the object, the side formerly perceived as the facade turned out in our immediate perception to be the back of the house, and the anticipated back turned out to be the facade. Although this would lead to a new perception of the "old" facade and thus also of the entire house, these reorganizations would take place within the same noematic system.

2.1.2 The presentation of processes

If we transfer this analysis of the world of things to the world of temporal processes, i.e., to temporal things "that are not only units in time but that also contain temporal extension in themselves" (Husserl, Time: p. 24), we have to account for an essential difference. Time objects as events in a temporal sequence pass away again immediately in the process of their coming into being, while a space thing can present itself to me again. The beginning of an experience cannot be given again in immediate perception, but a house can be walked around and the facade can be looked at again. In the sequence of individual acts of an event, on the other hand, the past acts only exist for me in my memory, their immediate perception is gone forever. However, this difference between the perception of things and of processes exists only on the level of the re-presentation of temporally past experiences (the "secondary memory") and the potential re-perception of objects and not on the level of the act of perception itself. In the process of perceiving a temporal event, structurally the same thing takes place as in the process of perceiving a thing: in each case, the current perception involves retention, i.e., consciousness of what has just been directly perceived (primary memory), and protention, i.e., anticipation of what is to come in the future (Husserl, Time). "We have the analogies: for the spatial thing, its insertion into the surrounding space and spatial world; on the other hand, the spatial thing itself with its foreground and background. For the temporal thing: its insertion into the temporal form and the temporal world; on the other hand, the temporal thing itself and its shifting orientation in relation to the living now" (ibid.: p. 57). The visual perception of a spatial thing, which is composed of many individual perceptions in the process of looking, is itself a temporal act.

The difference in the perception of spatial and temporal Gestalts does not lie in the act of creating a whole with regard to the directly perceived part, but rather in the fact that what is presented as a whole on the one hand already exists, while on the other hand it is in the process of coming into being. Directly presented events, which stand out as units from the stream of experience through the reflexive act of the perceiver's attention, arise in the process of perceiving. It follows that these detached units – and only through this do they become an experience as a mode of being that differs from others (cf. Schütz 1932/1974: 67) – initially do not yet have a form, but are only anticipated as such. Whether that which initially presents itself as part of a whole is part of a Gestalt is only proven in the process of the succession of further parts. If we hear two tones, for example, we can perceive them as sounds belonging to a Gestalt, and thus as the beginning of a melody, in anticipation of other tones to be heard subsequently. Only the tones that follow, or do not follow, will confirm this perception, or show that we only heard someone touching the piano keys while dusting. When we anticipate a melody, we expect further matching sounds. Whether we perceive the next sound as belonging to the first sounds, or as being independent of them, depends on the factor of "meaningful continuation", which has been discussed by Gestalt theorists in respect of spatial Gestalts (Wertheimer 1923) and temporal Gestalts (Koffka 1935/1963: 423 ff.). Thus, neither the sounding of a car horn – apart from experimental music – after the sounding of a piano key, nor the sound of the closing of the piano lid would be a meaningful continuation. The tones or sounds belong together only if they present themselves to the listener as belonging together and not simply following each other, and if they mutually constitute each other in their meaning. Parts of a processual event do not form a Gestalt just because they follow each other: "A melody, a rhythm, a spoken sentence, are not analogous to beads on a string" (Koffka 1963: 437). Whether we perceive a house or a melody, in both cases we are dealing with organized entities (in the language of Gestalt theory: figures, and according to Gurwitsch: themes) which result from the perception of units that stand out against a background. The front of a house is experienced as part of a whole, a house, only because the house stands out against a background that is more or less irrelevant to it, while the front is experienced as essentially belonging to the house as an organized unit. The same is true of sound. Only when it stands out from the background of other sounds, or silence, and is experienced as belonging to a whole, is it perceived as part of a melody or a word. Thus, the difference between spatial and temporal figures does not lie in the structure of their organizedness. In both cases, in Gurwitsch's terminology, we are dealing with the presentation of a theme that stands out from the thematic field belonging to it, which in turn is surrounded by a margin that is irrelevant to the theme. If I consider the thing which presents itself to me as a house in a villa district, the other villas are the field relevant for the perception of my thing. The thematic field "villa district" prevents perception of the thing as a theatrical dummy. The color of the sky or the passing cars, on the other hand, are circumstances that are co-present but "have no reference to theme and comprise in their totality what we propose to call the margin" (Gurwitsch 1964/2010: 4).

The assumption of the organized nature of static objects of perception, their respective specific structure of theme, thematic field and margin, can now be transferred not only to temporal objects of perception, but to all acts of consciousness. It applies not only to immediate perception, but also to remembering, to thought processes, to imagining and fantasizing (cf. Wertheimer 1928: 51). Furthermore, the formal factors for Gestalt perception, which have been empirically proven by Gestalt theorists (cf. Wertheimer 1923; Köhler 1969) in the field of perception of optical objects, can be transferred, at least partially, to temporal processes, to remembering, imagining, and narrating (see below). The formal or "objective" factors condition the perception of a Gestalt; they can be understood as structural aspects that are immanent to perceptual images or processes. In the case of visual entities, these factors are *proximity, equality (or similiarity), closure, and meaningful good continuation*, where each factor is more dominant than the one previously named (Gurwitsch 1964/2010: 145). While Gurwitsch (ibid.: 146 f.) assumes that at least the factors of coherence and good continuation also apply to temporal figures, Koffka (1963) tries to prove the validity of all four factors for temporal figures using the example of melodies.[2] Let's take the example of the tones and the car horn: if a car horn sounds immediately after the first piano tone and the second piano tone sounds some time later, the factor of "similarity" between the two piano tones will lead to them being perceived as belonging together, and thus be more dominant than the proximity of the first tone to the car horn.

The dominance of the factor "meaningful good continuation" over the factors of similarity and proximity is illustrated by Koffka (1963: 423 ff.) in the following example: If two sequences of tones overlap in one tone, resulting in a long tone, it is nevertheless heard as two short tones, each belonging to the closed unit of one and the other melody. While this example illustrates both the factor of coherence, in the sense of separating one figure from the other, and the factor of good continuation, in the sense of what is perceived as belonging to a figure, these factors cannot be defined so easily when applied to social processes, especially if we reject the assumption of qualities that are inherent to the things themselves. The transferability of these factors to Gestalts, which are interactively generated as they happen, therefore requires a precise empirical analysis (cf. chapter 4.4).

Let us first stay with the question of the formal differences between spatial and temporal figures, which, as shown, are not to be found in their organizedness. So does the difference lie in their directedness, i.e., in a direction that is given in temporal processes but which is absent in spatial Gestalts (Koffka 1963: 439 ff.)? I can go from the front of a house to the back, and from the back to the front. Likewise, when looking at a painting, I can let my gaze wander from right to left, from left to right, from the center to the edge, whereas when listening to a melody, or when perceiving a course of action, the direction is imposed on me. Do I not hear the second tone in the melody as a continuation of the first, and do I not experience the second action as being conditioned by the first? If I hear the second tone, the first one is still there in my consciousness. It still resonates and thus qualifies the second

---

2 Alfred Schütz considered Koffka's transfer from the visual to the acoustic to be "nonsense". He wrote to Gurwitsch (Grathoff 1985: 227): "Every sketchbook of Beethoven, indeed every variation and every development proves Koffka's theory to be pure nonsense" (translated from the German). Unfortunately, Schütz does not elaborate on the extent to which it is nonsense – thinking mainly of the factor of "good continuation". Since I am not concerned with proving that this factor is important in the field of music, or that it influences music, but rather, as I will try to show later, in the remembering and telling of life histories, Koffka's remarks on music may be ignored here.

tone. But the still resonating first tone is also qualified by the second one. This happens, for example, if no melody was anticipated with the first tone and only with the second tone was the first one perceived as belonging to it. As in the perception of optical entities, the individual parts modify each other. In temporal processes we can assume that there is a tendency not only to perceive the second action as following the first one, but also to perceive it as being caused by the first one. But likewise, a noema that has just existed can be reorganized by the non-fulfillment of an expectation in such a way that it is incorporated into a new noematic system and thus acquires a completely new meaning. This reorganization can lead to a temporal modification in which the first action presents itself as being conditional upon the second action. Such temporal modification, i.e., a reorganization of temporal processes, plays a considerable role in memory processes and the present perception of past events.

Strictly speaking, looking at an object is an irreversible temporally directed action which depends on retention and protention; this can be seen in the fact that the area of "sharply focused" seeing is very small. Only by a mental effort does the whole facade of a house appear to us to be "sharply focused". The way our gaze "shifts" and the temporalization of the act of looking can be observed experimentally by gaze-recording devices.

2.1.3 The presentation of social processes

To illustrate the reorganization of past acts that still exist in retention, let us discuss an example from the social world. Let us imagine that we observe a man approaching a child and extending his hand to him at the level of his cheek. We can interpret this single gesture only by seeing it as part of an anticipated whole. For example, we can perceive it as the beginning of an affectionate gesture and anticipate that the man will touch the child's cheek and caress it. According to the rules of our culture, we could perceive this as a "meaningfully good continuation", an action which would be completed by the stroking of the cheek and withdrawal of the hand. So, without knowing the motives of the interactors, we perceive the single gesture as part of an action which we typify as a loving action. Thus, this part offers itself to our perception as a "hand, stretched out for a loving gesture". If, however, something else follows this gesture, namely that the man pulls the child violently by the earlobe, a reinterpretation of the first gesture is imposed on us by the continuation of the action. The overall action now no longer presents itself to us as loving, but rather as punishing. The first observed gesture, present in retention, is modified retrospectively when the man begins pulling the child's earlobe. If, on the other hand, the man's first gesture is followed by the child taking fright and running away, we can perceive this as a reaction by the child to a threatening and unpleasant touch, although the man's intention might have been to show his affection. With this reading, the outstretched hand could be understood as a follow-up action to the perception of a frightened child and not as the beginning of this sequence of actions.

In general terms, we can say that even in temporal processes we cannot assume that the presentation of the sequential order of individual acts, or an understanding of individual components due to their situatedness in the process, exist independently of the perceiver. The organizedness and thus meaning of a temporal process is constituted by the noematic and the noetic sides of perception, just like that of a static entity. As will be shown, a social event, just like a static entity, presents itself differently depending on the way the observer focuses on one component. At which point of a social event an observer starts to observe at all, whether he perceives an imagined whole at the first observed act, upon which the other act follow analogously – in the sense of anticipated subsequent action, or whether he only sees the Gestalt of a process on observing the third act, and accordingly reorganizes the first and the second act, depends on his approach to the social event, and on the presentation resulting from it – and vice versa. Even though a specific evolving sequence is preset in temporal space as opposed to a static object, I assume that the perception of an object is structurally no different from the uninvolved observation of a process. Although the temporal sequence imposes certain presentations of the event rather than others, these are not determined by the sequence alone, but rather by the focusing of certain parts, i.e., from which part the whole is inferred.

The perception of a social event by those who are themselves involved in the interaction is to be distinguished from uninvolved observation. The uninvolved observer has no direct access to the intentions of the interaction partners, and thus no influence on the progress of the action. While the uninvolved observer depends solely on typification for the interpretation of an action, and attributes certain intentions and goals to the actor on this basis, the involved observer uses typification to anticipate the intentions of his interaction partner and s them a component of his own actions (cf. Schütz 1932; engl. 1967). In the interaction with another person, we plan our own action in the light of the anticipated action of the other person, so that this anticipated action already becomes a component of our own action.

The actual action of our interaction partner is in a mode of fulfillment or non-fulfillment with respect to what we expect of him, just as my action is in a mode of fulfillment or non-fulfillment for him (Schütz 1932/1974: 239). Thus, on the one hand, the involved person can test the designs and motives of the other person in actual practice, whereas the observer can only check his perceptions by continued observation. On the other hand, the involved person also has a share in the fulfillment of his assumptions even if these do not coincide with the original intentions of the interaction partners.

Formulated from the noematic side, being involved differs from being uninvolved in that the observer involved in the interaction can help the presentation of his interaction partner's preceding action to be fulfilled by his own action. By contrast, the uninvolved observer has no influence on the progress of the action and thus no part in the fulfillment of the anticipated overall action.

Let us now transfer these considerations to the example of the interaction between the man and the child. Let us assume that the child perceives the outstretched hand of the man as the beginning of an unpleasant contact. This results in the child being startled and running away. With this action, the child has co-constituted the meaning of the gesture, quite independently of the man's motives. As a result of this behavior, the man's gesture can no longer develop into a loving touch. His outstretched hand presented itself to the child as threatening, and the continuation of the action (being frightened and running away) prevents a possible reinterpretation of this gesture for the child. Such a reinterpretation would be possible only if the child were to take another look at the gesture, but this would require special motivation, since it is not imposed by the course of action (unless the man talks to the child about it). Without this readdressing, the man's gesture will continue to present itself to the child in secondary memory as the beginning of an unpleasant contact. Thus, the rememberer will not only interpret the gesture as unpleasant, but it will continue to present itself to him as such.

In contrast to the uninvolved observer of processes and things, an involved person thus plays a role in the fulfillment of the designs or protentions. The uninvolved perceiver has no influence on the house as a thing, nor on whether a gesture develops into a loving or a punishing one. In contrast to an involved person, he also has no influence on whether a process develops into a Gestalt and a social event. In the case of involvement, on the other hand, if an action by one person is perceived by the other person as the beginning of an overall action, this alone can have a Gestalt-producing effect. If the agent perceives gestures made by the other person as referring to himself and initiating interaction, as George Herbert Mead (1934) discussed with his concept of significant symbols, and if he responds to this with a significant gesture, a social action results from this, regardless of whether the first gesture was intended by the other person to be significant. Thus it becomes possible that we can understand our action as caused by the interaction partner, although his behavior did not refer to us: it only presented itself as referring to us.

The progress of a social event is thus essentially determined by the point at which the participants locate the beginning of a social action, and how this beginning of action presents itself to them. Every beginning of an action is thus always a restriction of the potential possibilities of the continuation. If the continuation fulfills the protentions of the agents, there is no need for them to revise their perception, seen from the noematic side, i.e., without motivations coming from other sources. The noematic side imposes reorganization only if expectations are not fulfilled, while seen from the noetic side, the agent can question the course of action by voluntarily addressing it.

2.2 The intention of the agent

With our last remarks we moved increasingly to the noetic side of perception. Whether certain circumstances or events are given to the subject "cannot be determined by physical examination of the individual real objects, but only by considering the relation of these objects to the organism", writes Kurt Koffka (1915: 33, translated from the German) in his discussion with Benussi, in which he rejects the assumption of constancy of both stimuli and sensations. Depending on the attention I pay to the given, it appears to me in different ways. Which noema in which noematic system presents itself to me *also* depends on the way I approach it. And yet this approach is constituted by the noema.

Normally, however, in theories of action in the tradition of Max Weber, which give preference to intentionality, attention is ascribed a special egocentricity ("Ichhaftigkeit"): "From the ego emanates a 'ray of vision' which throws light on the object" (Waldenfels 1983: 19; translated from the German). Despite Alfred Schütz's (1932) efforts to overcome this intentionalist bias in

Max Weber, he himself remains stuck in Weber's rationalist model and in the dominance of noesis. How I perceive something, and thus how it presents itself to me, depends, according to Schütz, solely on the attention I pay to it, my interest and my relevancies.

In his theory of relevance, Alfred Schütz (1970; 1966: 116 ff.) analyzed these noetic points of view differently from Aron Gurwitsch. He names three types of relevancies: Motivational Relevance, Thematic (or Topical) Relevance, and Interpretive Relevance. How a window presents itself to an architect is different from how it presents itself to a window cleaner. The different motives of the architect and the window cleaner determine which aspects of the house are of interest to them. Because of their different relevance systems and their different operational knowledge, their motives differ. The structural design of the roof may be of interest to the architect, whereas the accessibility of the windows may be of interest to the window cleaner. The respective interests of the agents thus determine which aspects of the world surrounding them they draw upon to define their situation of action. These aspects of the world surrounding them can come from the immediate world of perception as well as from the imaginable world of memory. If I think about my past, my interests will influence the way I select experiences from my memory (cf. chapter 3.1).

A person's interests are embedded in a superordinate life plan: "Motivational relevance sets behavior in the current situation in meaningful relation to life plans and daily schedules, and this applies to routine decisions as well as to 'extraordinary decisions'" (Schütz/Luckmann 1979: 256; translated from the German). The motive of any interpretation is determined by past experiences: If the architect was once responsible for a problematic roof construction in a similar house, she will, for this reason alone, take a closer look at the roof of this house. The "because motive" of her action is her wish to avoid such mistakes in the future, and the "in-order-to motive" shapes her action, which has the goal of closely inspecting the roof which she now perceives.

"While the in-order-to motive, starting from the intended project, explains the constitution of the action, the because motive explains the constitution of the project from past experiences" (Schütz 1932/1974: 123; translated from the German). The thematic relevance determines that something becomes a topic, i.e., is in need of interpretation, because it can no longer be automatically brought into congruence by the agent with his previous stock of knowledge, i.e., the routine course of experience comes to a standstill. If a window strikes a window cleaner as difficult to clean because of its covering, it becomes an issue because of the anticipated blockage in the window cleaner's course of action. Again, the interpreter's past experience plays a role: so far, he has not been able to incorporate into her knowledge stock anything that would lead to an automatic interpretation of the situation. For the interpretation of the problem that now exists, those aspects are relevant that can contribute to its solution. Here Schütz speaks of interpretive relevance.

These three relevance structures cannot be thought of as separate from each other and occurring in a particular order. They are intertwined. "Only in reflective access can one or the other relevance emerge 'first', in which case it can be conceived as the 'basic' relevance, while the other two relevance structures appear as conditioned by it" (Schütz/Luckmann 1979: 277; translated from the German). In the context of the present study, the relevance concept will not be used analytically because it unilaterally favors the ego side, or intentionality. Instead, a non-egological variant of the constitution of order is preferred here, which does not exclude noesis as achieved by the biographer, but also does justice to the noema as a precondition for this achievement.

2.3 The formal organization of what is presented

2.3.1 On the origin of organization

Decisive for conceiving the relationship between noema and noesis as a Gestalt is the consideration that the different organizedness of the facade for the two observers is not only the product of their intentional action, looking at the facade, but that the noema predetermines a structuredness. Dualistic conceptions can be overcome by making a Gestalt analysis of the noema, a phenomenological analysis, and consistently rejecting the assumption of constancy. Although Husserl abandoned analysis of the world of things with the dichotomy of sensuous givens on the one hand and order-creating noetic acts on the other, the constancy assumption crept back into his conception of noema and noesis. According to Husserl's understanding, organizedness is imposed on the noema from the outside, and the organization of the total perceptual noema is attributed to "noetic factors" (Gurwitsch 1964/2010: 261). Thus, in Husserl we also have "stratification of *inferiora* and *superius*. Upon an underlying matter a 'higher' datum, a, 'quality of the second order' is founded" (Gurwitsch 1929/1966: 253).

This idea that something is added to a given, where the given, depending on its nature, appears in a different light, can be found in the theory of William James (1905). James cannot completely free himself from dualism, despite his criticism of the dualism of elementaristic and atomistic theories. While rejecting these, he conceives every act of consciousness as a unified and undivided whole and discusses the meaning of what is perceived as constituting itself from its placement in the stream of consciousness. He assumes that organizedness comes from outside into the stream of experience (Gurwitsch 1964/2010: 23 f.). Only ostensibly is the independence of the event-world from the experience-world thus given up. As long as an indissoluble interrelation is not assumed, the illusion of a promising search for the things and processes *per se*, without the "additional" subjective, continues to exist. Behind the concept of "subjective perspective" or "subjective experience", which is so popular in the social sciences, we too often find the dualist concept of an event that is independent of the perceiving subject and his different experiences. According to this concept, the observer or involved agent perceives the "objective" reality in a particular way, in the sense that something is added to it: it is seen more brightly or more dully, some parts are overlooked while others are overemphasized in their importance, and so on. Each observer or involved agent perceives the reality differently. In this conception, if the perceiver modifies his perspective, the perceived object remains unchanged, it only appears in a different light. Gurwitsch (1929/1966: 265) objects: "Attentional modifications must, therefore, not be considered as changes in illumination; nor is the comparison with the moving beam of light appropriate at all. On the contrary, attentional modifications affect the material content of the noema to such an extent that a radically different noema results".

To illustrate this intervention in the factual content of a noema, its structurally different presentation depending on the particular noesis, Gurwitsch (1929) discusses the impressive example of how Chinese characters are perceived by a person who can read Chinese, on the one hand, and a reader who cannot, on the other hand. Each of these observers sees the characters in a completely different way. According to the 'illumination assumption' this can be explained by saying that for the person who knows how to read Chinese, meaning is added to the strokes, which are also perceived by the one who does not know how to read them; he thus sees more than the one for whom the strokes are meaningless. Thus, according to this understanding, both are presented with something which is identical but which has more or less meaning. To counter this, we can say that in both cases the formal inner organization of the perceptual noema alternates. That which is "immediately given to either of us, what either perceives, is not the same object" (Gurwitsch 1929/1966: 255).

The ambiguous figures so popular in Gestalt theory are another example. Figure and ground can change here; what at one time I see as the figure, I may see another time as the ground. This is the case in the following image discussed by Edgar Rubin (1921):

Chart 2
Source: Rubin (1921)

We can see both a white cross on a black background and a black cross on a white background. One time we make the white the center of our interest and another time the black. By paying attention to one part, this part offers itself in its character as a figure and thus stands out from a background. As long as I focus on the black cross on a white background, the white cross is absorbed in the background; its visual form is non-existent (cf. Köhler 1947: 107). The alternation, however, cannot be understood as an intellectual activity that is added to the perception of the images, by which individual parts of the image are regrouped. The picture presents itself as a particular Gestalt, depending on whether it is centered on black or white. The noetic act thus does not create the Gestalt-like quality of the figures through the composition of individual elements, but by concentrating on white or black, the picture imposes a perception on the viewer. This ambiguous image is a so-called unstable figure in which both perceptions are of equal importance and can be changed back again at any time (Wertheimer 1923: 339). In other ambiguous images, one figure may tend to dominate. The example of the Chinese characters, on the other hand, is an image in which, once one figure has been seen, the other can no longer be perceived. Changing back to the image of meaningless characters that was once perceived is no longer possible. With learning to read, the characters are presented in a completely different way and can no longer be seen as strokes, as before, but only as signs. With the acquisition of new "ways of seeing", or, in the language of Jean Piaget, new "schemata", not only does what was previously presented change in its structuredness, but the change can become irreversible. This is always the case when a formerly perceived chaos is transformed into something ordered. Once we have succeeded in perceiving what is presented to us as a Gestalt, we can no longer see it otherwise (Koffka 1963: 507). Once we have learned the signs – such as the Latin letters that we can read – we can no longer see them in the same way as before the learning process, despite any attempt to see them from our previous perspective. If it is hardly possible to break down individual words into their letters again, it is completely impossible to break down the letters themselves into strokes.

Experience does not come into play additionally in perceiving, but with experience, what is perceived is reorganized. In perceiving social processes, we can change perspectives and thus view them differently, but here too we can assume a dominance of the present perspective. If we see something that was previously hidden from us, or if something becomes ordered that was previously incomprehensible, we will not retreat from this perception, provided that what is now perceived is not subject to psychological resistance. As adults, we experience again and again in our interaction with children how difficult it is to regard an object or a process in the same way that we once perceived it in the past. Perhaps we can still remember that we too once had difficulties in forming formal logical groups and, when looking at five red and two yellow flowers, that we saw more red flowers than the total number of flowers. But we cannot see the flowers in this way again today, since they present themselves to us as a coherent group. We probably don't even remember seeing them differently as children. If anything, we remember that we were blocked in our actions because our mother was annoyed by our perception and thought we were pulling her leg. What we remember are the situations in which there were disturbances, i.e., the experience of crises in learning new schemata, and not what was presented to us at the time (cf. chapter 3.1). This applies both to the area of cognitive competence, for example the competence to form groups, and to the social competence which allows us to assume roles or to make moral judgements (cf. Kohlberg 1974). To some extent, this consideration can also be applied to the interpretation of social phenomena. If the behavior of our mother, which we once saw as caring and protective, is now presented to us as oppressive and aggressively intended by her, the old perception will be absorbed by the new one. We can still reconstruct the old perception, but we can no longer see or remember our mother's behavior accordingly.

Because it argues that perceived objects present themselves to us differently, and because it rejects the idea that experiences in the present lead to the addition of new meanings, Gestalt theory has been accused of ignoring history. Jean Piaget (1973:383), who wanted to make Gestalt theory "more mobile" "by replacing its a priorism with a genetic relativism", objects to it as attributing the reorganization of perception exclusively to the maturity of the individual and thus as independent of his past. Piaget's criticism of Gestalt theory can be agreed with insofar as it opposes the existence of Gestalts and their organized nature independent from the act of perception or their rootedness in the nervous system of the organism. But even if the question of the origin of organizedness in Gestalt theory remains mostly unanswered or contradictory, this does not mean that the basic assumption of Gestalt theory ignores history, that in the current situation of perception and perceptual organization, earlier experiences do not additionally come into play. Rather, past experiences are understood as determining the organized nature of what is presented, and thus the past extends into the present without being seen as an additional component.

Gurwitsch (1964/2010: 344 ff.) then argues against Piaget's conception of the application of schemata acquired in the past that there must first be a "something" that can be included in a schema in order to be able to apply a schema at all. Piaget discusses the *reorganization of schemata* in the process of accommodation, the change of structures under the influence of the environment, in contrast to traditional learning theory, in which learning is only seen as being able to do more and not as being able to do differently. But the *reorganization of objects* escapes him. If we perceive the characters we have learned to read, they present themselves legibly "without an explicit recall of the situation of action in which the object was reorganized and acquired its functional character" (Gurwitsch 1964/2010: 97). Husserl (CM: p. 111) discusses the following example: when a child learns the use of scissors, it "understands, let us say, for the first time the final sense of scissors; and from now on he sees scissors at the first glance as scissors but naturally not in an explicit reproducing, comparing, and inferring. We are dealing here with a double reorganization: on the one hand, the child learns the new behavioral scheme of using scissors and, on the other hand, the object "scissors" restructures itself with its newly acquired instrumentality. The influence of the past on the perception of the object as scissors "must be accounted for in terms of reorganization and reconstruction. When a perception is experienced after some reorganization has occurred, the corresponding percept depends *as a whole and for its entire structure* upon both the present stimulation and the previous occurrence of the reorganization in question" (Gurwitsch 1964/2010: 256 f).

While Gestalt theory emphasizes the structure of the perceptual field, Piaget gives the perceptual field its structure through organizing activity. Both conceptions, with their concentration on one side, harbor a dualism that could be circumvented in their intermediate area. Just as we cannot consider noesis independently of the noema, we cannot consider the noema independently of noesis. The orderliness with which the noema presents itself is thus inherent neither in the noema nor in noesis, but is constituted by the interrelation between the two. Here, correspondences can be found in Piaget's dialectical conception of the interaction between environment and organism: "No subjects without an influence on the objects, no objects without a structuring that is brought about by the subject" (Waldenfels 1980: 136, translated from the German). Bernhard Waldenfels discusses Piaget's structuralism as a conception beyond subjectivism and objectivism and refers to Maurice Merleau-Ponty (1942/1976: 200), for whom the dialectic of human practice consists in the ability to "transcend created structures in order to create others from them". Merleau-Ponty's special merit in this context is that he tries to undermine the dualism of inside and outside, of body and soul "by having recourse to the lived and experienced unity" (Waldenfels 1980: 36 f.). Merleau-Ponty (1976), who also uses concepts from Gestalt theory in his theory of perception, locates organizedness or structuredness in the "intermediate area of ambiguity": in this ambiguous in-between area, the world merges into the I and the I merges into the world. The structure is neither thing nor idea, neither does it belong to a purely external world or to a purely internal world. In this way, he rejects the idea of structuredness achieved by consciousness and structuredness residing in things, as he still sees it represented by the Berlin Gestalt theorists. Contrary to this criticism of Gestalt theory, Waldenfels at least traces reflections in Koffka (1963: 11–16) on an inner togetherness between inside and outside, and tries to understand this togetherness as both separateness and belonging together, using the concept of behavior, following phenomenology, especially Merleau-Ponty. In behavior he sees (1980: 65) a "unification that presents itself as internalization of the external and divestment of the internal". Waldenfels – like Merleau-Ponty – rejects a view in which inside and outside coincide; rather, he understands behavior as entanglement in the sense of "unity in difference". By this is meant: "a partial congruence, an overlapping of different spheres or, conversely, difference on the ground of an immediate unity and in the horizon of a unity to be mediated" (Waldenfels 1980: 65; translated from the German). He thus argues for a dual, but not dualistic conception. Inner and outer are conceived here neither as separate nor as coinciding spheres, but as mutually determining and relativizing moments of a structuring process.

Ludwig Binswanger's critical discussion (1931/1955: 147 ff.) of Erwin Straus' (1930/1978) only partially successful attempt to overcome the dualism of event and experience, and thus to reject qualification of the event as objective and experience as subjective, is another very convincing step toward a dialectical conception. "The concepts of individuality and world, inner and outer life history, and the concepts of experience and event, which emerge from the same antithesis, stand in a dialectical reciprocal relationship, insofar as in thinking one concept the other must always be thought along with it and vice versa, and insofar as the actual construction of human individuality can be 'comprehended' at all only from the living penetration of this dialectic" (Binswanger 1955: 148; translated from the German). Binswanger argues against Straus that meaning can neither be taken from an event nor put into it, since there is no event in itself. Rather, everything that happens is always an event that has already been interpreted. Although Erwin Straus (1978: 30) assumes a "compelling bond between event and experience", he nevertheless discusses the existence of events – such as borderline situations in the terminology of Karl Jaspers – that impose a certain experience, the compulsion to a certain "taking of meaning". In this way, he once again gives the event the status of something that is independent from experience. Binswanger, on the other hand (1955: 155; translated from the German), completely rejects the existence of events independent from experience: "We have seen that there is no such thing as 'the happening' or 'event', because everything that happens or occurs has already been interpreted in such and such a way".

Whether something is perceived at all, and how it is perceived, depends, as Straus has discussed, not on the intensity of the sensory stimuli, but on the observer's biographically conditioned perception, on the meaning that the perceived has for the perceiver. Just as the event does not imposes a certain meaning that can be extracted, one cannot speak of an "insertion of meaning". "But the 'meaning' is not something between two poles; rather, it is always a way of understanding and interpreting the world 'from the perspective' of an individuality; here it should again be noted that individuality and world are by no means 'absolute' but dialectical opposites, in accordance with Hegel's lapidary comment: "individuality is what its own world is" (Binswanger 1955: 157; translated from the German).

2.3.2 Organizedness: theme, field, margin

As explained above, the field of experience – whether of perceptual objects or processes, of memories or fantasies – presents itself as already ordered. It can only be perceived as being structured. In the intentional act of considering the world, an intention to consider "something" is required, which, since we intend to consider it, is already given to us. "The seizing-upon is a singling out and seizing; anything perceived has an experiential background" (Husserl, Ideas I: p. 70). In order to emerge from the diffuse horizon and appear as something, it requires a division into shape and background: the only condition "that the something in question must be segregated and detached from its environment" (Gurwitsch 1964/2010: 41). A field without differentiation gives no starting point for an act of perception. The something that stands out from a background is in a multidimensional horizon of reference to the past, the present and the future. We grasp it as a something with a certain meaning, and a horizon of potentialities opens up in which "the current Gestalt never exhausts all possibilities and leaves room for reshaping and new shapes" (Waldenfels 1980: 66, translated from the German).

In the beginning there is not chaos, but difference. Gestalt theorists empirically demonstrate that the figure-ground relationship is an irreducible structure of perception. Their analyses show that neither a figure without a reason nor a reason without a figure can exist: "Mere ground would be equivalent to no consciousness at all" (Koffka 1922: 566). The above example of the black and white cross makes clear that the figure has no identity. Rather, the enclosed and enclosing surfaces can be interchanged. The difference between figure and ground as the phenomenon of a structure that is not constituted by individual elements but by their position in relation to each other implies a fundamental openness to transformation. The structure does not change quantitatively by the addition or removal of individual elements or by shadowing, depending on external influences, but is subject to qualitative restructuring. "Accordingly, the course of experience can be interpreted as a process of structuring and restructuring", writes Waldenfels (1980: 136, translated from the German), following Piaget. Aron Gurwitsch, using Gestalt theory, discusses organizedness as an "autochthonous" trait of consciousness. Formal organization is an invariant of *all* fields of consciousness. No field of consciousness – regardless of its content – exists without this organization. It is always divided into *three* specifically structured areas: "theme", "thematic field" and "margin". What was referred to as a figure by Edgar Rubin (1921), with regard to the perception of optical structures, is transferred by Gurwitsch, with his concept of theme, to all processes of consciousness, i.e., to immediate perception, as well as to memory or fantasized imagination. The theme is that with which we occupy ourselves at a given moment, that which is at the focus of our attention, and is in each case embedded in a thematic field. Gurwitsch, in a further development of Husserl's distinction between an inner and outer horizon, the horizon that co-determines the mode of perception and the open, endless horizon of co-objects "which I am not now actually turned but toward which I can turn at any time" (Husserl, EJ: p. 33), makes a further division of the background. The thematic field does not coincide with the totality of the theme. Only those circumstances co-present with the theme, "which are experienced as materially relevant or pertinent to the theme", are constituents of the thematic field (Gurwitsch 1964/2010: 4). The margin, on the other hand, includes those circumstances that are only temporally co-present.

If we look at a painting and hear noises in the background, they are given in time, but unlike the blue background of the figures in the painting, they have no inner connection to the painting. The noises belong to the margin. If, on the other hand, our thoughts drift to other paintings, we continue to move in the thematic field, which we may call "painting". With the presence of other paintings, we move from one part of the field to the next, we move from theme to theme – as in the telling of stories that all belong to one thematic field. The margin can also move to the center of our attention at any time. In this case, however, there is not a modification within the field, as in moving from theme to theme, but alternation from one field to another. If, for example, we identify the sounds as a melody, we make the change to another thematic field, that of music. Then the picture moves to the periphery,

On the Gestalt nature of experience

provided we do not combine painting with music, i.e., do not see them as parts of a common field. In the flow of perception, modifications of theme, field and margin can thus take place constantly.

Gurwitsch's achievement lies precisely in the fact that he discusses not only the organized nature of the individual aspects of the theme, but also that of the field. Potential further themes of the field are not simply added to it – like the margin – but have an inner relationship with it and a specific arrangement. This relationship is based on relevance, and not, as in the case of the margin, solely on the temporal relationship, inherent in every act of consciousness, to the actions that have preceded it or will follow it (Gurwitsch 1943b/1966; 1964/2020). The contents of the field are related to the theme because they are relevant to it. The contents of the margin, on the other hand, are co-present with the theme, but are not substantially related to it; they are irrelevant to both the theme and the thematic field.

We are dealing with three different types of connections. In the case of the constituents of the theme, Gurwitsch follows the Gestalt conception of *unity through Gestalt coherence*, i.e., the continuous interrelation between all components of the Gestalt. The connection between theme and thematic field, on the other hand, is based on *unity through relevance*. By contrast, the connection between the thematic field, the theme and the margin is purely temporal. The two first-mentioned types are Gestalt-like wholes, where one unity presupposes the other: unity through relevance is only possible between Gestalt formations that are themselves connected by coherence. Let us recall the ambiguous figure of the black and white cross: here the white background is determining or relevant for the presentation of the black cross, but it is not a component of it, i.e., it is not connected to it by Gestalt coherence. The conditions of the white surface are not included in the components of the black figure. But this white background, this field, in contrast to the margin surrounding it, which in Rubin's work is gray, is related in itself through Gestalt coherence; it is a Gestalt unity for itself. The connection between theme and field is a Gestalt one, even if it is not based on Gestalt coherence. The thematic field is not an arbitrary accumulation of items, but these are in a certain arrangement with the theme and substantially related to it. Their connection is a Gestalt connection. "Appearing as units, delimited and detached from one another items of the thematic field exhibit the same organizational structure as the theme and also independence in the same sense of consolidation and segregation" (Gurwitsch 1964/2010: 356).

In contrast to the egological conception of thematic relevance according to Alfred Schütz, relevance here means relevance for the theme and not for the subject. For Schütz, something becomes relevant as a theme because the subject can no longer easily transfer it into the state of the unproblematic. Gurwitsch himself demarcates his concept from Schütz's: "According to Schütz, relevancy denotes a relationship in which objects and items stand to the Ego with regard to Ego's plans and designs, not, as with us, the relationship of mutual pointing reference of these items" (1964/2010: 333). In this respect, Schütz's self-understanding (1966: 126) that Gurwitsch's concept of relevance is a special case of his "thematic relevance" is misleading (cf. Embree 1979: 75).

If, for example, we consider the theme of "My father, who was cruel" in the thematic field of "My childhood", this theme refers to other items in this thematic field, such as "My mother", regardless of whether or not we intend to deal with them. Schütz, on the other hand, would speak of thematic relevance when the mother's behavior becomes a theme because the autobiographer cannot accept it as unquestionable, and considers, for example, whether the mother tried to prevent the father's cruel behavior. Questionlessness or questionability as categories of the noetic side of perception, however, have an effect on the noematic side, since both sides always determine each other reciprocally. When Gurwitsch distinguishes between "definite" and more or less "vague" and "blurred" in respect of the items in the thematic field, this will be determined by the attitude of the perceiver, the direction of his interest and attention, just as the embedding of a theme in a specific field already is. On the noetic side, whether the theme "My father, who was cruel" is associated with the theme "My mother, who was unloving" in a relatively close and definite way, or whether the latter is vague and far removed from the former, depends on how I approach the theme, which in turn is determined by the field in which I embed it on the basis of my interest and motives. On the noematic side, on the other hand, it is determined by the references given in the theme. William James (1905, Vol. 1: 258 ff.) discusses these references using his concept of "fringes": "Let us call the consciousness of this halo of relations around the image by the name of 'psychic overtone' or 'fringe'" (ibid.: 166). Each theme is surrounded by fringes that create a web of relations and references of which we are only vaguely aware. The fringes link the individual theme (noema) with the systematically organized association of themes. They thus represent the link to the things themselves, since this link is established through the relationship between the individual noema and the systematically organized association. The fringes link the things ("topics of thoughts") with the noemata ("objects of thoughts"), since the reference to the "topic" is included in the reference to the context.

If, for example, I concentrate on the memory of a situation in which my father was cruel to me, and if, among other things, the behavior of my mother who was present at the time becomes present to me again, this theme refers to the theme immediately adjacent in the field: "My mother's behavior". In our example, where my mother was present in the experienced situation and behaved in a certain way, this further theme is not only given because of my attention to him, but the theme referring to this situation refers independently to my mother.

Because of the references of the theme, it always presents itself in certain contexts. In each case, different, albeit limited, contexts are given. The theme can be embedded in different fields, but these are not arbitrary, since the theme contains certain references and excludes others. The adjacent themes in any particular field determine the theme that is central at the moment of my paying attention to it. This indicates that a dialectical relationship between theme and field must be assumed: the field determines the theme and the theme determines the field. With the change of a theme from one field to another, the theme is modified, just as with the embedding of the theme in a specific field, this field is modified (cf. chapter 2.3.4).

2.3.3 The questionable identity of the theme

Aron Gurwitsch's discussion of the reciprocal relationship between theme and field shows some contradictions and indeterminacies. From the phenomenon that the theme stands apart from the field, as a "self-contained unity" "within well-defined boundaries" (1929/1966: 207), he derives not only a relative independence from the field, but he goes so far as to speak of an "identity of the theme" (1964: 345). From the embedding of the theme in different fields, he concludes that the theme would be preserved in its "core". If we persist in the natural approach, and do not believe in the identity of things, this assumption, supported by examples from the world of things, makes sense, since in our philosophical naivety we see "things" as simply given and as existing independently of the observer (cf. Bertalanffy 1966). It therefore takes some effort to strip the examples Gurwitsch took from Husserl – continuing the intention of these two philosophers – of their unquestionability; for example, when both authors assume that the "noematic nucleus" of an inkwell that was previously on the desk and is now on the piano remains the same in both places. One of the other examples chosen by Gurwitsch is the sentence: "Columbus discovered America in 1492". Regardless of whether I read this sentence in a book about the history of America or in one about the great geographical discoveries, it remains – according to Gurwitsch – the same. This example is also chosen in such a way that one accepts it too quickly without questioning it. By contrast, the idea of embedding this sentence in a book title such as "The Biography of Columbus" already raises doubts, since this focuses on a different aspect. In the terminology of Alfred Schütz[3] it is not the discovery of America but Columbus himself that is thematically relevant here. And we can generally assume that a different aspect of the theme is centered depending on the way it is embedded in a thematic field. This modification can be understood as meaning that we are dealing with a different theme. The inkwell on the desk in my study presents itself as a completely different theme from the inkwell on the piano in an art exhibition like the "Dokumenta" (an exhibition of contemporary art which takes place every five years in Kassel, Germany). Neither the inkwell nor a sentence in a book, nor the memory that comes to my mind remain identical in different contexts – if we follow a strictly noetic analysis and include the belief in the existence of things.[4] The inkwell or the sentence are preserved only in the sense of a formal unity, but the thing or the sentence cannot be identical with the theme, since the theme must be determined as the theme of "something". It carries meaning, and this is only constituted in the reciprocal dialectical relationship between theme and field. Depending on the field, the inkwell or the sentence can become an aspect of a superordinate theme, and is thus no longer a detached entity in the sense of the theme described by Gurwitsch. Thus, Gurwitsch himself writes: "Whenever a theme is given in a thematic field, this situation by its very nature implies the possibility that through a new act the entire field of consciousness is made a unitary theme to which, in turn, a new thematic field then belongs" (1929/1966: 249).

---

3 See also the problematization – according to Schütz in his correspondence with Gurwitsch – of what the theme or aspects of this movement are (Grathoff 1985: 242).

4 For a discussion of the structural similarity between the perception of physical and mental phenomena, between the external and internal worlds, see the very entertaining article by Ludwig von Bertalanffy (1966).

Let us return to Gurwitsch's conception of identity. For him, depending on the field, not only the sentence quoted above remains the same, but also the theme. Thus, something is added to the field in which it is located. To quote Gurwitsch (1964/2010: 313 f.): "the theme appearing in the light and under the perspective of the field", or "by a shift of attitude, one thematic field may supersede another, and yet the theme remains the same". In contrast to his conception of the structuredness of the theme as a Gestalt, he reintroduces here, unnoticed by himself, the assumption of constancy. However, since he is actually concerned with refuting it, and his own analyses contradict it, he gets caught up in inconsistencies and vagueness. In the end, however, he cannot free himself from the idea of an identity of the subject. Thus, he takes from Husserl (Ideas I: § 91; § 130) the problematic division of noema into a "noematic character" and a "noematic nucleus" which is invariant, unlike the character. The character refers to the noema's mode of being in terms of perception; in Husserl's "Ideas", this means first of all whether it is intended in immediate perception, in memory or in imagination. The core, on the other hand, is the factual content that is given in this way and remains the same even when given in different ways. In this way, Husserl describes the independence of the noema from the thing, i.e., the noema is not affected by the changes that the "real thing" can undergo. Even if the perceived tree has been felled, for example, it is still given to me in memory: "Still the tree can be remembered and imagined as appearing from a certain side, under a certain aspect, briefly, as presenting itself in that manner of appearance corresponding to a previous perception" (Gurwitsch 1964/2010: 173). The nucleus of the noema is still the same, but its character has been modified; it is now no longer given to me in perception, but in memory. In "Logical Investigations" (LI II § 20), Husserl discusses the example later taken up by Gurwitsch: the existence of people on Mars can be asserted, negated or imagined, and in each case the noematic character changes, but not the nucleus.

In my opinion, Husserl can be agreed with to the extent that the tree remains as an intended thing, whether it is perceived or remembered as a formerly perceived thing, since both perception and memory noemata refer to this one intended tree. Different noemata in a noematic system thus overlap because they are linked by their respective relation to an intended object, whether perceived, remembered or imagined. We also have overlapping of the noemata in the conception of people on Mars, whether asserted, imagined or negated. Isn't every negation, like the assertion, based on imagining? With the distinction between variants and invariants within the noema,

60 ON THE GESTALT NATURE OF EXPERIENCE

Husserl locates invariance in the noema itself and not in the relation of the noematic system to the perceived or remembered objects. The concept of the "nucleus" and the associated idea of something that surrounds it, but does not change it, must also be rejected. Otherwise we lapse again into a conception of something constant, to which, depending on the illumination, something is added, against which Gurwitsch so convincingly argued with the help of Gestalt theory. Thus Husserl (Ideas I: p. 224 f.) also speaks of changes of illumination in attentional modifications, different modes of the subject's attention in relation to the noema, which "do not change the object in its own meaning", i.e. the core, "but brightness and darkness modify the way it appears".

In the following sentence, however, he takes back this assumption of constancy: "Obviously the modifications in the noema are not such a kind that mere outward adjuncts are added to something which remain unvaryingly identical; on the contrary the concrete noemas change through and through, it being a question of necessary modes belonging to the mode in which the identical is given". It is not the noema or its core that remains identical, but – in a convincing overcoming of the assumption of constancy – the object to which it refers. Gurwitsch himself also oscillates – first in his dissertation published in 1929 and later in "Field of Consciousness" published in 1957 – between accepting and rejecting the conception of a constant theme understood independently of the field. His oscillation is evident, for example, in formulations such as "this invariance is not absolute" (1929/1966: 228), where he refers to certain "shapings of consciousness" – such as the color of a figure that changes by being embedded in another background – in which "the theme itself also suffers modifications of some kind". His attempt to define the type of connection between field and theme also illustrates his contradictions. First, he thinks (1929/1966: 233) that the connection corresponds to the "additive sum" described by Wertheimer, the pieces put together in arbitrary linkage[5], only to revise this statement in the very next sentence: It is not a matter of an "additive sum" in the "pure and pregnant sense", but rather of Koffka's "'and-connection' of isolated ... fully articulated partial wholes". He

---

5 "What appears to be joined together, at the same time, next to each other, one after the other, is in principle arbitrary; for the being together, the 'content' or the togetherness of contents is actually irrelevant. No factual moments are conditional for the being-together, but rather non-contentual, 'fact-external' factors, such as, for example, often having been together, simultaneous observance, etc." (Wertheimer 1922: 50, translated from the German).

ON THE GESTALT NATURE OF EXPERIENCE   61

then formulates his further definition in the subjunctive: "Perhaps one does justice to this state of affairs only by considering the Gestalt connection binding up the thematic field to the theme as somehow relaxed. However, there is an appreciable difference between a Gestalt connection, however relaxed, and a pure 'additive sum', and just this difference prevents us from speaking here of an 'and-connection'" (ibid. 234).

2.3.4 Theme and thematic field of a narrated story

How can theme and field be determined? The theme is based on a self-contained unit, but formal syntactic units like sentences, or pragmatic ones like narratives, cannot be identical with the theme. A sentence or a narrative refers to "something", and this "something" has yet to be determined. A sentence or a narrative only presents itself as a certain theme on the basis of the sentences or narratives surrounding it. If we were to assume that the sentence or narrative is the theme, theme would be a meaningless category.

In order to clarify this relationship between formally determinable units on the one hand, and themes and fields on the other, I will discuss the above-mentioned example of a narrated story about a "cruel father", which is based on the narrative of the daughter of a Nazi doctor who was involved in euthanasia crimes and was guilty of crimes against humanity (Rosenthal/Bar-On 1992).[6] So the autobiographer tells a story. If I now want to say what the story is about, I have to assume a theme. While assuming a theme is easy, reconstructing the theme as it was intended by the narrator is a much more difficult undertaking. But let us first assume, without quoting from the story, that it is a story about a situation in which the narrator, who was four years old at the time, smashed a glass door with her fists out of anger, and her father beat her so badly that she had to stay in bed afterwards. The theme is "My father who beat me up", which stands out as a memory noema with a narrative as a delimited unit from a thematic field. This narrative of the violent father can now be embedded in different thematic fields, and yet it is preserved both as a narrated story with a beginning, a plot block, a further

---

6 The narrative comes from a biographical narrative interview I conducted with Ms. Stegmann, as we call her. Previously, Dan Bar-On had interviewed her as part of his research on children of Nazi perpetrators (Bar-On 1989). For a comparison of the two interviews, see Rosenthal/Bar-On 1992.

course and an end[7], and as a memory unit of an experience, as a memory noema. It is questionable, however, whether the theme of the narrative also remains identical. Let us play through the following two fields as a thought experiment: "As a child I was irascible" or "My father, the Nazi doctor". The contents of the two fields would then be different. The first field would include, for example, "My aggression against my brother" or "My outbursts of rage at school", while the second field would include the father's deeds, such as his responsibility for the sterilization of forced laborers, or the sending of children to Hadamar and thus to death by gassing. With the narrative about the violent father, the two fields each take on a specific meaning. While the field "As a child I was irascible" is given the meaning that irascibility was severely punished, the field "My father, the Nazi doctor" is given the meaning "My father, the Nazi doctor, was also cruel to his own daughter". But to what extent do the fields modify the theme? If we carry out a thought experiment to change the attitude from field 1 to field 2, then "the violent Nazi perpetrator" is not just presented in a different light from the "violent father", but the violence appears more cruel, even sinister. If we then hear the narrator's assumption that her older, disabled brother was killed by his parents, the beatings present themselves as life-threatening! In field 1, we had perhaps considered the aspect that the daughter must have provoked her father considerably, but now our attention is focused on the aspect that the daughter had to stay in bed. With more knowledge about the further content of the two possible fields, it would become more and more obvious that the theme becomes strongly modified, and – this is my central thesis – that the theme can be a very different one depending on the field. The only thing that would remain "constant" would be the experience underlying the narrative and intended in the noema of experience.

By "constant" I mean neither that the narrative would be told identically depending on the theme – although I will also play this out below, at least as a thought-experiment, nor that the experience given in the memory would present itself in the same way regardless of the attitude to it of the narrator. Rather, what is meant by "constant" is that the experience presented in the memory and the narrated story – they are two sides of one process – each refer to one and the same experience actually had and sedimented in form of a Gestalt, which has certain references inherent in it (cf. chapter 3).

---

7 On the overall structure of narratives, cf. Labov/Waletzky (1967).

How the past experience presents itself is an immanent component of the noema of memory. What I mean is that an experience presented in a narrative relates to several possible fields, as the example mentioned above belongs to both the fields I have discussed. On the noematic side, the father cannot present himself to the biographer and possible readers in any other way than with reference to his crimes in the "Third Reich", insofar as the biographer and the readers are aware of these crimes. Likewise, the narrative that refers to an angry child has references to the field "As a child I was irascible". Here, it is clear that these references are by no means based on the experience at the time alone, but also on knowledge that comes later and thus on new classifications in the narrator's stock of knowledge. The crimes committed by the father only later, which the autobiographer perhaps only learned about as an adult woman, determine the references, as does a biographical global evaluation that was not yet established at the time: "I was irascible as a child". The noema of memory is thus constituted by the narrator's present; a present that results from the past, but which must not be understood in the sense that it is added to the past. But before I go into the relationship between what is experienced in the past and what is remembered in the present (chapter 3), it should first be clarified what the difference is between narrative and theme.

Here is the transcription of the narrative with Ms. Stegmann, as we call her:

"The second memory is a negative one. My eldest brother wasn't supposed to let me in through the door of the practice – my parents were away – but I was supposed to go in through the side entrance. The main idea – I heard later – was that the handle on the entrance door for the patients might be contaminated with bacteria or whatever if they touched it, and my parents feared infection, so we were supposed to go in through the side entrance. But the main entrance was so beautiful, it had a big glass door. And I was four years old and he wouldn't let me in, he was six years older. And then I broke this big double glass door with both fists, out of sheer anger that I had to enter through this stupid side entrance. When my parents came home, they didn't look to see if I was hurt. Surprisingly, I wasn't hurt at all, but I was miserably beaten up. According to my father, my temper was beaten out of me by his own temper. And my mother must have saved me from these beatings. Because at some point he stopped. But I was still lying in bed. I don't know how long that was. For me it was a very long time that I was injured, really injured and had to stay in bed. Whether that had to do with being saved by my mother, I don't know. But in my memory it had to do with the fact that I had been beaten so badly. And in retrospect I have the feeling that from then on I was a very good child" (translated from the German).

We can now imagine the course of this event: The older brother refused to let her enter by the main entrance, which also led to the father's practice, the girl smashed the glass pane, the parents came home and the father beat her up; the mother's behavior remains undetermined. This course of events does not yet make sense. Nevertheless, it can be assumed that every reader of this narrative will "find" a meaning without making any effort to impart or extract meaning that goes beyond comprehension of the event or is added to it, and thinks that he or she understands this narrative. But how can we understand a narrative without knowing how it is embedded in the overall context of the narrative? It presents itself to us as meaningful only if we assume a context – even without knowledge of the overall context – by determining the thematic field in which this narrative is embedded, and thus also its theme. By assuming a theme, we also, conversely, determine the thematic field. Without this assumption, the event has no meaning, neither for the child at that time, nor for the narrator today, nor for us as readers.

This embedding happens through the references to possible fields contained in the narrative, as well as through knowledge of, or presumptions about, external contextual data. With the information that the father, as a doctor, was involved in crimes against humanity, our perception of the narrative is already pre-structured when reading it. As discussed earlier, in the referential context "This Nazi perpetrator was also cruel to his daughter", we focus on the aspect of the violent father. In this case, the father is the theme of the narrative, around which the other aspects are arranged. We could just as well make the older brother's behavior, or his sister's suffering under him, the central component of the narrative. This reading might suggest itself to us if we ourselves suffered from an older brother. The thematic field would then be "My suffering under my older brother". This field is not only possible because of our imagination, but also the narrative contains this reference: the anger of the four-year-old was initially directed against the behavior of her brother. Likewise, we could focus our attention on the parents' fear of germs, and with the background knowledge that their behavior was determined by Nazi racial theory and ideas about hygiene, the meaning of the narrative would again undergo a reorganization.

As it turns out, the story told and the theme are by no means identical: a different theme is constituted depending on the embedding in a thematic field of the story told. It is not a matter of illumination changes, but the theme presents itself differently, similar to the way the Chinese characters present themselves differently to the person who can read Chinese and the person who cannot. It could be objected that despite the centering of different aspects, we are always moving within the same theme, which is composed of different aspects. The theme is, after all, the entire narrative or the experience underlying the narrative. This objection is only justified insofar as we understand the narrated story as a formal category. However, if we give the narrative or the experience a *meaning*, we also determine the arrangement of the individual aspects. If we follow the Gestalt conception of a unity of theme through Gestalt coherence, this means that a different theme results, depending on the arrangement. With every change in the arrangement of individual aspects of the narrative, which takes place depending on the centering, the whole structure changes. The same elements remain, but different Gestalts emerge from their different arrangement.

The apparent identity of the theme, or the apparent independence of a narrative from the thematic field of its context of origin or use, as well as the ease of a supposed understanding of the narrative, has far-reaching practical consequences for research. It leads to the narrative being subsumed under fields (i.e., categories) conceived by researchers, and not to a reconstruction of the fields in the context of origin. Precisely because a narrative, or other units of a text (such as arguments in respect of a certain topic), have a certain autonomy as self-contained entities, even social scientists who use hermeneutic and reconstructive methods are frequently under the illusion that they understand the meaning of these units in the context of origin without having reconstructed that context.[8] Whether the embedding of a narrative in a field anticipated by the interpreter corresponds with the field in the context of origin, and thus with its latent and manifest meanings for the narrator, can, as also in our example, only be conjectured on the basis of the references. Based on the references, we can develop various hypotheses about possible thematic fields, but their empirical verification requires the reconstruction of the text surrounding the narrative. Only then will it be possible to distinguish between what the narrator expresses today with this narrative according to her present-day perspective, and what this experience meant to her at the time. In addition, the references that are not elaborated in the rest of the text but are contained in the narrative make it possible to develop hypotheses about the reasons for their avoidance, i.e., to ask why the narrator could not or cannot take up these references. These questions can be

---

8 Thus, a detailed sequential analysis in the style of structural hermeneutics (cf. Oevermann et al. 1979; 1987) lacks, in my opinion, a systematic step of the analysis for reconstructing the sequential embedding of the text passage to be analyzed in the overall Gestalt of the text.

66 ON THE GESTALT NATURE OF EXPERIENCE

pursued by making a thematic field analysis of the overall text, in other words the biographical self-presentation in which this narrative is embedded.

2.3.5 Thematic field analysis of a biographical narrative[9]

In order to reconstruct the thematic field to which the narration of this story by Ms. Stegmann belongs, we need to have knowledge of what preceded the narration and what followed it. First, I ask my interviewee, who was born in 1934, to tell me her life history. In response to this invitation, she first asks whether she should also talk about her "many *siblings*", to which I reply, "if that is important to you". Ms. Stegmann then begins with a brief description of her *"first memory"*. It is about the happy time of her childhood, about the sun-drenched kitchen in her parents' house. A mood picture, in which no persons appear, is presented here, with no narration of experiences. Our first assumption is that Ms. Stegmann will subsequently say more about her happy childhood, and that perhaps this is the thematic field of her biographical narrative.

After explaining the order of her siblings, she says that her three older siblings, on the one hand, and she and her younger brother, with whom she no longer gets along, on the other hand, formed two separate units. Does this now mean that we are in the thematic field of "My happy childhood", to which belong a sunny kitchen and a good relationship with the younger brother, and from which the present is different? As her presentation progresses, this reading becomes implausible. What follows is her *"second memory"*, the narrative of how she was beaten by her father. Mother and father are introduced here into the biographical self-presentation with their problematic meaning for the autobiographer: we get the impression that the father was a brutal man; whether the mother helped her daughter remains unclear. If we look at the structure of the text, we notice that Hiltrud Stegmann expands her "second memory" narratively, while her "first" memory was only a brief mood picture. From this, the following hypothesis can be derived: the contents of the thematic field of her biographical self-presentation are not positive, but negative experiences. In order to confirm this reading, Ms. Stegmann would have to focus primarily on memories of painful situations in the course of her biographical narrative. The plausibility of this reading would be further sup-

---

9 On the procedure of sequential text and thematic field analysis, see chapter 6.2.

ON THE GESTALT NATURE OF EXPERIENCE 67

ported by the fact that negative experiences are narratively expanded, while positive ones are only hinted at. The thematic field could now be either "My sorrowful life", or, more restricted: "My sorrowful childhood" or "My suffering under my parents". Let us see how she continues. As her *next memory*, Hiltrud Stegmann illustrates with an exemplifying narrative[10] how she was *"dethroned"* by her younger brother. She says that her father played with her brother, while she just stood by and watched. Here the meaning of the question posed at the beginning, whether she should speak about her siblings, becomes clear. She not only formed a unit with her younger brother, but also suffered from the way he was given preference. She suffered from a father who beat her and put her at a disadvantage compared to her brother. Furthermore, the clearly ordered presentation of her childhood history is striking. Ms. Stegmann herself orders her presentation according to her "first", "second" and "next" memories. This is by no means an unprepared impromptu narrative, but the presentation seems prepared and as if she has frequently told it. Is engaging in a stream of storytelling, and thus re-experiencing, perhaps too threatening for her?

But first let us see how she continues. In the following sequence, another component of her "suffering" is introduced. She argues that in the so-called "Third Reich" girls did not count for much, and that she was conceived only because of the "Mother's Cross". She thus presents herself as fulfilling a function for a Nazi family. Does she perhaps see herself as a victim of the Nazi ideology or as a victim of a "Nazi family"? So we have some indications suggesting the reading that the contents of her thematic field are negative experiences, and presumably this field is based on the biographical overall view: "My suffering under my parents" or "My painful childhood".

The next sequence makes it clear that the suffering mainly refers to the parents. After a *short* remark about her happy school days, her preference as the daughter of a respected Nazi and as a blond and blue-eyed girl, there follows a long description of her suffering under the bombing raids that took place on her hometown, starting in 1942. So there are some pleasant memories of childhood, such as her schooldays, but even this is related to National Socialism and her Nazi parents. However, these memories and this positive side of Nazism in her life are not fleshed out by Ms. Stegmann in her self-presentation. They do not belong to the inventory of the thematic field she has designed. If one considers her reasoning that she suffered so much from

---

10 For the definition of text types, see "Criteria to define the sequences" in the Appendix.

the bombings because she did not feel safe with her mother, this further reinforces the reading that she embeds all her sorrowful childhood experiences in the framework of suffering under her parents. That she sees this suffering in the context of her parents' Nazism also becomes clear in this sequence. Ms. Stegmann thinks that her mother did not take care of her during the bombing raids because she was too busy in her function as a local leader of the Nazi Women's League (Kreisfrauenschaftsführerin). We can thus further concretize the thematic field as "My suffering under my Nazi parents".

In the following sequence, Ms. Stegmann reports that in 1944, unlike her older brother, she passed the entrance examination to a Reich school of the SS, a National-Socialist boarding school (abbreviated as Napola). She justifies her parents' decision to send her to this SS boarding school – her own motivation can only be read between the lines – with her own fears of bombing raids. She then only briefly reports on the one year she spent in this Napola on Lake Constance, which was housed in a building previously occupied by mentally handicapped children. She evaluates the time as follows: "I was quite happy at school there". Here, too, she does not narratively expand on these happy schooldays. By contrast, she then tells of her despair over Hitler's death. When she heard about it on the radio, she had cried bitterly for a long time: "The world in which I was and which I had left behind, it was broken". In this narrative, another reality shimmers through, different from just her suffering under her Nazi parents: "The world I had left behind" probably also refers to the positions of her parents under National Socialism (her father was head of the Reich Medical Association of his district) and the privileges that grew out of it. She can talk about the collapse of this world in the interview situation, since this situation fits the thematic field of her suffering. But does this sequence perhaps herald an alternation of the thematic fields in this biographical self-presentation?

She then reports that after the German capitulation she was housed for several months, with no contact to her parents, with farmers at Lake Constance who treated her badly as the daughter of a Nazi family and made her work hard. The hardship of this time and her suffering under the farmer's family is thematically related to her suffering from her Nazi parents. While the privileges she enjoyed as the daughter of a Nazi family up to 1945, as well as the way she identified herself with this system, are pushed to the unthematic margin, here she is able to focus on her parents' Nazism, since she herself now had to suffer from it. If we assume that the farming family was against the Nazis, then Ms. Stegmann could also consider whether she was rejected by them as a Napola schoolgirl. But it seems increasingly plausible that her narrative is located in the thematic field "My suffering under my Nazi parents", and thus that she is presenting herself as a victim of these parents and dethematizing her own identification and fascination with her Nazi parents and National Socialism. She marginalizes things that for her do not belong in this field; at the same time, the things she focuses on present themselves to her only from this point of view.

The climax of the narrative about the end of the war is then a story about how she returned to her mother and how she was received after being separated for one and a half years. This situation is expanded narratively. The mother opens the door to her, but does not immediately take her daughter, now 11 years old, into her arms; rather, she is horrified to notice the lice in her hair. Immediately, she is given a so-called lice pack. This story is evaluated by Hiltrud Stegmann as follows: "And from then on I no longer believed I would receive affection from either of them".

In addition to the narrative about being beaten by her father, this story is the second detailed interaction story in this interview. In other words, these are the two central stories of her narrative so far. We can now assume that the thematic field of this biographical narrative is "My suffering under my parents". Ms. Stegmann selects experiences from her memory which plausibilize the perception of her childhood as one in which she had to suffer from lack of attention or even cruelty on the part of her parents. She does not recount experiences from her positively experienced school years, nor situations in which her parents had behaved affectionately toward her. One might now think that she never experienced affection and that her parents were always cruel to her. But in the part of the interview where the interviewer asks questions, several situations are mentioned in which she experienced affection during her childhood, and which point to a positive identification with her parents, especially with her father. However, Ms. Stegmann is focused on showing the unkindness of her parents and not admitting other levels of reality. This also explains why she cannot engage in a stream of re-living and storytelling. She tells her fixed story, with which she wants to show how she suffered due to her parents' behavior, and limits the positive experiences in her life to early childhood – to the first four years of her life, the time of brightness.

This structure does not change as she continues with the description of her time as a student, and the founding of her family, up to the present; rather, the thematic field "My suffering under my Nazi parents" becomes more firmly established. Ms. Stegmann tells how she suffered under her disempowered father, who was sentenced to several years in a labor camp after 1945, and how she could hardly cope because, in addition to her studies, she had to help in his reopened practice. The narrative about her marriage and her children is also related to this. She sees her difficulties as a mother as well as the death of her son from leukemia and her chronic sleep disorders, which have increased since the birth of her children, as the result of her parents' Nazi past. Her entire biographical self-presentation is situated in *one* thematic field; there is no alternation with any another field. However, she does not make the connection between her "suffering under her parents" and their Nazi past explicit until the narrative about her time as a wife and mother. We also learn nothing about her father's crimes in the main part of the interview; they are only perceptible as threatening shadows in the background of the narrative. However, all sequences are latently pervaded by the theme of "My suffering under my Nazi parents".

If one begins to read the text from this perspective, the link between her suffering and National Socialism – and, more pointedly, its victims – can be impressively demonstrated. If we look, for example, at the two extended stories of interaction, how she was "beaten by her father" and given a painful "lice pack" by her mother it is striking that these narratives evoke associations with the brutal practices of the Nazi perpetrators. In her account of the beating scene, the emphasis is on her parents' fear of germs, her father's brutality and his characterization as a "cruel father". But when she recounts the story of how her mother immediately "deloused" her after a long separation, we cannot avoid thinking of the so-called delousing of concentration camp inmates. In addition, when asked about it, Ms. Stegmann says: "I was downright afraid of extermination". She also says that as a child she imagined that the Jews were killed with lice packs. She also makes a connection with the victims of National Socialism when asked about the beating scene. She remembers that her father, while beating her, shouted: "I will drive out your temper", and that later, during confirmation classes after the war, she always associated the Bible verse about how "the Jews were driven out of Egypt" with this situation. Since Ms. Stegmann unconsciously connects her own suffering with the suffering of the Jews, she confuses the Bible words – the Jews were not driven out of Egypt but departed – and thus embeds this central act of liberation and founding myth of the Jewish religion in the framework of persecution.

As our detailed case analysis of this biographical narrative makes clear, this latent conception of a lifetime of suffering under her Nazi parents, based on her experiences, enables Hiltrud Stegmann to maintain the unconscious strategy of "pseudo-identification with the victims" (Rosenthal/Bar-On 1992). It is true that she also sees herself as a victim of National Socialism in the sense of "I, too, suffer"; however, she hardly ever adopts the perspective of the victims of violent National Socialist crimes in the two interviews. With this strategy she tries to limit her own feelings of guilt, which are based on biographical entanglements with the fate of murdered children. She unconsciously feels guilty for the fact that, as a Napola pupil, she inhabited rooms previously occupied by mentally handicapped children who may have been murdered. She unconsciously links the possible murder of these children to the crimes of her father, who was responsible, among other things, for the deaths of mentally and physically handicapped children. Her pseudo-identification with the murdered children then also leads to the fact that, from this present perspective, all the injuries she suffered at the hands of her parents present themselves to her as "cruelty". This retrospective reinterpretation of her suffering as that of a victim persecuted by the Nazis is, however, not separate from her own experiences.

Our case analysis shows that as a child Hiltrud Stegmann was afraid of being considered by her parents as not worthy of living, due to physical deficiencies such as being short-sighted. We may well regard this fear as realistic.

The memory noema of the experience of being beaten up by her father, and its inherent reference to him as a Nazi perpetrator, are indeed constituted by the narrator's present-day perspective, which is linked to later situations and information. Nevertheless, it is *also* based on a situation that was traumatically experienced at that time, and which became one of the building blocks of her present-day perspective. At that time she developed a fear, which later developed into a "fear of annihilation", and which persists to this day – even after the death of her parents – and probably contributes to her chronic sleep disorder. I wish to emphatically emphasize here that I have no wish to imply that Hiltrud Stegmann was not a victim of her Nazi father.[11] Rather, as the analyses by Judith and Milton Kestenberg (1987) clearly show, we can assume that many Nazi fathers showed violent behavior toward their own children. However, as long as her self-presentation serves Hiltrud

---

11 I would like to take this opportunity to thank Judith Kestenberg for her important suggestions.

Stegmann to exonerate herself, she cannot perceive how realistic her fears of annihilation were. A few years after the interview, on the other hand, she was able to admit the memory that her father had almost murdered her youngest brother as an infant.

3. On the Gestalt nature of memory and narrative

3.1 Experience – Memory

While something that has just happened, the contemplation of a house or a telephone conversation, is still vivid in my memory, days or years after the experience I have to "call it back to mind", as Edmund Husserl (Time: pp. 206 ff.) puts it. While the metaphor of "calling back" contains the image of something stored and deposited in memory, it is precisely Husserl's merit to have rejected the assumption of constancy with his analyses. In his conception, remembering is not just retrieving what has been stored, but is based on a process of reproduction, in which the past is subject to constant modification depending on the present situation and the anticipated future: "... memory flows continuously, since the life of consciousness flows continuously and does not merely piece itself together link by link into a chain. Rather, everything new reacts on the old; the forward-directed intention belonging to the old is fulfilled and determined in this way, and that gives a definite coloring to the reproduction" (Husserl, Time: p. 54).

Husserl understands reproduction as something that is free from experience: not only can we remember faster or slower, more clearly or more confusedly, but the temporality of our perception differs from that of memory. This phenomenon of the difference between the order of experiencing and the order of remembering needs special reflection in the field of biographical research (cf. Fischer 1982; 1985), and especially a separate reconstruction of experienced life history and narrated life story (cf. chapter 6.2).

Although, besides the work of Husserl to which little attention has been paid by psychologists, a groundbreaking study in the field of memory psychology by Frederic C. Bartlett appeared in 1932, in which remembering was discussed as a process of reproduction, and although constructivist approaches have since been developed (cf. Schmidt 1991), it seems that many memory psychologists are not yet able to free themselves from the conception of storage. Conceptions of memory as a collection of things that are stored, and thus constant, can still be found; and despite the obsession of some social scientists with the natural sciences, they fail to see that they have developed into reflexive and dialectical concepts. Debates, especially in neurobiology, center around the reflexive modelling of memory and the associated rejection of the notion of traces fixed in memory (cf. Rosenfield 1988).

Let us first consider the "storage conception", in which memory is conceived as a kind of deficient tape (cf. Fischer 1987). The tape is deficient because it does not correspond to the ideal conception that everything experienced was recorded in sequence and should be playable at any time (Fischer 1987: 465). Questions such as: How well or how poorly does the narrator remember? or: How honest are his statements? result from this conception. The memorized is recalled in a "distorted" way due to diverse influencing factors, such as fatigue, or certain emotional states in the present of the narration which do not correspond with the past (cf. Snyder/White 1982), or the conditioning factor of social desirability. This distortion is considered as secondary, because what has been stored in the memory is deficient in comparison to what "objectively" took place, so that both the process of perception and the later process of remembering are defective. When remembering this already deficiently stored image of what once happened, this distortion of what objectively took place, its reproduction becomes even more distorted, crippled and limited by influencing factors in the present of the narration. And psychologists then plague themselves with searching for the distorting factors, the so "difficult to control source of error" (cf. Strube/ Weinert 1987: 150). Innumerable studies have investigated the question of the conditions under which memory performances are better or worse. For example, Marigold Linton (1979) kept a daily diary from 1972 to 1977 and tested her memory gaps one month later.

If the storage conception takes into account that memories are subject to change, then only in the sense that something is added to what was has already been stored. Thus one speaks of "superimposition on the original" (cf. Chassein/Hippler 1987: 454). Again, the researcher then sets out to find the conditions that will make the "memory process better" (ibid.). In other words, one looks for the tools that help in scraping off the superimposed layers and allow the image first drawn to emerge.

Atomized vs. Gestalt-shaped memory

Something that has been more or less well stored, which can be more or less coherently "retrieved" depending on present influences, is seen in these conceptions as an accumulation of individual elements that can emerge from memory in the present of remembering with the help of associations. By "associations" or "chains of associations" is meant that a stimulus in the present corresponding to one part of the past experience causes the recollection of further parts of the past experience. According to this conception, the association with a single element of a stored unit, such as an experience, leads to the memory of further elements of this unit. For example, if I see a child breaking a window pane, this may remind me of an experience in which I myself broke a pane of glass. But what elements of that situation come back to me? If I remembered all the elements associated with this situation, I would be flooded with the abundance of elements that every situation contains. Rather, remembering is always a selection process, following rules which cannot be reconstructed on the basis of atomistic or associationist conceptions.

Despite cognitivist attempts to model networks, there is as yet very little in "mainstream" psychology to suggest that Alfred Schütz (1945/1962: 109) was right with his optimistic prognosis that, with a consistent phenomenological "insight into the through and through connectedness of our stream of experience", so close to Gestalt theory, there would come "the definite overthrow of the psychology of association" and "an entirely new theory of memory and experience in inner time". The well-founded critique of atomistic or associationist conceptions of perception and memory by Gestalt theorists at the beginning of this century and their alternative conceptions have, in my opinion, lost none of their relevance. Wertheimer (1922: 49) comes to the joking conclusion that his friend is associatively connected with his telephone number, based on the association hypothesis that if content *a* frequently occurs together with content *b*, there is a tendency to remember *b* whenever *a* occurs. He places beside the idea of an associative connection of individual elements that of a Gestalt connection: "Remembering involves essential Gestalt-forming processes; memory ties itself primarily to whole-properties and structural connections; the essence of memory processes (or of 'experience') is not exhausted in the idea of sum and sequence, nor in that of wholes, but they are basically summative part-wholes" (Wertheimer 1922: 55 f., translated from the German).

On the basis of a large number of studies, the Gestalt theorists (Köhler 1918; Koffka 1922; 1925) were able to empirically reject the notion of an and-association of memory contents "which are associated externally by mere repetition, and reproduced on the basis of these external associations" (Koffka 1925: 567; translated from the German), and show that they are "uniformly Gestalt-shaped entities" from the beginning. In contrast to the associationist argument, one does not assume here that units are remembered on the basis of an element appearing in the present. Instead, one assumes organized processes or units, which in their whole-property recall the whole-properties of memory units (cf. Köhler 1947). If I see a child breaking a window pane, and if my perception of this present situation is organized in terms of the child's helplessness in the face of locked doors, if the situation has this meaning for me, this will remind me more of situations in which I was helpless or excluded than those in which I broke a glass pane out of anger. If, on the other hand, I see an angry child trampling a flower bed, this will probably remind me more of a situation in which I was angry and broke a pane of glass. According to Gestalt theory, the broken pane of glass did not enter my memory as a single element, but in its relation to the experienced situation, in other words in its meaning. Thus, whether present experiences are linked to past ones does not depend on the similarity of their elements, but on the common meaning that links them together. The selection of a past experience from one's memory "depends upon the similarity of pattern between excitation and trace, and this implies again that an excitation must be patterned before it communicates with the trace system, for otherwise it would not be capable of selecting the proper one among the many traces which are constantly being left in the organism" (Koffka 1935/63: 464).

One could object that this idea of Gestalt-shaped units corresponds exactly to the new theory of memory, based on the idea of networks in which individual components of a situation that is regarded as a memory unit are interconnected (cf. Anderson 1976; Collins/Quillian 1969). Bower (1981), for example, explains his plausible empirical findings, consistent with other research, that one best remembers those situations that correspond to one's present feelings, as networks between present emotional states and associated memory units. If I was angry when I broke a window, and I am in an aggressive mood today when I see a child breaking a window, I am more likely to remember my experience than if I am in a depressed mood. My present emotional state thus leads to the association of situations stored in my memory in which this feeling prevailed or of which it was an element. The feeling has here the status of an element, which in this conception has an and-connection with other elements present in the memory unit, and is just not a functional component of a Gestalt-shaped unit. Furthermore, network theorists do not see that remembering is a constructive, Gestalt-shaping process undertaken in the present of remembering; instead, they argue that the rememberer is subject to his or her networks. Even in the constructivist approaches (cf. Schmidt 1991), which, with their conception of ordered combinations, argue similarly to the Gestalt theorists, the links are based on associative connections that are independent of the sense-making processes of the rememberer.

By contrast, instead of assuming that memory is made up of networks with and-sum-like units, and a rememberer who is subject to these networks, a Gestalt-theory view based on Aron Gurwitsch's thematic field analysis makes it possible to see a dialectical relationship between more or less Gestalt-like memory units formed in the present of remembering, and – through interaction with others – Gestalt-forming communication processes. This conception can also explain the phenomenon that we initially remember not so much the elements of individual original situations as their patterns, and, on the basis of these, reconstruct their functional components (cf. Koffka 1935/63: 460). For example, I remember how angry I was when I broke the window, and only in a second step do I begin to reconstruct the past situation on the basis of this pattern. This reconstruction work, begun on the basis of a part of the past situation and based on a pattern or schema, is also described by Bartlett (1932: 209), who, according to Koffka (1935: 518 ff.), does not really differ from Gestalt theory: "and the event is then reconstructed on the basis of the relation of this specific bit of material to the general mass of relevant past experience or reactions, the latter functioning, after the manner of the 'schema', as an active organised setting".

Formulated in terms of Gestalt theory, a component of a present situation reminds me of a past situation only if it already carries traces of the whole (Köhler 1947), i.e., its functional significance for the whole situation is recognizable. The empirical finding that one remembers more easily experiences which correspond to one's momentary mood can be explained in terms of Gestalt theory by the reciprocal "communication" between present and past Gestalts. However, this communication takes place only when the mood is a functional component of both the present and the past situation. The meaning of the experiences in their entirety, and not only the component of the emotional state at that time, controls the selection of experiences from one's memory. One does not remember all the situations in one's life which correspond to one's present feelings, but only those which have a thematic connection with the present situation, or are in the same thematic field. The rememberer then also remembers those components of the past experience which have a functional significance for his theme. If, for example, in the present of remembering I am feeling angry about my inability to express my aggression, and I want to reassure myself of the truth of the statement "I find it hard to show my aggression", I will select corresponding situations from my memory, and just not the one in which I broke a glass pane out of anger. Since, starting from Gestalt-shaped units, we remember past Gestalt-shaped units, and thus relate wholes to each other in their meaning, there is no need for correspondence between the individual components of the respective units. We can recognize a melody as one we have already heard, although we first heard it in a different pitch. We have memorized the pattern of the melody and not its individual tones. Which experiences are linked to each other can therefore by no means be derived from the sameness of their elements.

Wolfgang Köhler's (1918) learning experiments with chimpanzees and chickens show how even animals memorize Gestalts and not the individual components of a situation. In a first experiment, the animals were presented with a light-colored and a dark-colored key and learned that they received food when they pressed the dark one. In a second experiment, they were presented with the familiar dark key and an even darker key. In most cases, the animals chose the darker key. The greater the time interval between the two experiments, the greater the learning success. Thus, the animals had memorized the pattern "light-dark" and not the individual elements of the setting, the light and the dark key. The memorization of patterns or Gestalts also has the consequence that we remember the overall impression of an experience more easily than its individual elements or sequences of actions. Instead, we have to reconstruct these on the basis of our overall impression.

So can we only remember something that was already shaped as a Gestalt during the experience? Empirical studies on memory performance show that such Gestalt-shaped experiences can be memorized much better than the perception and experience of chaos (Koffka 1963: 522 ff.; Wertheimer 1922: 55 f.). Chaos enters memory at most as an impression of chaos, and thus without any attribution of meaning. Crucial for the "survival" of memory traces is thus the prior structuredness of the experience. It is easy to remember things that we have stored as organized units in our memory, and "organized memory depends upon organized experience" (Koffka 1963: 520).

How difficult it is to memorize unstructured things is shown by trying to learn nonsensical syllable sequences (cf. Müller 1917: 43 f.). If something is difficult to learn, we won't remember the unstructured content, but we will remember the effort expended. If one were to ask the "test subjects" of such learning experiments about their experiences years later, they would not remember the syllable sequences, but they would remember their learning difficulties at that time. In this case, when reproducing past experiences, the act of perception and the primary memory act are recalled, but not what was perceived. This differs structurally from memories that reproduce what was perceived at that time, and where we cannot remember the act of perception: "I remember the illuminated theater – that cannot mean: I remember having perceived the theater. Otherwise, the latter would mean: I remember that I perceived that I perceived the theater, and so on. I remember the illuminated theater means: 'in my interior' I see the illuminated theater as having been. ... But I must not do it in such a way that I represent the perception; rather I represent the perceived, that which appears as present in the perception. Memory therefore does actually imply a reproduction of the earlier perception" (Husserl, Time: p. 60).

If we cannot remember the perceptual noema without further effort, the memory of the perceptual act may help us to reconstruct what was perceived at that time. Experiments by Kurt Lewin (1922) show the interesting phenomenon that "test persons" who were asked to remember a learning situation in which they had to learn pairs of syllables were quicker to name the other syllable when given one of a pair, than other "test persons" who were only asked to name the syllable that occurred to them when looking at a given syllable. If we transfer Koffka's consideration about the probable disappearance of unstructured memory traces to social situations, then it applies here only if the unstructured, the "chaos", has not become a problem or a theme for us and we have not suffered from it. What we experience in the drifting of everyday time without dividing lines or markings is not memorized any more than our incoherent, fragmentary daydreams. Thus we all know the phenomenon that, if someone asks us what we are thinking about, we find the question difficult to answer, even though we have only just stopped "thinking", because we can recall only incoherent scraps of thoughts.

Now there are also situations that we experienced as chaos because they had to be endured without any real changes in space and time, and were therefore hardly distinguishable from other situations, and in which our options for action were limited. What about these very painful and sometimes traumatic situations? Do we simply forget them? This cannot be what Koffka meant. Provided that we have not repressed these experiences, or are not trying to deny them, we remember these phases – which cannot be divided into separate situations – through impressions, individual images, fragments and our feelings at that time. We have trouble, however, to join these fragments together into unified Gestalts, or even to shape them into communicable stories. Thus, these fragments are subject to the danger of being increasingly forgotten in the course of time. More and more we will have trouble to remember them. Above all, since the fragments are not communicable, they will sink into the realm of speechlessness. Fragmentary remembering means that it is difficult to form these individual fragmentary parts into stories. Stories presuppose the memory unit of an experience, i.e., that the experience "receives a new mode of being through attentive consideration and recording" (Schütz 1932/1974: 67; translated from the German). The unit of memory thus refers to something that is "distinguished", "singled out". While the degree of orderliness of stories or of narrative chains can vary widely, stories always require the overall Gestalt of a temporal process with a beginning and an end. Chaotic patterns, on the other hand, have neither well-defined boundaries that hold them together and delineate them, nor internal stability (Koffka 1963: 507).

Empirical analyses of the life stories of World War I veterans (Rosenthal 1991/2019; 1993) show this phenomenon of narrative difficulties due to "chaotic experience" very clearly. While these veterans can easily talk for hours about their experiences in World War II, in which they also participated as soldiers, they usually give only a succinct paraphrase of their experiences in the trenches of World War I, which often lasted for months and years, using metaphors or arguments. They are unable to communicate these experiences in the form of stories. Their narrative blocks are due, among other things, to the difficulty of putting their diffuse and chaotic memories of the constant noise of explosions or of their everyday life in the trenches into a sequential order.

We can understand the difficulty of remembering one's time in the trenches better if we accept the assumption of Gestalt theorists that our memories are organized spatially rather than temporally, and that the memory of sequential sequences follows the changing environment. One trench looked like the other. If our surroundings do not change, our consciousness of time is lost (cf. Gurwitsch 1943a; James 1905: 619 f.). The year or years spent in the trenches shrink to a single picture or brief evaluations, since the rememberers cannot reconstruct particular experiences that stand out during this state of emergency that continued unchanged from day to day. In order to be able to easily remember temporal sequences of individual unrelated experiences (not sequences of action within a single event), a spatial orientation is required, since time is spatialized in memory. This phenomenon, already known to Gestalt theory, has also been discussed by neurobiologists (cf. Rosenfield 1988: 162): "Time is not an absolute quality in memory; it is an ordering of people, places, things, and events. There are no calendars in the brain." For example, if we try to remember our trip through Italy, the first things that come to mind are the marketplace of Siena, the olive groves, and the walk along the Arno River. If we think of the temporal sequence of this trip, this knowledge is based on the spatial patterns attached to the remembered experiences (cf. Koffka 1963: 446). On the basis of the sequence of different places, we can reconstruct the order of our experiences or the times when we were in Siena and when we were at the Arno. In this respect, there is more freedom in the reproduction of past experiences, the reinterpretation of their temporal anchoring in the course of life, than in the reinterpretation of spatial circumstances. "The knowledge of their temporal relations seems much more to be a dynamic relationship which connects them with my Ego than one which holds them together among themselves" (Koffka 1963: 446). However, this presupposes that we are dealing with temporally and logically unconnected events, for there may well be temporal events that are remembered in their sequentiality without requiring spatialization (this is also conceded by Koffka, ibid).

Another factor leading to difficulty in remembering, and thus in narrating stories, in addition to those already discussed, (a) chaotic experience and (b) the lack of change of environment, is (c) the routinization of situations. If I experience certain situations again and again, it is difficult for me to recall individual ones even if they stand out very much from everyday life. My memory condenses them to an overall picture. Narratives by members of the civilian population about the bombing raids in the Second World War show this phenomenon (Rosenthal 1993). The situations in the cellars and bunkers, which are repeated day and night, are narratively expanded only in the case of outstanding attacks, otherwise they are described in condensed terms – the way it always was. This condensation is not only due to the difficulty of distinguishing the individual, recurring situations from one another, but also results from the fact that we tend to remember only unique situations in which action blocks occur. In the case of recurring traumatic experiences such as the bombing raids, the death of comrades at the front, or – for former prisoners in the concentration camps – the daily roll calls, it is usually the first of these situations, in which an abrupt change occurred, that is memorized and recalled today.

Experimental confirmation of the assumption that action blocking is better remembered than routinized procedures is found in a study by Zeigarnik (1927). He had "test subjects" solve various mathematical tasks and interrupted the solution process. The unsolved tasks, i.e., those whose processing was interrupted, could later be remembered significantly better than the solved ones.

Recall or Reproduce

Gestalt theory also contains ideas of deposition and storage. Thus, it admits the idea of traces – Koffka regards his theory as a revised version of the "trace theory" – which enter memory as Gestalt-shaped experiences and are updated in new situations. They resemble in their totality the organized totality of the new experience. Frederic C. Bartlett (1932) goes further with his proposal to abandon the concept of "traces". He argues instead for a concept of reconstructing the past by means of "schemata", where the term schema denotes an organized group of elements. However, looking at his use of schemata, it is striking that he means both the "forces" that influence reconstruction and the form by which the material is preserved. Thus, I. H. Paul (1967) points out that, contrary to his intention, Bartlett does not do without "traces". Even if we understand the concept of schema as referring only to present organizedness, Bartlett introduces the "trace" at the moment when he speaks of a schema being applied to a "detail" of an experience that emerges from memory. What, then, is this "detail" but a trace? Paul then also argues for a conception in which both traces and schemata are integrated, since every act of memory is based on an interaction between the two. Following Reiff and Scheerer (1959), who use the schema concept in Piaget's sense as a "mode of functioning with traces", Paul understands remembering as a reconstruction of a previous experience: "in such a way that it can become integrated into the functional schemata of the person at the time of remembering" (Paul 1967: 256). Another prominent representative of the reconstruction hypothesis and vehement rejection of the "trace theory" is Maurice Halbwachs (1925) with his analysis of the so-called collective memory. Halbwachs assumes that memories represent a recurrent reconstruction starting from the present and are not stored as mental states. He explicitly rejects the Freudian conception of stored psychic experiences in the unconscious or preconscious. Against the notion of something stored within, he prefers the idea of externally constructed memories: "There is nothing to look for where they (the memories, G.R.) are, where they are stored, in my head or in any corner of my mind to which I alone would have access; they are, after all, called to mind by me from without, and the groups to which I belong offer me at every moment the means of reconstructing them, on condition that I turn to them and that I adopt, at least temporarily, their mode of thought" (Halbwachs 1925/1985: 20 f.).

Apart from the (from a sociological perspective) undifferentiated nature of the concept of collective frames of reference offered by social groups, Halbwachs, in my opinion, jumps to the other side of dualism with his justified criticism of the deposition theorists. If some scholars – mostly psychologists – insist on the "fixed interior", Halbwachs, as a sociologist, argues for the "fixed exterior". While we can fully accept Halbwachs's thesis that we reconstruct our past from our present position, we need to understand the present as being constituted by the past. This past of ours, however, cannot be equated with the collective past of a milieu; it is rather the experiences which are peculiar to us in each case, even if they are to some extent collectively shared, which constitute our present and our memory. With the reconstruction of the past, therefore, it cannot be meant that memory processes are set in motion solely from the present. Not only that something from the past is presented during the process of remembering; during the process of remembering, impressions, feelings, images, sensual perceptions and components of the remembered situation also appear which do not fit into our present perspective, of which we were no longer aware, and which can be absolutely incompatible with the reconstruction frame of the rememberer and his milieu. But Halbwachs (1985: 71), who cognitivistically reduces memory performance to a "constructive and rational activity of the mind", rejects the notion of a subject experiencing himself in the course of his memories. For him, something does not emerge from memory; rather, with cognitive effort and with the help of our collective frame of reference, we must laboriously turn to memory and reproduce the past. This one-sided conception is contradicted by the experience of being overwhelmed by our feelings from past situations – without any conscious, intentional effort to remember them, as well as all the bodily memory processes that are based on the bodily memorization of experiences. The body memorizes sensations of pain and discomfort, which can be actualized without any conscious effort in certain related situations. This process is used in body therapies to trigger memory processes through bodywork.

In his critique of psychoanalysis, Halbwachs overlooks its reconstructive parts, which were already discussed by Sigmund Freud (1899; 1901; 1910), namely the idea that memory traces are organized in the memory process. The interaction between traces and the memory process is then more strongly elaborated in later psychoanalytic studies (cf. Kris 1956; Rubinstein 1965), especially in ego psychology – with increasing emphasis on the active role of the present in the memory process and the dynamic process of reorganization in focusing different memory traces: "the present selects, colors and modifies. Memory at least autobiographical or personal memory, i.e., the least autonomous area of memory function, is dynamic and telescopic" (Kris 1956: 55 f.).

Moreover, in recent psychoanalytic research, similar to Piaget's tradition, increasing importance is given to the ongoing transformations of memories through recurrent memory processes (cf. Cohler 1982: 212). In studies from cognitive structure theory (Paris/Lindauer 1977; Riegel 1977), based on Piaget's (1977) accommodation and assimilation model, the transformation processes of memory patterns that occur as a result of new information are discussed. However, these efforts to conceptualize the interaction between past and present, linked in psychoanalysis to the distinction between traces and memory processes, remain ultimately dualistic, as do the proposals of Paul or Reiff and Scheerer and their concepts, traces, and schemata. By contrast, a view of the interaction between sedimented and present Gestalts based consistently on field theory and Gestalt theory makes it possible to circumvent such dualistic conceptions of something that is stored in memory, on the one hand, and something that is remembered in the present, on the other. It is true that the idea that an organized trace is actualized on the basis of a present Gestalt risks being misunderstood in the sense of the assumption of constancy – with the argument that two Gestalts or figures do not have to reorganize themselves mutually in the interaction with each other. But an approach based on Gestalt theory, as in the case of thematic field analysis, inevitably involves the conception of the mutual constitution of "old" and "new" figures, i.e., a constant reorganization. Thus Koffka (1963: 524) writes, "that the reorganization of the pattern interferes directly with the recall of the old pattern, i.e., it exerts a direct influence upon the old trace".

As an example, Koffka cites the perception of a house that has been remodeled and whose shape before the remodeling is difficult to remember because the remodeling determines the "old trace". While in this case we can still try to reconstruct the former object of perception, just as we can reconstruct our perspective at the time in the case of social events, there are also irreversible changes, as, for example, when something that I initially perceived as chaos can no longer be remembered as chaotic after being perceived as orderly. If, for example, I have recognized the image of a face in lines that were initially unstructured for me, it will no longer be possible for me to see the disordered lines. The first trace is irrevocably destroyed. I can only remember that the object of perception once presented itself to me "differently" – namely as chaos. However, this irreversibility of reorganization is limited. It is possible to reverse a reorganization, and after being repeatedly remembered, the noema in the memory can be closer to the noema in the experienced situation than in the initial memories. It must be considered that the once experienced event or the perceived object is not changed by the memory process, only its respective noema in the memory, which again refers to the noematic system, and thus also to the experience noema. As the memory noema refers to a past experience, and to the noematic system as a whole, i.e., also to the experience noema, the past has an effect on the present. Thus, it is quite possible that the experience presents itself in the memory in a different way than it did at first, namely "closer" to what was experienced at the time. This assumption requires closer consideration, since it is contrary to the recurring criticism of biographical research or "oral history" that their "sources" are unreliable, since what is narrated lies far back in the past and is thus far removed from the event. It can be countered that the time span between experience and narration says nothing about the degree of modification of the narration. Whether one year or twenty years after the experience, its noema in my memory is determined by the attention I pay to it; there is no structural difference between the two memory noemata. As Alfred Schütz (1932) analyzed in detail, the meaning of the event, the unit that stands out in my reflective attention from the stream of experience with a before and an after, is based on the classification of this unit in the context of the experience. My attentive gaze can only be turned to a delimited event (ibid. 1932/74: 69). This does not take place during the event, but is directed at it, when planning it or after completing it. This process of meaning-making, which takes place after the event by placing it in an experiential context, is structurally comparable to the modifying attention paid to this event after years of experience and its embedding in new memory contexts. My view of what has just been experienced can be far more "limited" in perspective than my view of it after decades. Jean Piaget and Bärbel Inhelder (1973), for example, show in their empirical studies how memory codes change in the course of cognitive development, and how memory improves due to the new acquisition of schemata. They presented children with geometric arrangements of wooden sticks and asked them to memorize their arrangement. Those children who did not yet have the cognitive competence to form rows could not remember the arrangement, but reorganized it according to their schemata. Only after acquiring the appropriate schemata and recalling the memory a second time were they able to correctly reproduce the original arrangements. This phenomenon can also be observed in respect of social events. Here, too, it may be possible that with new schemata, or when psychic blockades are eliminated or become superfluous, what is remembered may be closer to the experienced situation than in earlier remembering situations – an assumption on which psychoanalytic practice is based. In other words, by becoming conscious of repressed or denied experiences, or even isolated components of such experiences, the analysand can see and re-experience "more" than before.

Let us return to the conception of interaction between a Gestalt-shaped memory unit and a Gestalt-shaped present unit. If we consider this as an interaction not between two figures, but between figure and ground, and, following Gurwitsch, as an interaction between theme and thematic field, then the viability of a dialectical conception of memories as in Gestalt theory becomes clear. The experience selected from memory in the present represents our theme, which is embedded in the thematic field constituted in the present. As already discussed (chapter 2.4.4), the field constitutes the theme and, vice versa, the theme constitutes the field. The present perspective and the present life practice of the rememberer thus allow an experience to present itself according to its Gestalt, just as, conversely, the presented experience constitutes the present. In order to remember something, or in order to perceive something emerging from my memory, I must regard it from the perspective of my present situation with my present system of relevance and interest. I need a memory frame or, in other words, a contextualization of memory. If we do not succeed in contextualizing, or if we have lost the ability to do so, for example due to brain damage, this has far-reaching consequences, as Israel Rosenfield (1988: 26 f.) demonstrates, for example, with the case of a patient described by Cirandeau in 1882. Before this patient could answer a question, it had to be repeated three times. Her answers then mostly referred to the context of the previously asked question. Rosenfield, who uses many other examples to very convincingly refute the localization theory within brain research, sees the patient's described incompetence as being due to her inability to establish a context in which the words and sentences she heard would make sense to her. We usually do not realize how much we need contexts, since they arise without any further attentional effort. However, we are familiar with the phenomenon that we can remember telephone numbers or names only in certain contexts or with a certain contextualization. Rosenfield discusses memory performance in terms of the Darwinian model of variation and selection: according to this conception, memory functions according to a system based on an indefinable variety of selection possibilities, in which the individual units are never constant but change according to context: "We recollect information in different contexts; this requires the activation of different maps interacting in ways that differ from those of our initial encounter with the information and that lead to its recategorization" (Rosenfield 1988: 192).

But how does this context emerge? Halbwachs introduced the concept of the collective memory framework, thinking of a framework imposed on the individual by social groups. He differentiates according to social groups, but not according to the different biographical background of the remember. Against this, Wolfram Fischer (1987: 466; translated from the German) objects: "The reconstructive activity of remembering is guided not only by 'external' milieu schemes, but in the first place by the biographical overall concept of the person who remembers". This biographical overall concept, the frame of reference constituted biographically through interaction with the social world, and the interests and moods pursued in the present of remembering, define the memory frame. Against the background of this frame or thematic field, I turn to my memory and select corresponding experiences or themes accordingly.

Turning to my past can be motivated by a need for self-assurance and self-understanding, as well as by the need to establish an identity which I can present to others (cf. Kohli 1981). These motives, as well as my present feelings, bodily sensations, and relevances, determine the selection of my memories. However, the present situation and biographical overall perspective determine not only the attention paid to specific experiences, but also their memory noemata, i.e., how they are organized depending on which specific aspects are focused on. If we are feeling dejected, we not only select a depressing experience from the past, but our approach to this experience, which we might have experienced as a happy one at the time, constitutes the experience as a depressing one by placing its unpleasant components in the center of our attention. In another thematic field, this experience might present itself in a completely different way. The thematic field, for instance "my dejection", determines the reconstruction of certain memory components, and the fading out of other components, as well as the organization of the components. Without this selection mechanism, we would be flooded by a disorganized accumulation of individual parts. But our memories are mostly consistent entities resulting from the act of attention and the organized nature of the memory unit, and are further organized in verbalization (cf. chapter 2.5.2).

The theme in turn constitutes the thematic field. Depending on which experience I turn to, this turning leads to different reorganizations of the field. Thus, when recalling an experience, components from the past situation can reappear that are incongruent with the thematic field and components of the margin become the theme.

3.2 Memory – Narration

To what extent is the narration of a self-experienced event based on a memory noema? Is it merely a verbalization of the memory? Following Rush (1987), could we not assume that the shaping of the narrative is based on patterns that are structurally similar to the memory noema, i.e., on a coherent pattern of action sequences with clarification of causal and temporal relations? First of all, it can be objected that not every narration of a self-experienced event is based on a memory noema that presents itself to me because I turn to it. I can construct a story in the present of the narration, based on fantasies about what happened at that time and on stories told by others. Likewise, I can simply retell a story that has long since become an anecdote. The part played by memory in the process of storytelling may thus vary.

Let us consider the case of a narrative that is based on a memory, in order to illustrate the mutual constitution of narrative process and memory process[1]. In contrast to the irrevocable fusion of the presented object of perception with the perception taking place through the intentional attention of the subject, in this case we have to assume a difference between narration and memory which is perceptible for the narrator, as well as for the recipient of the story. The memory noema is not subject to the same interactional requirements as the narration of a story. The mere translation of my idiosyncratic memory into an intelligible and comprehensible form for the listener (or reader), who as a rule was not involved in the events of the time and does not share my memory, implies a not inconsiderable difference. I can make do with vague, opaque, inconsistent, contradictory memories that are nevertheless comprehensible to me, while the interactional demands of a narrative make it necessary to resolve vagueness and contradictions or else to explain them. Moreover, in the process of their "translation" for the listeners or readers of my story, the memory noemata that at first seem plausible to us reveal their fragility and inconsistency, and above all the incompleteness of their Gestalts. The storytelling process, more than the process of remembering, offers an opportunity to uncover fragilities and to become aware of hitherto "unseen" memories and parts of memories. The narrative process, provided it is stimulated and not blocked by the listeners, motivates the search for, and reconstruction of, further memory parts: "Finally, aspects of events and structures of social processes emerge in the narrative process, strangely enough, which the narrator had simply not perceived or not understood as an actor at the time, because they concerned hidden tendencies, the unmanageable overall framework of events, or even unknown processes taking place unnoticed at the time" (Schütze 1987: 84; translated from the German).

On the other hand, the narrative process encompasses less than the memory process. The requirement to tell a consistent and self-contained story with a beginning and an end means that all the contradictions, unclear parts and contradictory feelings and bodily sensations found in the Gestalt of the memory noema are not verbalized, and the stories that are constructed tend to bypass it. The communicative sharing of memories, the narrative schema, imposes on the autobiographer certain constraints of plausibility and rationality, and thus leads to a consistent story, while the inconsistent parts are pushed into the background. Through repeated narration, the memory noema that organizes itself in the course of these

---

1 Cf. the numerous narrative analyses by Fritz Schütze (1976a; 1976b; 1984; 1987; 2007a; 2007b), and Kallmeyer/Schütze (1977).

narrative processes becomes less and less susceptible to reorganization. Nevertheless, I do not share Rush's (1987: 374) assumption that stories cannot be changed "because it becomes increasingly difficult to think against the persuasive power of a complex consistent system, and because it would mean an ever-increasing effort, and finally the impossibility of willingly giving up the consonance, security, and pleasure gained by such a system".

Not only do such constructivist approaches underestimate the liquefaction of structures in communicative settings, i.e., they assign too little importance to social interaction for the constitution of narrative process, but these statements are also less applicable to biographical narratives, which are told not only for pleasure but primarily for better self-understanding.

With regard to the three constraints of narration described by Fritz Schütze (1976a), the differences between memory and narrative processes can be further systematized. The compulsion to detail those sequences of actions or events which require explanation, and which are regarded as indispensable for the understanding of the listener, does not apply to the same extent to memories that are recalled in "silent solitude", although if I want to be certain about myself and how I became what I am, I also need a certain amount of detailing. Likewise, when remembering, I can more easily evade the need to complete the Gestalt, the social expectation to finish a story or to recount all its important parts (Schütze 1976a: 224). However, this difference must be qualified in the sense that our process of remembering, understood as a process of interaction with ourselves, does not follow different rules, in structural terms, than the process of interaction with others. It is admittedly easier to abort a memory process than a narrative process; but when aborting a memory we feel compelled to justify this to ourselves. If, finally, we consider the compulsion[2] to condense a narrative – the limited time available and the limited attention of the listener compel the narrator to establish relevancies and to condense the story, then there is no qualitative, structural difference, but only a quantitative difference between the narrative and the remembered situation. In the process of remembering, I

---

2 Gerhard Riemann (1987: 25 f.) discusses the implications of these constraints for the proximity of the narrative to the structure of the "actual action and experience". Among other things, he makes clear that the condensation constraint can result in the uncovering of discrepancies between "on the one hand, intended actions and realized actions, and on the other hand, earlier intended actions and evaluative attitudes regarding a problem with later intended actions and evaluations regarding the same problem" (translated from the German).

can abandon myself to the stream of memories emerging from my memory with an abundance of details that I would never bother a recipient of my story with – unless I were lying on my psychoanalyst's couch. Nevertheless, as already discussed, condensation also takes place in remembering – just as in telling – due to the thematic focusing or splitting of the stream of consciousness into theme, field, and margin inherent in every perception. Not even the rememberer has unlimited time and attention capacity at his disposal to allow an unrestricted alternation of theme, field and margin.

Besides this quantitative, and not structural, difference between the restrictions imposed on the rememberer who abandons himself to the process of remembering without any communicative intention, and those imposed on the narrator, we must now examine more closely the differences between the memory noema of an experience which becomes present during the narration, and the narrative unit of a story. The narrated story contains both more and less than the memory noema:

1. Not everything is told that the narrator remembers at the moment of telling.
2. Components are included in the narrative that do not belong to the memory noema of the experience. In addition to components of other memories or argumentative explanations, foreign narratives can also be interwoven into the story, in other words narratives that are not based on the narrator's own experience, but which have been told by others.

Omissions

Some things that emerge from the memory, or certain components presented in the memory noema, which either a) cannot be embedded in the story because they are not understood or are experienced as inconsistent, or b) are a cause of embarrassment and shame or do not correspond to cultural norms, or c) have been denied and repressed and d) do not belong to the narrator's intended theme, may not be directly expressed, although they may become apparent in paralinguistic ways or be indirectly referred to in the narrative. Images, thought fragments, feelings, sensual memories of smells or sounds mostly remain in the prelinguistic realm. The same applies to bodily sensations that occur during the narration and cannot be classified by narrators, but which present themselves to them incoherently and unrelated to the theme, or which are difficult to convey linguistically (such as sensations of pain). While verbal omission of bodily and sensory sensations tend to be due to the difficulty of translating them into language, narrators, to the extent that they can control it, tend to withhold embarrassment and unpleasantness. These omissions become noticeable to the listener mostly in the skipping of details, the change from a narrative schema to an argumentation or descriptive schema, and – paralinguistically – through hesitation and breaking off. In order to ensure that these differences between memory noema and narration are not completely lost to the social scientist, an analysis procedure is needed that is not limited to the manifest linguistic content of the texts.

Insertions

On the other hand, the narration contains more than the memory noema or the memory unit. If the narrator notices vagueness and gaps or inconsistencies, he can fill up the story with memories from other situations, with mental constructions, or with components reported by other people who experienced the situation. Fritz Schütze (1984: 97 f./1989: 57) introduces the concept of "background constructions" in this context. These have the function of eliminating vagueness and opacity not only in individual stories, but especially in narrative chains. Background constructions can be descriptions or explanations, as well as narratives of other experiences that serve to make the main story more plausible. They are incorporated into narratives primarily when ambiguities occur as a result of withheld and hidden aspects, but the narrator realizes that without them his narrative is implausible.

Let us return to "fillings" in the narration of a story, of which the narrator need by no means be aware. For him, they may have already become part of his memory noema. Especially in the case of memories from early childhood, which – as sufficiently discussed in psychoanalysis – are often subject to childhood amnesia (Freud 1905), we sometimes find it difficult to distinguish between what we remember ourselves and what others have told us. This also means that we may mistake narratives by others for memories, even if they are contrary to what we experienced at the time. In any case, the inclusion in my story of parts told by others will lead to reorganization of my memory noema. While such narratives refer to situations in which we ourselves were involved, a narrator can also incorporate into his narrative components from situations that he did not experience himself, but that were told to him by others involved in the situation. The prerequisite for narrating

On the Gestalt nature of memory and narrative

an experience as it presents itself from the perspective of another participant is the process of perspective adopting: "In the narrative process, the interaction standpoints of alter ego can be recalled to memory or reconstructed retrospectively in a density of experience that may not have been possible in the immediate interaction situation at the time" (Schütze 1987: 69; translated from the German). With the subsequent adoption of the perspective of my interaction partners in situations that are not identical with the one I remember but relate to it, a different presentation of my experience becomes possible: the adoption of the perspectives of a participant in the situation leads to the reorganization of my memory noema.

If the juxtaposition of memory noema, on the one hand, and narrated life story, on the other hand, remains attached to a dualistic argumentation, it gradually becomes clear that we have to assume reciprocal reorganization – if we consistently follow the perspective of Gestalt theory and field theory. In order to vividly illustrate this reciprocal shaping of narrative and memory and, above all, of the past experience represented in each narrative, I would like to return to the example of Ms. Stegmann's narrated story. For a better understanding, here again the quotation:

"The second memory is a negative one. My eldest brother wasn't supposed to let me in through the door of the practice – my parents were away – but I was supposed to go in through the side entrance. The main idea – I heard later – was that the handle on the entrance door for the patients might be contaminated with bacteria or whatever if they touched it, and my parents feared infection, so we were supposed to go in through the side entrance. But the main entrance was so beautiful, it had a big glass door. And I was four years old and he wouldn't let me in, he was six years older. And then I broke this big double glass door with both fists, out of sheer anger that I had to enter through this stupid side entrance. When my parents came home, they didn't look to see if I was hurt. Surprisingly, I wasn't hurt at all, but I was miserably beaten up. According to my father, my temper was beaten out of me by his own temper. And my mother must have saved me from these beatings. Because at some point he stopped. But I was still lying in bed. I don't know how long that was. For me it was a very long time that I was injured, really injured and had to stay in bed. Whether that had to do with being saved by my mother, I don't know. But in my memory it had to do with the fact that I had been beaten so badly. And in retrospect I have the feeling that from then on I was a very good child" (translated from the German).

Which noema of memory underlies this story? Depending on which theme Ms. Stegmann pursues with the narration of her story, what she wants to assure herself or her listeners of, what she wants to gain certainty about, her memory will present itself to her differently. The way she approaches the past is constituted by her present perspective (Fischer 1978), in other words her present interests, needs and biographical overall view, the situation in which she currently finds herself, and the degree of attention with which she remembers. Depending on how she turns to this experience, a different noema will present itself to her, and depending on the presentation, her attention will become modified. On these reciprocal processes depends which components will emerge from the memory, and whether this will lead to a reorganization of the theme and of the thematic field. Let us assume that Ms. Stegmann recounted this experience, among other things, to illustrate the cruelty of her father in contrast to the caring behavior of her mother. Let us further suppose that in the process she tried to recall her mother's behavior at the time, and suddenly remembered that her mother verbally supported her father. A dramatic reorganization of the memory noema, and thus also of her narrated theme and field, would be the consequence, and the experience might now present itself to her in the way that was traumatizing for her at that time. Perhaps the mother's behavior was so hurtful and threatening that she had to suppress it from her consciousness.

In this example, the narrative process, with the attempt to visualize the situation at that time, led to the emergence of previously concealed things, and thus to reorganization of the memory noema, although this was not in the interest of the narrator. Thus, during the narration, components of action sequences in the situation at that time may well emerge from memory that are contrary to our present narrative interest. The "memory dynamic" released by the impromptu narration sets "an inner process of self-assurance in motion ... in which the solidified layers of experience, which the narrator carries around with him in his present life and action in static, selective, excerpt-like images, is again liquefied into sequences of experience" (Schütze 1977: 40; translated from the German). If we get involved in a memory process, we cannot do what we want with our past; we cannot invent stories. If we want to invent stories or equip ourselves with a past that fits our present, then we must not surrender ourselves to a narrative process based on memories, but must construct stories without memories – preferably without the pressure of communication situations.

In the case of Ms. Stegmann's narrative, too, one can wonder whether she was engaging in a process of remembering or telling a story that has already been told many times and fixed in static form. On closer examination of her story, one begins to wonder whether she can remember anything at all. Right at the beginning, she adds to the story the parental motive for the ban, which she only learned about later. Why is there a need for information about her parents' fear of bacteria? Is Ms. Stegmann still trying to understand this ban, which was opaque to her at the time, or does she think she has to make the ban plausible to the listener? Perhaps she became so angry because she did not know her parents' motives at the time. When a story is enriched by later knowledge, this can be a sign that lack of understanding or vagueness led to difficulties at that time (cf. Schütze 1989: 57).

If, on the other hand, we assume, according to thematic field analysis (chapter 2.3.5), that her narrative is in the thematic field "I am a victim of Nazi parents", we can also see this enrichment in the light of "racial hygiene ideas". Thus, Ms. Stegmann inserted into her story an aspect that only became relevant to her much later; as a four-year-old, she probably did not see her father in connection with Nazi ideology. This insertion is a result of her present-day perspective: in the memory noema that presents itself to her, her father appears as a Nazi perpetrator who, as a doctor, put racial hygiene into practice in a murderous manner. But this reinterpretation is not independent of her experiences at the time. Even if she did not see him as a "Nazi perpetrator" at the time, his ideology, as well as his position and participation in Nazi crimes, determined her everyday life during the Nazi era: his parenting style was based on this ideology, and his actions outside the family were part of his identity. In retrospect, Ms. Stegmann today sees the connection between her parents' exaggerated ideas of hygiene, their related attitude toward the patients who consulted her father (her mother worked part-time as a nurse in the practice), and her own bodily socialization in the family, including her fear of being considered not worthy of living by her parents because of her physical inadequacies (Rosenthal/Bar-On 1992). Generally speaking, this means: Even if a memory noema presents itself to the rememberer on the basis of her present perspective differently from the experience noema in the situation at that time – and we can generally assume this – this noema refers to the same experience, which is now presented with other emphases, but ones which were contained in the situation at the time. The experience is not changed, but only seen and understood differently today. Today's view can be regarded as having co-determined the experience at that time, even though this has not been realized before now.

If we continue to consider the story of Ms. Stegmann, it is noticeable that we learn relatively little from the perspective of the then four-year-old. It is clear that she broke the glass pane out of anger. But she conveys neither her feelings then, nor her feelings now, in the face of her father's unbelievable beating. She only sums up, "And in retrospect I have the feeling that from then on I was a very good child". This statement, however, does not present a feeling, but is a retrospective interpretation, i.e., seeing this experience as an "interpretive point" (Fischer 1978) that separates her life before the event from her life after it. This story marks the beginning of her life as a "good child". But what emotions are hidden behind the story? Listening to the tape recording, although the facts of this narrative are startling, one does not sense any expression of emotion by the narrator. Rather, it is like something experienced by another person, reported from a factual distance. This failure to revive former feelings, and thus to verbalize them, could be due to the interview situation: perhaps the narrator is trying to control herself and not surrender to the stream of re-experiencing. Another possibility is that this lack of emotion is a sign of the isolation described by Sigmund Freud (1926/60: 264) as a defense mechanism: "...the experience is not forgotten, but it is stripped of its affect, and its associative relations are suppressed or interrupted, so that it stands there as if isolated and is not reproduced even in the course of thought activity" (translated from the German).

If, on the other hand, a narrative is accompanied by feelings, or if these are reactivated by the narrative, this does not necessarily mean that they refer to the story being narrated. They can belong to completely different experiences, but be connected to the narrative by the defense mechanism of "displacement". Perhaps, for example, Ms. Stegmann has shifted her fear of her father, and her feelings of hatred toward him, to someone or something else – for example, to her brother – and now becomes aggressive when speaking about her brother.

The assumption that Ms. Stegmann is isolating something in this experience becomes even more plausible at a later point in the interview. Asked by the interviewer whether she can remember being beaten by her father, she says that she remembers the room, and her father's words, but[3]:

"these blows (1 second pause) so can so- the uh the direct blows I don't know (1) mhm ((exhales)), so I don't feel them (2) 'I don't feel them' (2) if I think about it, if- I've never really thought about it but, if I do, then I remember the, the whizzing hands (3)" (translated from the German)

It is clear that she is trying hard to remember, but only the "whizzing hands" are present to her. The blows, the pain, the fear, on the other hand, remain

---

3 Because I deem it necessary for the interpretation, the text is given with the corresponding transcription symbols (see appendix).

in the dark. This is also clear in the narrative quoted above, when she says that "at some point" her father stopped. She cannot remember the end of the beating nor how long she stayed in bed.

Let's look at another aspect of the story that Ms. Stegmann cannot remember, namely the behavior of her mother: "Whether that had to do with being saved by my mother, I don't know". Why does this memory remain closed to her? With the formulation "and my mother must have saved me from these beatings", she tries to ascribe assistance to her mother. Perhaps she wishes for this behavior and thus covers up her lack of support.

We get another impression if we consider a passage from an interview conducted with Ms. Stegmann a year earlier by the Israeli psychologist Dan Bar-On:

"and I have this faint memory of being a bit angry with my mother for not standing by me in that situation, taking me away when he hit me and saying, 'Well, that's enough'."

Again, the narrator tries to fill in the gaps in her "faint memory" with conjecture. However, in both narratives it is not really clear how her mother behaved; the only thing that is clear is that Ms. Stegmann has doubts about her mother's behavior. Perhaps these doubts arose only at a later time, when her relationship with her mother had become a problem for her, and she examined her childhood memories in search of clues to her mother's behavior. Thus, we know from her presentation of her life story (chapter 2.3.5) that she negatively evaluates her mother's unloving greeting when she returned home in 1945, with the story of the "lice pack" and the remark: "from then on I no longer believed I would receive affection from either of them". Perhaps this situation, experienced seven years later, was the turning point in her relationship with her mother and the beginning of a reinterpretation of the past.

Overall, this story shows how much the experience is painstakingly reconstructed by the autobiographer and filled out with conjecture. The narrative is not a process of recollection that starts to flow during the telling, not an unprepared impromptu narration, but rather something that has already been reported frequently. The isolation of her feelings is clear, as well as her fruitless attempts to talk about them. For example, Ms. Stegmann continues after the above quotation:

"Those were my feelings when I thought-, it wasn't a particularly pleasant feeling."

The structure of the text reveals to what extent a narration of self-experienced events is a memory process in flux, and thus a developing and reorganizing memory noema, or whether it is the reproduction of a quasi static, fixed memory noema.

But what value do such fixed stories and fixed memory images have for a biographical analysis? What do such attempts at construction tell us? The informative value of such texts becomes apparent if we do not try to discover "how it really was at that time", but ask: "Why does the autobiographer present the experience in this way and not differently?" In analyzing an interview of this type, we need to ask why the autobiographer cannot abandon herself to the stream of re-experiencing and thus of narrating. This is because the memory traces, the narrative blockades and the breaks give us clues to what the narrator has to protect herself from, with which biographical strategies she succeeds in doing so, and what function these strategies have (cf. chapter 2.3.4). This requires a thematic field analysis that reveals the background of individual sequences of biographical self-presentation. This, in turn, requires a biographical grand narrative, since we need more than the telling of one story to reconstruct the thematic fields. We need the narration of several stories against the background of a thematic field created by the autobiographer – and not by questions asked by the interviewer.

4. On the Gestalt of narrated life stories

4.1 Biographical preconditions for shaping a life narrative as a Gestalt

Before applying the above analyses to the Gestalt-forming factors of a narrated life story, we need to discuss the preconditions for such a Gestalt-forming process. We cannot assume that every person in our society has at every point in his or her life a life history that presents itself as a Gestalt and that can be presented in words. Apart from interactional preconditions in the situation of narrating a life story – above all the presence of a listener who leaves the creative process to the autobiographer (cf. chapter 6.1), the *experienced* life history of the potential autobiographer must fulfill certain preconditions so that his life presents itself to him as a Gestalt and he can talk about it without further effort. The most essential biographical preconditions for this are:

1. patterns internalized during socialization for shaping the biographical presentation as a Gestalt, the cognitive competencies necessary for this, and a biographical necessity for the narration;
2. an experienced life history with a certain degree of biographical freedom to act and changes of lifestyle;
3. congruence of experienced life history and biographical overall evaluation;
4. a biographical coherence that has not been "destroyed".

4.1.1 Learned patterns, cognitive competence, and biographical necessity

With the social necessity for increasing biographization of our lives (cf. Fuchs 1983: 366), rules or patterns have become institutionalized which are offered to the autobiographer by his social environment for the interpretation of his life. The meaning-making process, i.e. the embedding of experiences in a context, their reorganization when they are thematized at a later time, and the memory frame constituted in the present of biographical self-presentation, are all based on institutionalized patterns and rules. How biographical experiences are interpreted and reinterpreted over time is socially constituted, as is the manner of their presentation. In the course of socialization, one learns which areas of life are narratable in which situations, which are better kept quiet, and which forms of presentation are appropriate. Some of these rules for the presentation of a life story are latently conveyed to the individual during the socialization process; in other words, these "collective unconscious rules of behavior" are, for him as well as for his socialization agents, "rules of behavior rendered speechless and not admitted into language" (Lorenzer 1979: 139, translated from the German). The "speechless body" in biographical narratives, which usually appears as a theme only when embedded in a history of illness, but hardly ever in experiences of pleasure, is partly an expression of such a rule[1]. If we then explicitly ask autobiographers to tell the story of their bodily experiences, as we did in some cases in our project "Biography" (Rosenthal 1989), we get interesting descriptions and arguments about different "body areas," but this prompt rarely evokes narratives. Either the body is subsumed under reflections on the self: what one has already said about oneself is presented again as a bodily feeling – as for instance in the case of Hans Gruen, who feels "divided in two" as a homosexual (cf. chapter 4.4.3). Or the innocuous topics that are permissible in our society are listed, such as giving up smoking, changing eating habits[2], or adopting new dress habits or regulations, as in the interview with a nun.

The manifest and latent learning process of presenting one's own life story, or parts of one's life, takes place in the most diverse contexts. One of the oldest institutions, which still exists today, that literally demands biographical thematization in the sense of reflecting on one's own past

---

1 In my opinion, this rule regarding exclusion of the body in our culture, which is not expressed in words, also has an effect in sociology, in which, apart from a few studies in the sociology of medicine, the body is treated as a sociologically irrelevant phenomenon or is not thematized at all. Even in studies of the body, the experience of pleasure is often excluded. For example, Herbert Plügge (1967), in his impressive phenomenological study of the body, assumes that the body only makes itself felt as something disturbing or foreign, as an experience of non-lust.

2 Cf. the statements made by Simone Hildebrand, chapter 4.3.3

actions and intentions, is confession in Catholicism which has been practiced since the 12th century (cf. Hahn 1982). In Protestantism, too, there are forms of self-confession; instead of telling an official person endowed with special privileges about one's actions and their biographical genesis, one confesses here to one's Christian brother or entrusts oneself to one's diary as an institution of "confession enabling biographical self-assurance" (Hahn 1982: 429). Thus, even today, a diary is an appropriate gift for a confirmand. Going beyond confession, the initiation of biographical narratives has become fashionable in both Catholic and Protestant pastoral care prior to official acts. Before conducting a wedding ceremony, for example, priests and pastors invite the couple to tell the story of their lives and the story of how they came to know each other, and sometimes then refer to these narratives in their sermon during the wedding. Or before a funeral they visit the relatives of the deceased and ask them to tell the family history (Schibilsky 1989a, 1989b). "We need a different basic understanding of the official acts. An important element is the biographical approach. And in the training of theologians .... this has been neglected for generations" (Schibilsky 1989b: 3, translated from the German).

In the secular sphere, we are not only asked to submit our CV when applying for a job (cf. Hohn/Windolf 1988; Schuler/Stehle 1986), but also to speak about our past life in the job interview. Physicians initiate biographical thematization during their anamnestic interviews, albeit in a mostly very limited form due to standard questions and answers. In court, defendants are asked to talk about their biographical background and the history of the development of their criminal career.

The biographical approach, in the sense of an understanding of the life narrative as a learning process, is also becoming increasingly popular in adult education and social work (cf. Nittel 1991; Mader 1989). Based on the seminars on so-called "guided autobiography" (Hateley 1985) developed by James E. Birren (Hateley 1987) in the USA in the 1970s, which are used in adult education, seminar participants in the Federal Republic of Germany are now also motivated to write their biographical experiences on the basis of a relatively closed guideline on certain areas of life, such as "the history of my family" or "the history of my attitude to food and drink", and are helped to do so (Mader 1989).

In job interviews and in court, a biographical narrative is demanded of the biographer and much depends on how he presents it. In confession, it contains a disciplinary and obligatory element. In pastoral care, in medical and psychotherapeutic anamnesis, in adult education and in social work, it serves to support the biographer and to "prevent and control biographically risky courses" (Brose/Hildenbrand 1988a: 22, translated from the German). Against this cultural background of the different settings in which, in our culture complex, we recount our life story or phases of our life, the biographical narrative stands between the poles of control and relief, between being judged and being understood. If a life story is to be told in the context of a biographical interview, as a form of relief and being understood, this requires an appropriate way of conducting the interview (cf. chapter 6.1).

In our culture, an adult is required or allowed to speak about his life in the most diverse contexts.[3] On the one hand, he is expected to have a "life history" – in the sense of a sequence of important dates – and, on the other hand, to make phases and events of his life comprehensible with temporalized accounts related to his identity, i.e. with biographical thematizations. In modern societies, not knowing one's date of birth, the number of one's siblings, or the date of one's marriage, as well as an inability to tell stories, would under certain circumstances entail the risk of psychiatrization.

How the social expectation of orientation to dates, which differs from society to society, can manifest itself within a life narrative is shown by the life story of a woman who emigrated to a modern society from a cultural area in which people are less aware of dates and often do not even know the year of their birth. It is the life story of a Jewish woman from Libya who came to Israel in 1949 when she was about 31 years old.[4] Liora Guetta was asked by Amalia Garon, psychology student: "Please tell me your life story. Anything that is important to you." Whereupon the biographer made clear how she understood this by asking "What I suffered and what I enjoyed?" and then spoke in detail about her childhood and youth, the death of her father, the birth of her three children, the war years, the Arab attacks on the Jewish population during the British occupation, her emigration to Israel and her life there. What is interesting about this interview is that the woman, who does not know in which year she was born, mentions no dates in connection with her life in Libya, but only her respective age – in contrast to her account of her

---

3 On the various types of biographical thematizations, see Allport 1942, chapter 6.

4 This biographical-narrative interview is from a project carried out by Dan Bar-On at Ben Gurion University in Beer Sheva, Israel. It was translated from Hebrew into English by Julie Chaitin. Initial joint interpretations took place in the seminar on biographical analysis I conducted in Beer Sheva. For a case analysis of this life story, as well as the life stories of Liora's children and grandchildren, see Bar-On (1994).

life in Israel. She introduces historical data only with the bombing of Tripoli in 1940 and the two pogroms against the Jewish population in 1945 and 1947. The first biographical dates she gives – such as her emigration to Israel, the death of her husband, or a trip to Italy – are related to her life in Israel. While we can interpret the mentioning of historical dates as an expression of the intrusion of world history into her life (Bar-On 1994), the fact that she mentions them in her narrative of her life in Israel reflects the importance of dates in a modern society and their official recording – as in the case of her husband's death certificate or the visa endorsement in her passport for the trip to Italy.

While it is easy to adopt the practice of memorizing dates, because this is required by the bureaucratic acts of a modern society and because they have to be given so often, storytelling, which is practiced especially in cultures less dependent on writing, requires far more skill. In modern societies the telling of family stories plays an important role in the family-specific appropriation of social reality (cf. Hildenbrand/Jahn 1988), and children develop competence in recounting biographical experiences in the family. At school – especially in German lessons – writing essays on biographical topics is used as a way of teaching stylistic means for presenting events experienced by oneself and others. In addition to the narrative, students learn how to write a report, minutes, or a description. In addition, they practice the basic ordering scheme for a life story in our culture: following the temporality of the life course, i.e., its chronology, which was discussed by Karl Jaspers (1923/1973: 567) as a specifically biographical order. Giving important biographical dates in the right order, i.e., in chronological order, is probably one of the first rules – besides the rules acquired with the competence to tell stories – that a child or adolescent in our society learns for telling a life story.

Excursus: life stories narrated by children?

How children and young people respond to the invitation to tell their life story gives us insight into these learning processes. My youngest interviewee is seven years old. Dirk, who knows about my interviews with "old" people, is eager to be interviewed himself. However, my request to tell me his life story overwhelms him, and so he initially protests: *"Why, what's the point?"* This not only allows him to reject my request for the time being, he also indicates how implausible this request seems to him. The request is incomprehensible for a seven-year-old child, because he does not yet have the concept of time (Piaget 1955/1974) and the cognitive competence for telling a life story, which are necessary for its meaning. He cannot establish a connection between individual events experienced in the past, nor can he reconstruct their sequence, nor understand the present and future in the mirror of the past. Just as he does not feel compelled to plan for the future beyond the present, he does not need to reflect on his past life. He is not faced with the need to make biographical decisions, nor does he have to reinterpret and weigh up past events.

When I then ask Dirk, "Tell me what you can remember", he answers, "Yes, quite a lot," and begins a long narrative about his train journey and his visit to relatives the previous day. This child is stuck in his immediate past, for him what is relevant is what has just been and is still going on, not what happened long ago. Since Dirk does not yet have a concept for presenting a life story, there are no further hesitations in his narrative flow. Rather, he can abandon himself to his relevancies and tell me about his journey, which stands out from the routine of his everyday life.

His 13-year-old brother Knut, who is present during this interview, finds this narration wrong and rebukes Dirk: *"That was pretty stupid, you didn't do it right"*. Knut probably already has an idea of the right way to tell a life story, or at least of the way it should be shaped. He responds to my request to tell his life story with the remark, *"My whole life, that's too much"*, verbalizing a problem we all have to solve. Every autobiographer must make a selection from the abundance of events in his life. He needs a thematic field, a framework that provides him with certain criteria for his selection. Let's see what Knut selects after I asked him to tell me whatever comes to his mind:

"I was born on 5.4.1975 in Munich. And then I was in the hospital for a week, then I was at home and (20 second pause) then when I was two, my parents separated. And what else? Then I started school. Was with the childminder the whole time" (translated from the German).

After this, he mentions the schools he went to and the moves with his mother. In contrast to Dirk, Knut has already learned what could be expected of him: 1. to report in the chronological sequence of events, and 2. to refer to biographical data such as birth, divorce of his parents, and enrollment in school. At the beginning, he gets into trouble with his attempt at making an objective report. He cannot remember his birth and his first years and therefore falters. When he realizes this, he makes large temporal leaps without telling stories about each turning point. Only later, when asked specifically about certain events, which relieves him of the problem of having to choose, does he recount specific experiences.

In another interview with 12-year-old Simon[5], the same phenomenon appears. He, too, reports the biographical "key data" and then repeatedly asks himself what else he could tell. In the interview with Simon, the effort that it means for a twelve-year-old to present an account corresponding to the request to tell his life story becomes obvious; the problem for him is the uncertainty that he does not know exactly which topics belong to the narration of a life story. The two older children try to meet a social expectation and are not able to abandon themselves to their own relevancies, as Dirk does with the story of his journey. However, when I ask Simon to tell me about his holidays, which he introduced right at the beginning when giving his biographical data, as what he "did in between", he embarks on a long narrative flow without pauses. Now he can recount experiences which have relevance for him, but which he had been unsure whether they belonged to telling his life story, or which he did not subsume under it.

Now Knut's and Simon's difficulty in finding a thematic guide for the selection of topics and stories by no means follows only from their uncertainty about what is expected of them or from the form of presentation, which at this age is more like a CV than a life story. Rather, the lack of narratives is also due to the absence of a "biographical overall view" – understood as a latent pattern, of which the biographer is not necessarily aware, with which he looks back on his life. Likewise, a twelve-year-old has not yet been able to develop a "biographical overall evaluation" – in the sense of an intentionally represented view of his life – that would express his evaluation of his past and future life, and determine the selection of experiences from his memory. An early adolescent who is still at the beginning of developing a sense of identity, the certainty of inner unity and continuity, is not yet able to present his life under a certain "motto" or from a certain perspective. He cannot yet look back on his childhood as: "A happy childhood in the country" or "An unhappy childhood caused by the divorce of my parents". However, if an autobiographer turns to his or her experienced life history without the potential of a specific perspective, it cannot present itself to him or her as a Gestalt. In this respect, these children are still faced with a disordered reservoir of individual memories. Unlike adults, they still need the questions of a listener to help them structure and select their experiences.

---

5 The interview was conducted by two sociology students, Evelin Strüber and Andreas Wüseke, as part of the teaching project "Biography", which I directed.

In contrast to the seven-year-old, the two older children already have the necessary cognitive competencies for telling a life story. In terms of their cognitive development, they are making the transition from concrete to formal operations, i.e., to hypothetical and deductive thinking (cf. Piaget 1933/1954). This enables them to think about the possible and the future, about the long-term consequences of their actions in the present, or even of their actions in the past, and to understand the present as lying between the past and the future. But even they do not feel a biographical need to sum up their past lives. Although Knut, for example, has already experienced biographical turning points relevant to his life, such as his parents' divorce, he does not yet conceive of himself as having a present that is distinct from the past. "Any narration of self-experienced memories refers, at least partially, to a change of the narrator's self" (Schütze 1984: 82, translated from the German).

In addition to the lack of cognitive competencies, which can be held responsible for the inability to tell one's own life story, the biographical necessity for biographical thematizations that refer to a temporal process is still relatively low in childhood and early adolescence. Everyday life is relevant, situations as they are currently experienced, and not reflection on how they came about. In the interview with twelve-year-old Simon, this self-definition, which is rooted in the present, manifests itself in self-descriptions to which, however, he does not give a biographical dimension. He does not tell or explain how he came to be what he is. He presents himself with his characteristics, his eating habits, his clothing preferences, his dreams, and his daily routines.

Self-*description* as a possible component of biographical self-presentation is seldom chosen by adults in our society, but the dominant form of life *narrative* in our culture, which follows the chronological order of events, is by no means the form chosen in all historical epochs and cultures: "Rather, the temporalization of a self-presentation is obligatory only where identical presents are the endpoint of extremely different pasts, that is, where the present does not make enough of the past transparent" (Hahn 1988: 98, translated from the German).

If one reads, for example, the description of the life of the Italian citizen Girolamo Cardano from the 16th century, it does not show a temporal Gestalt, "but, so to speak, a sectoral one" (Böhme 1990: 142, translated from the German). The life is divided into chapters such as "Home and Family" or "Of My Health", and it includes areas unfamiliar to the contemporary imagination such as "Shape and Appearance". This type of biography conceives "the wholeness of life according to a kind of bookkeeping with various headings" (ibid). Gernot Böhme (1990: 142) further refers to the account of Isocrates, who likewise deals with different circles of his bios one after the other: "The figure of life is here the figure of the person himself. It is not a development but his being that constitutes this figure". Hagiographies (biographies of saints), written to instruct and strengthen the reader's faith, also do not follow chronology. The biographers of the saints are rather concerned with "the didactically meaningful grouping of legends and (miracle) stories around an extremely thin biographical framework" (Alheit/Dausien 1990: 18, translated from the German).

4.1.2 Biographical freedom to act and changes in lifestyle

The need to thematize biographical experiences does not arise from a drive inherent in the individual. Rather, the motive – like all motives – is socially constituted. A self-referential view of one's experienced life history is socially imposed on members of society by the enormously expanded freedom to act that has developed in the course of the social process of modernization, by increasingly uncertain careers, by the lack of institutionalized trajectories, and by changes and breaks in people's lives (Fischer/Kohli 1987). Biographical thematizations are "provoked not by the self-evident normality of the life course, but by contingency experiences – by events and actions that call for classification, processing, normalization" (Kohli 1988: 40, translated from the German).

If, on the other hand, we look at biographical self-presentations of members of society who have had a pattern of events socially imposed on them without any biographical planning of their own, it becomes apparent how difficult it is to tell the story of a lifetime spent in an institution. Long-term inmates of total institutions (Goffman 1961), such as a psychiatric hospital, a prison or a convent are restricted in their agency and have little active involvement in planning and shaping their future. Their life path is institutionalized; other people determine both their future and the interpretation of their lives. Gerhard Riemann (1984; 1987) uses the example of psychiatric patients to show how their own biography can become alien to them precisely because experts take over the power to define their life story. This alienation from one's own biography and being subject to decisions taken by others can lead to "the partial or complete loss of a narrative relationship to one's own life story" (Riemann 1985: 381, translated from the German).

Excursus: narrated life stories of nuns and monks?

Another example is nuns and monks who, after entering a monastery or convent, are no longer able to make decisions concerning their own life. Our analysis of biographical self-presentations of nuns and monks can give further insights into the social constitution of the narrated life story and its lifeworld conditions. These biographical self-presentations were made in the context of biographical narrative interviews conducted by representatives of the secular world, where the possession of a life narrative is, so to speak, socially expected. In looking for the conditions that make it difficult for nuns and monks to tell their life stories, we encounter – as with psychiatric patients – the lack of individual life planning. Although nuns and monks, unlike psychiatric patients, decided voluntarily – at least according to their self-definition – to enter the total institution, they lose their individuality upon entry. Instead of individuality, they are expected to strive to be and live like all nuns and monks. The place for the expression of individuality in the monastery is the confessional. This classical context for biographical thematization and self-assurance serves – in addition to the creation of meaning – as a form of discipline (cf. Hahn 1982), for it is here that deviations from monastic norms are thematized. For the nun and the monk, this thematization of deviations is restricted to confession, and is not part of interactions outside the institution, especially not with representatives of the secular world. Here, we can quote Leitner (n.d.: 41 f., translated from the German) who writes about narrative taboos in the case of violation of norms in institutions whose practice is regulated by ceremonial procedures (from the family to the criminal trial): "For the narrative would present deviation as a strategic possibility much more emphatically than the norm itself does … At the very least, however, the narrative would indicate that one could do otherwise, that this was one among other possibilities".

Now, when nuns and monks are asked to tell stories about their life in the convent or monastery, we may expect that they will have no stories to tell – unless they belong to a religious order that emphasizes the individuality of its members. This is because stories are generally about exceptions to the rule, about something that did not go as would normally be expected. Instead – and this is also evidenced by our interviews (Beneker/Driever 1989)[6] – life in such institutions is portrayed through descriptions of the ceremonies and execution of the norms. The aim here is to "show something: reality as it meant to be" – and not how it is actually lived (Leitner n.d.: 44).

In addition to creating commonalities with other people, telling a life story, that is, telling stories about events that are unexpected and deviate from predetermined roadmaps, is a way of making a dense and detailed presentation of a unique life that is shared by no one else. Every person who presents himself or herself faces the insoluble problem of living up to the ambiguous expectation of being "like everyone else and yet like no one else" (Goffman 1963). This problem is exacerbated when two worlds interact, the monastic and the secular, each of which emphasizes different aspects of this expectation. Within the monastic world, which primarily requires "sameness", nuns and monks still have opportunities to express their "otherness". In addition to confession, there are niches here, as in every total institution, in which they can preserve their individuality – for instance in their personal identification with the biographies of particular saints. But what possibilities do they have in interaction with members of the secular world to present themselves differently from the others without breaking the rules of their order? At the same time, they must also comply with certain rules of the secular world in order to make communication possible at all. The nun and the monk must know how to navigate between a non-self-centered portrayal of religious life and the portrayal of an individual life path in order to be able to tell a life story at all.

A typical biographical strategy for dealing with this problem can be seen in the case study of Sister Maria Bernadette[7] presented by Hanna Beneker and Ute Driever (1989). This nun belongs to a religious order in which the nuns work not only within the convent but also externally in charitable institutions. Up to the point of entering the convent she presents her life history through narratives, and then moves to an account or description of monastic life – both the "career" of a nun and daily life – that is not tied to her person. In the approximately one-hour narrative about the pre-monastic phase of her life, she presents herself as the actor at the center of the action, but at the point of her biographical self-presentation when she

---

6 The biographical interviews were conducted within the framework of the teaching project "Biography".

7 The name is anonymized.

enters the monastery she immediately disappears as an actor from her life story. This break becomes manifest when she talks about how she left her personal belongings behind in her parents' house: while the autobiographer initially still appears as an individual actor, she then switches to a descriptive presentation in which the personal "I" is replaced by the impersonal "you" (German *man*):

"I left my watch at home (5 sec. pause). I put it (4) in the drawer and then my parents found it. You get new clothes (4) and then you have to do what your superiors tell you. And then you're taught the rules and regulations for daily life. And then you can't go out as much as you want, you have to ask for everything" (translated from the German).

She also presents being dressed as a nun – arguably a biographically relevant turning point – in a descriptive style that is independent of her person:

"And in August we were given our nun's clothes. So you first get (2) yes (2) it's a kind of trial period (2) and then you get this dress, like the one I have on now. Then you get a white veil, this is because I work, a white veil. So you get, you get a dar- black dress, as you know, and then you get a white veil for two years. So that's the outward sign that you're a novice (3)".

This description begins the account of her life in the convent, which lasts only about ten minutes in the interview; the predominant mode of presentation of this phase of her life is description. Embedded in this is the narration of the biography of the founder of her order, which is not untypical for a nun, as well as an argumentation about the happy life in the monastery. Finally, the 63-year-old nun gives a brief account of the various stages of her working life and then ends her presentation with the remark: *"That was my life"*, which refers neither to the present nor to the future. With her entry into the convent, Sister Maria Bernadette disappears as an actor from her biographical self-presentation. She does not explicitly justify her decision to enter the convent; rather, she presents her experienced life history as a path leading to this decision. Thus, she does not give her decision the character of an individual achievement, and at the same time avoids presenting herself as a praiseworthy person who, for example, took a vow (there are indications of this in her narrative about her experiences in World War II). Nor does she characterize herself as someone who had the grace of enlightenment.

Furthermore, it is interesting that this woman, who was born in 1925, concentrates on the war period in her account of her pre-monastic life and speaks about it in great detail, although she was already 14 years old at the beginning of the war and, moreover, continued to work for several years after the war. She thus presents the uniqueness of her life by reporting on the phase in which the secular world, the "big story", broke into her life; her pre-monastic life thus appears not as autonomously controlled, but as heteronomously produced. In wartime, however, Sister Maria Bernadette showed great drive and courage and was by no means driven by external circumstances. By embedding her activities in a time of passive suffering, she can present herself relatively covertly as an active and competent woman. We can therefore assume that this concentration on the war period – apart from the high biographical relevance of this time, which was presumably decisive for her later entry into the convent – has further significance for Sister Maria Bernadette's biographical overall view. By framing her biography within the collective biography of all those German Christian women who suffered war and expulsion, she succeeds in presenting the uniqueness of her biography without explicitly presenting herself as an active shaper of her life, but as one of many who had to suffer in the same way. While this *collective biography* can still be told, the *we-biography of the monastery* is then only presented through description of the rituals.

On the basis of this life story it becomes clear that the biographical self-presentation does not represent an individually created pattern emerging from a unique situation, but is a response of the autobiographer to the social constellation in which she lives, constituted according to social rules. We can say that the generation of regular autobiographies requires a life that has involved many changes and individual biographical decisions; at the same time, a life in which the autonomy of action of the subject is restricted to a considerable degree and everyday life is highly routinized tends to hinder the generation of an autobiography.[8]

4.1.3 Possible congruence of experienced life history and biographical overall evaluation

It is true that the presentation of one's life story is based on cultural rules and patterns that are internalized in the course of socialization. However, this cannot be understood in such a way that the autobiographer superimposes learned patterns on his or her experienced life history and thereby gives it order. Rather, the experienced life history imposes a specific order on the

---

8 Cf. my analyses of the structural differences in experiences of World War I and World War II and their effects on the generation of narrated life stories (Rosenthal 1991; 1993).

autobiographer depending on how he approaches it. In other words, just as the narrative has a structuring effect on the memory noema, the presentation of at least partially ordered memory noema has a structuring effect on the narrative. If, on the other hand, an autobiographer tries to force his experienced life history into socially desired or learned patterns, although no corresponding memory noema presents itself to him, he will not succeed in creating a biographical grand narrative. This failure of biographical grand narratives due to patterns or biographical global evaluations that are incongruent with the experienced life history can be observed, for example, when – as already indicated – extraneous theories for their lives are imposed on the biographers, as in the cases of psychiatric patients analyzed by Gerhard Riemann (1985; 1986; 1987). Riemann discusses the type of biographer who has assumed the role of a psychiatric expert when speaking about himself, with the consequence that in the biographical self-presentation the narrative scheme is replaced by argumentation.[9]

A completely different form of substitution of the experienced life history by justifications and argumentations is discussed by Lena Inowlocki (1988; 2000) on the basis of biographical interviews with right-wing extremist youth. Here, as in other analyses of biographical self-presentations of these young people (Michel/Schiebel 1989; Schiebel 1991; 1992), a consistent lack of narratives becomes apparent. Inowlocki is able to show on the basis of her research how these young people substitute collective historical references and historical experiences handed down in their families for their own biographical perspective.

The analysis of biographical self-presentations of members of society whose past or present is socially unrecognized, or problematic for themselves, also reveals the phenomenon of a lack of narrative (Rosenthal 1989). Whether it is a prostitute who, as a dominatrix, wants to present herself in an appropriately dominant, commanding manner and without any breaks in her life course (Ahrens et al. 1989), or a woman who can no longer have children but normalizes her problematic life course as well as her infertility (Diekhöhner 1989), they cannot abandon themselves to the flow of the narrative because their biographical experiences do not present themselves in a way that fits the desired presentation.

---

9 As further reasons for the lack of biographical narratives in psychiatric patients, Riemann discusses the lack of distance to the problematic time or getting lost in delusions.

On the Gestalt of narrated life stories 113

Excursus: narrated life story of a dominatrix?

Erving Goffman (1961: 151) expects criminals, alcoholics, and prostitutes to tell a "sad" life story, since – so he assumes – they will try in this way to gain understanding and recognition for their life path from the listener. While this idea is plausible for criminals – especially those with experience of being tried in court, and it is known that alcoholics seek to justify their alcohol abuse by talking about all the problems in their lives, this assumption is likely to apply to prostitutes only in certain biographical constellations. A prostitute will only make her involvement in prostitution plausible with a sad story if, in the interaction with the listener, she accepts the social rejection of her profession, sees her entry into prostitution as problematic[10], and regards her current work as a way of earning money that is not freely chosen. If, on the other hand, she stands by her profession, she will have to struggle with social rejection and will therefore try to justify herself, but this is likely to prevent her from telling a story of suffering. A sad story will be inappropriate if the prostitute does not suffer in her present working situation, but enjoys the autonomy it gives her, and especially the high earnings, like the call-girl Julia Rüwald[11] we interviewed in the context of our project. Julia Rüwald, for example, explains that she "entered the trade" because she had huge debts that she was unable to pay off, without, however, telling this as a sad story.

A story of suffering can be expected even less from a dominatrix whose task is to humiliate, torment and torture her clients. In the case of Lena Preusser[12], the aggressive presentation of her career as a prostitute and especially as a dominatrix predominates in the interview (Ahrens et al. 1989). In the case of this autobiographer, her self-portrayal as a woman who determines what happens – including the course of the interview! – and makes others accept her will as their own desire, coincides with her biographical global evaluation:

"I had found a way to exercise power in sexual matters, so that I wasn't in danger of being the underdog, in a literal sense"(translated from the German).

---

10 Harald Greenwald's study of "call girls" (1958) – to which Goffman refers – and his finding that they told elaborate "sad tales" is based, in addition to interviews, mainly on the psychoanalytic treatment of call girls. However, in therapy sessions, probably everyone has "sad tales" to tell.

11 The name is anonymized. Julia Rüwald was interviewed by Evelin Strüber and Rita Volpert in connection with the teaching project "Biography".

12 The name is anonymized. The interview is from the project "Biography".

Lena tries to squeeze her entire life – at least from the time she was 7 years old (!) – into this image of a woman exercising power, which reflects her sexual career. She worked as a street prostitute for a short time when she was 24 years old, after giving up her studies in social education, and after two and a half years of casual work, and since then has worked as a dominatrix in various establishments. Her biographical self-presentation, however, begins with the information, which suggests some degree of suffering, that her mother left her with her grandparents after her birth and "went away with the man who was my father". As an unwanted and unloved child, she had developed a wide variety of survival techniques. In this context, she then expresses the all-encompassing view of her life:

"I can remember deciding at about age seven: men and sexuality no. And if I did, I would never let a man gain power over me sexually".

Now it may well be that Lena thought such things at the age of seven. But what kind of suffering could have led a seven-year-old to make such decisions? Did she feel obliged to shield herself from male violence at the age of seven? However, this woman does not want to talk about her suffering; she wants to present herself as a woman who exercises power and dominates everything, who masters difficulties autonomously and competently in all situations. Therefore, she must not get caught up in stories, since stories deal with action blockages and thus reveal suffering. It is characteristic of Lena Preusser's self-portrayal that she nevertheless succeeds in conveying the impression that she would share intimate things from her life, that she would also be willing to tell stories (Ahrens et al. 1989: 75). A sequence that initially begins as a narrative makes this clear: when asked whether she actually got to know her mother, Lena Preusser answers that she found out her mother's address at the age of eighteen and visited her. She narrates in detail the story how she rang the doorbell, how her mother opened the door and, without hesitation, addressed her by name. The reader of the story now expects a narrative about the interaction between daughter and mother. Instead, Lena provides extensive background information about her mother's siblings, the number of children now living with her, and her marital situation. Embedded in this is the argument that the many children prevented her from asking her mother "about things that were important to me". Instead of talking about the meeting with her mother, about her disappointment because of the conversation that did not take place, and thus revealing her unfulfilled hopes and longing for affection – which for Lena presumably means weakness – she skips the complication part of the story. Rather, she ends with an evaluation that is consistent with her self-presentation:

"I had the feeling that they ((mother and siblings)) were really happy to meet me. So it was a great experience in that respect, just being taken in like that (3 second pause). Yeah, that was the time I met my mother".

Considering that she has not seen her mother again since then – and this means for 20 years – the evaluation of this meeting as a great experience can be interpreted as a considerable trivialization, as a defense mechanism. In addition to this interpretation of a defensive attitude towards her past suffering, her biographical self-presentation is also intended for the public. This woman has given interviews to the mass media several times and is interested in conveying a certain image of the dominatrix. Her presentation in the media coincides with the habitus of a dominatrix, i.e., the behaviors demanded of her in her profession and paid for. This habitus of a woman who dominates others, suggests a certain image of herself to them, and also deceives them (Lena always feigns coitus with customers), is probably not something she can easily discard. So she behaves accordingly in the interview, feigns intimacy, and controls the course of events. Structurally, she will not behave differently in her life outside her work. For example, in response to the interviewer's question about whether her sexuality with a partner differs from that with clients, she says: "With me, my own sexuality with my own husband is only different in some ways".

Apart from the special features of this woman who is used to public self-presentation, we can generally assume that the professional work of a dominatrix – as in the case of some other occupations – has an impact on the whole personality, and that in the present case it leads to dominating behavior in situations outside her profession. It is therefore to be expected that these women will portray themselves as self-confident women who do not suffer but are proactive – and a sad life story does not fit in with this. Lena Preusser's everyday theory that every person is responsible for his or her own decisions, actions and desires fits seamlessly into the portrayal of an autonomously constituted life path. This theory also provides legitimation for working as a dominatrix. Thus, it succeeds in attributing her activity as a tormentor to the autonomous decision of her clients, and not having to see herself as responsible for her own aggressive actions.

Excursus: the loss of the life narrative and its correspondence with modern reproductive medicine.

Let us further consider the biographical self-presentation of a woman who suffers from childlessness and has decided to undergo the costly, unpromising and painful process of extracorporeal fertilization (Dieckhöner 1989). One might assume that behind this decision is a long process of suffering. However, Ms. Tiemann[13] repeatedly asserts in the interview that everything was always normal and unproblematic for her. The extent to which this corresponds to wishful thinking rather than to the experienced past and, above all, the present, becomes manifest in one of her statements in the context of the topic "parental home," about which she knows nothing:

"Well, I never had many problems or I can't think –. Okay, everyone has problems sometimes, but (2) they don't stick. What sticks are the nice things. Let's put it this way. Or rather, I want it to stick" (translated from the German).

Yet her life story – especially from the perspective of her present infertility – contains a number of problems: an abortion at the age of 15, a divorce, a remarriage, a miscarriage after the seventh week of pregnancy, and fallopian tube obstruction. But in the interview these "data" are only dealt with in report form by Ms. Tiemann. When asked by the interviewer about her first husband, she talks, for example, about how pleasant it was for her to get to know him, about the initially misinterpreted symptoms of pregnancy, and about the visit to the doctor during which her pregnancy was diagnosed. Instead of now speaking about the following, certainly difficult, time, and about her abortion, there follows – as in all corresponding passages – a problem-avoiding, i.e., normalizing account (Dieckhöner 1989: 123 f.) in which she plays down her difficulties. With a laugh she tells how the pregnancy was diagnosed, and says:

"I say, but we've done a great job. That's why, I wouldn't know how to tell it any other way, it sounds a bit strange, but– You know how it is, one person wants it this way and the other– I see it positively. What am I supposed to do, I can't just look gloomy, I always say, if I didn't see it that way, I wouldn't be where I am today".

Interestingly, this normalization of the experienced life history and the concomitant loss of a life narrative is evident in another case study of a woman who also underwent this method of treatment. In her case analysis

---

13 The name is anonymized. The interview is from the project "Biography".

of an IVF patient, Kerstin Rießbeck (1988)[14] convincingly shows to what extent this evasion in respect of the "biographical processing" of childlessness corresponds to and supports the "reductionist perspective of modern reproductive medicine, which excludes the biographical contexts of meaning and significance of the symptom of involuntary childlessness" (ibid.: 179). The autobiographer presented here normalizes not only her unfulfilled desire to have children, which has already lasted eight years, but her entire life history. This is manifested in the textual structure of her biographical self-presentation. When asked to tell her life story and to start with her childhood, she summarizes everything up to her marriage at the age of 22 – the beginning of her unfulfilled desire to have children – with the global evaluation that *actually* she had a "normal and happy childhood":

"Well, what can I tell you about my childhood? Quite a normal childhood, actually. We were (1) I still have a little brother. He's ten or nine years younger than me. My parents have a terraced house. So everything is quite normal, actually (laughing). Nothing out of the ordinary. Actually quite a nice childhood. A good relationship with my parents. (2) Then I got married when I was twenty-two. My husband is twelve years older than me".

With this global evaluation of normality, however, stories cannot be told, since stories are more about blockages to action than about normal routine. Instead of recounting self-experienced events, autobiographers whose self-presentation is incongruent with their experienced life history lay emphasis on their global evaluations, which they try to corroborate with arguments and supporting narratives. In such cases, there can be no question of a "narrated life story". However, since narratives run the risk of becoming entangled in contradictions which belie the evaluations, they must be avoided. "The success of an autobiographical interview depends on the informant being able to abandon himself to the narrative stream of reliving his experiences, and that he does not take a calculated, prepared story, or a story that has often been told as a form of legitimation, as a narrative foil" (Schütze 1984: 78, translated from the German).

From the above considerations it follows that if there is a difference between the presentation interests of the autobiographer and the experienced life history, such that the experienced life history cannot serve these interests, then no life story with Gestalt quality will result without great effort on the part of the autobiographer. He or she must work hard to produce "some-

---

14 This case analysis was developed in the context of a diploma thesis I supervised.

thing" that is well ordered; to do this, they need their argumentation scheme and cannot abandon themselves to any narrative flow.

4.1.4 A life story that has not been "destroyed"

With adults, if they engage in a narrative flow and do not counteract it with incongruent overall evaluations, we can generally assume that the process of shaping the narrative does not require any additional effort and construction. However, if the autobiographer looks back on an extremely fragmented, torn and confusing life, if he has been traumatized by certain experiences, then some effort and construction are necessary so that the experienced life history as a whole – and not only single phases – can present itself to him as a Gestalt.

Excursus: survivors of the Shoah

This is shown in particular by my analyses of narrated life stories of survivors of the Shoah (Rosenthal 1995a; 1998/2010; 2010a). The persecution, the physical and psychological destruction of their environment and of parts of themselves, permanently destroyed their sense of continuity. The experienced life history of these people presents itself as "torn apart" and fragmentary, and a connection between the different phases – meaning the time before persecution, the time of persecution, and the time after surviving – can be established only with difficulty. Even within one phase, there may be considerable breaks between different experiences. And entire phases may sink into the realm of speechlessness and be accessible to the biographer only in the form of fragments, images and moods.

These phenomena require further analysis, as they give us insight into a) the conditions of Gestalt formation, b) the psychological consequences of Gestalt destruction, and c) the healing effects of biographical narratives (cf. chapter 5.2).

Some survivors are unable to present their memories from the time of persecution in the form of narratives.[15] They solve this problem with the fol-

---

15 In psychiatric literature they are described as the 'average type' (cf. Eissler 1963; 1968), whereas in my interviews they are rather an exception. This is probably due to the fact that I did not interview psychiatrized people and that they had volunteered to be interviewed. By contrast, most

ON THE GESTALT OF NARRATED LIFE STORIES

lowing presentation structure: they tell their life stories up to the beginning of the period of persecution, or up to the traumatic turning point during persecution, then skip the entire phase up to liberation, and continue with the time after liberation. This structure can be found, for example, in the life story of an Auschwitz survivor: Ms. Silbermann[16] from Jerusalem describes in detail the three extremely stressful years in the ghetto, during which – except for her mother – the entire family was murdered, and reports briefly how she was taken to Auschwitz with her mother in the summer of 1944. She then spans the temporal arc to the end of the time she spent in the camp. She tells the story of her survival in detail: she survived because she wanted to die. In January 1945, shortly before the SS left the camp with the prisoners, except for the most seriously ill, her mother was admitted to the sick block. This usually meant certain death in the extermination camps. After several failed attempts, Ms. Silbermann finally succeeded in being admitted there as well. She wanted to die together with her mother. The result was that mother and daughter did not take part in the "death march", which they would not have survived in their physical condition, but experienced the liberation by the Red Army in the camp.

In the interview with Ms. Silbermann, I tried several times to motivate her to tell more stories about the time in Auschwitz. I was unsuccessful. She could only respond with images like "The prisoners all looked deranged" or "Auschwitz was a madhouse", and could not tell any stories. For her, time in the camp has lost its temporality, it has shrunk to a timeless figure that can only be reproduced as an overall impression without particular elements, or particular experienced situations that led to the creation of this impression.

When I met Ms. Silbermann again a year later, in February 1991 during the Gulf War, the reason for this lack of narrative became drastically clear. When I asked her how she fared during the Iraqi missile attacks, sitting in a blacked-out room, she said:

"I feel like I did during the actions in the ghetto. I have this terrible, paralyzing fear, this pain in my stomach. Then after the all-clear, I feel all empty, all weak and lame, like in the ghetto" (translated from the German).

---

survivors with whom the psychiatrists spoke had to have these anamnestic interviews for the purpose of diagnosing "persecution-related harm" in the context of so-called redress of wrongs proceedings (Compensation for National Socialist Injustice). On the problem of inability to speak about extreme experiences, see Funkenstein (1993) and Greenspan (1992).

16 The name is anonymized like all others.

She dismisses my question, "Do you also feel like you're back in Auschwitz?"

"No, I don't think about that, I was almost dead by then, I didn't feel anything anymore".

To be almost dead, to feel nothing, to be in the state of a "Muselmann", as prisoners were called in the camp language who had given up on themselves and bore outwardly visible signs of death, meant the loss of any ability to plan one's actions and any future horizon. The prisoner only allowed himself to drift, functioning like a machine in the daily life of the camp, and was passively at the mercy of the traumatizing routines – such as standing for the roll call. The prisoner increasingly disappeared as an agent from his own life story, which thus became impossible to tell. This contrasts with the life stories of survivors who did not give up on themselves but fought for their survival with cunning and guile and who were not condemned to complete passivity due to their specific situation, such as those crammed into narrow hiding places. Such people often tell long and detailed, almost obsessive stories. Typically, Ms. Silbermann is able to tell her "liberation story" in detail. At this point, she had decided to do something, had become active, and, despite opposition from the camp doctors, achieved admission to the sick barracks.

Being unable to narrate one's own experiences due to forced passivity and persistent, recurring traumatizing situations is also evident in life stories of World War I veterans (Rosenthal 1988;1991). In the case of Mr. Span, this appeared very clearly. In the interview, he first talked for about half an hour about his childhood, his enlistment in the army in 1917, his training as a soldier, and his first days in the barracks. Then he described his deployment on the northern Italian front and began with a detailed description of the trench and the chapel that could be seen from there. Suddenly he could not remember any more, had a complete black out. He had been in the trench for a year, and although he wanted to remember, all he could remember was the picture of the chapel which he had drawn a few days before the interview, with the windows painted black, resembling grave crosses. Subsequent questions did not help him either; he could not remember any events, he could only remember the chapel, presumably a symbol of death. Only when he was asked about the end of the war did he start describing situations in detail again, this time about what happened during his imprisonment. This is an extreme example, but structurally it differs little from other interviews with men who suffered during World War I as soldiers in the trenches. The year or years experienced in the trenches shrink down to a single image, like the chapel on the next hill, or to terse evaluations, like "that was so terrible, you can't de-

On the Gestalt of narrated life stories 121

scribe it", which are helpless attempts to give expression to the feelings of mortal fear and despair embedded in one's memory.

In contrast to the life stories of war veterans, it is very clear that in the case of survivors of the Shoah not just one particular area but their entire life story is marked by their extreme experiences. In addition to the difficulty of narrating traumatizing experiences, which has been discussed many times in the literature in connection with the Shoah (cf. Eissler 1963; Niederland 1980), the life stories of survivors show that persecution can cause the time before and the time after traumatization to sink into the realm of storylessness. There are autobiographers who a) *cannot* say much about the time before their persecution, or b) *cannot* say much about the time after their persecution, or c) can *only* talk about the time of their persecution.

Ms. Weiss is one of those who can offer practically no life narrative before her transport to Auschwitz. At the beginning of the interview, she briefly gives background information about her origins, such as her parents' occupation and how many siblings she had, and briefly mentions when they entered the ghetto with the family. Then she gives a detailed account of the transport to Auschwitz, the circumstances of her separation from her mother at the ramp, and her time as "Mengele's guinea pig" together with her twin sister. In the question part of the interview, I try several times unsuccessfully to motivate her to say more about the time before the transport. My first question after her so-called main narration in this interview conducted in English (Ms. Weiss' "main language" is Hebrew; she no longer speaks her native Hungarian) is[17]: *"What can you remember about the time before the war?"* She answers:

"About the time before the war, eh–, you was, eh, you are– eh very– (2 seconds pause) eh– (2 seconds pause) happy family."

Her husband, who was present during the interview, corrects her: *"We was, we was."* Ms. Weiss:

"We was a very, a very happy family, eh–, and–, eh– (2 seconds pause) very rich family."

The confusion between "you" and "we", which is certainly not due to linguistic incompetence, gives us a first indication that her life story before Auschwitz is lost. It is significant that Ms. Weiss uses the first person plural personal pronoun in her narrative correctly up to the point where she was violently

---

17 The commas used in the transcript mean a short pause; and – – = abort.

separated from her mother upon arrival at the ramp in Auschwitz. In the course of her narration about the time in Auschwitz-Birkenau, where she was taken with her twin sister, while her parents and two older sisters were killed in the gas chambers immediately after their arrival, she loses the "we", which was irretrievably destroyed at that time. Ms. Weiss' childhood before Auschwitz – she was ten years old at the time of the transport – shrinks to the stereotype of the happy family and a few remaining photographs from that time, which she showed me. (One of these pictures, in which she is portrayed together with her twin sister, she gave to me). Childhood was cruelly and forever ended in that situation, when SS men tore her and her sister away from their mother's hands, because as twins they were to be kept "alive" for medical experiments.

One could object that this woman had very few memories of her childhood because she was only ten years old. But I also observed this phenomenon, which is reported in the psychiatric literature (cf. Grubrich-Simitis 1979), and which is described there as being due to the domination of memories of the time of their persecution, in some of my older interviewees. These people, all of whom were in an extermination camp, differ decisively from those who can talk about their life before their persecution. Unlike the latter, they have lost everything, absolutely everything, their entire life before their persecution: their families, their homeland, their language, their possessions; but also their plans for the future at that time, their chosen biographical paths, their hopes and their faith in God[18] as well as in themselves. Their former life line was abruptly and irreparably severed by the Nazis (cf. Niederland 1980: 229). The time before their persecution is no longer part of their narrated life story, or can no longer be integrated into their biography, because everything has been destroyed. There are no areas of their previous life to which they can still connect, no professional career and no family life. Formulated in terms of Gestalt theory: The figure of their life before their persecution cannot be integrated into the figure of their life after their persecution. There are no connecting lines between life before and after persecution.[19]

---

18 Ms. Weiss, for example, comes from an Orthodox family that kept strictly kosher. Like so many survivors, she thinks she lost her faith in God in Auschwitz; and since she couldn't keep kosher there, it didn't make sense for her afterwards.

19 Here the question arises how this applies to survivors whose life story began with their persecution, for whom persecution did therefore not constitute a break in their life. The life story of

Another reason for the loss of a life narrative before persecution can be that this time and the family members are idealized, and correspondingly all unpleasant feelings, thoughts and actions connected with the deceased are denied.[20] This idealized memory of a "happy time" or of tender, loving parents and siblings, which most often starts to develop during the time of persecution, can lead those affected to avoid telling stories in order not to jeopardize it.

Another argument in favor of the interpretation that life stories before persecution are lost due to the destruction of all continuities is that those people who tell stories about the time before their persecution narratively expand precisely those biographical strands that were taken up again after the war. For example, a survivor who was also in Auschwitz and lost her parents, sister and husband there focuses on the narrative of her educational career, which she was able to resume after 1945. Other biographical strands – such as her marital history – are introduced by her only briefly with the respective dates.

Moreover, the stories such people tell about the time before their persecution, as well as those about the time after it, are characterized by the fact that most often the entire biographical self-presentation is embedded in the thematic field of "persecution". In other words, the survivors can only see their lives within the frame of reference of the Shoah. Provocatively formulated: they have lost both the biographical strands of their life story and other ways of seeing their past experiences when they do not fit into this frame. Everything they have experienced and are experiencing, their entire attitude to life, and their biographical overall view is connected to the experience of persecution.

The thematic field of "persecution" varies from autobiographer to autobiographer with their different biographical experiences. It can be determined by the recurring question of why they did not emigrate in time, or, in the case of refugees, why they left their parents behind, or why they did not fight against anti-Semitism before the war. Dr. Prawda's biographical self-presentation (see below for details) is also framed in terms of persecution; he sums

---

a woman who experienced the most unimaginable abuse from the age of four shows how such a past can be remembered emotionlessly with all its details, as if it did not belong to her.
20 On the idealization of childhood in survivors, see Chodoff (1963).

up his entire life under the title "My Humanitarian Struggle Against Hitler's War of Annihilation".[21]

Accordingly, he presents his life before his persecution in the context of "my professional success despite anti-Semitism".

A survivor from Slovakia answers all my requests to tell me about her childhood and youth with stories that fit the thematic field of her main narration: "Why I did not emigrate". She tells me about good relations with Christians and that anti-Semitism was barely noticeable in her hometown. She tries to explain why she and her family did not foresee the coming persecution. When asked, "You have told me very little about your childhood so far. Maybe you can tell me a bit more about your life at home?" she answers:

"My family home, my parents were religious Jews. And as I told you, we were six children. I was the second one. We lived in a small town.... And at that time we young people were very happy. Maybe our eyes were closed. I don't know. Maybe we didn't want to see it. As a child, we didn't know what anti-Semitism was" (translated from the German).

The phenomenon of restricting the narrated life story to the thematic field of persecution, and being unable to leave it even when asked directly by the interviewer about other topics, is also evident in survivors' narratives about the time after their persecution. For example, Ms. Weiss, who survived Auschwitz as a twin, talks in great detail about her life after liberation. This life is a history of illness caused by the experiments carried out by Mengele and his helpers.

The possible objection that the thematic field of "persecution" results from the interview situation, in which the survivors want to present themselves as survivors of the Shoah, can be rejected if we compare these with other biographical self-presentations. In all of our interviews, the interviewees feel that they have been chosen because of one of their biographical characteristics, whether as a veteran of the First or Second World War, as the daughter of a Nazi perpetrator, or as a nun. But this determines the structure of their life narrative only when it is central to their biographical overall view. Otherwise, although they briefly address what they assume to be our interests, they shape their life narrative according to their own relevancies. Moreover, in the question part of the interview, they usually do not stay in the thematic field of their main narration. In these interviews, we must constantly strive not to determine the thematic field through our questions

---

21 Dr. Prawda asked me to give this title to his life story.

and thus break through the interviewees' relevancies. In interviews with survivors, on the other hand, this danger exists only when we try to focus on topics that are not relevant for the biographers, but not for a change of their thematic field. It can therefore be assumed that most Holocaust survivors, even in different contexts, are only able to tell their life story within the frame of reference of the Shoah. In my opinion, there is an opportunity here for effective assistance by listeners who can help the interviewees to reconstruct experiences that are not in the thematic field of persecution (cf. chapter 5.2).

What background experience prevents survivors of the Shoah – and this can presumably also be applied to survivors of other extreme situations – from narratively expanding their life story *after* liberation?

Mr. Prawda represents this type. At the time of the interview, the 81-year-old looks back on a very successful life. He came to Israel as a doctor in the early 1950s and embarked on another career – now already 41 years old – to become an internationally renowned university professor. He has four children and several grandchildren. After the death of his wife a few years ago, he married again.

These data alone suggest that this man could tell quite a bit about his life in Israel; his successful professional career also suggests a future orientation after his emigration. However, Mr. Prawda's life after his persecution is not the subject of his life narrative. He only talks about this phase of his life when prompted by detailed questions, and answers with only one story at a time. In contrast to the account of his life before liberation, about which he talks for eight hours in the course of two interview appointments, he does not get into any narrative flow. As I learned from his family, he has been telling his liberation story to the members of his family every Rosh Hashana (the Jewish New Year) for several years, ending each time – as in the interview – with the same story. This story is about a court case shortly after the liberation of his homeland, in which he was given the right to take back his daughter, who survived the Nazi occupation in the care of a Christian woman. The Christian woman did not want to return the child.[22]

Dr. Prawda's life narrative focuses on his dramatic escape from the ghetto and how he found his wife, who, independently of him, had also fled

---

22 Interviews with his children and grandchildren made it clear that the family dynamics revolve around this detail of the family history, namely the giving away of the firstborn daughter to a Christian and winning her back with the help of a court case.

the ghetto, staying with Polish peasants. Hypermnestically[23], all the details are still present in his memory. During the narration, in which he switches from German to his mother tongue Yiddish, and quotes literally what people said in Russian or Polish, he increasingly returns to the past. He repeatedly switches to the present tense, speaks more and more to himself, becomes more and more difficult to understand acoustically, is emotionally very agitated. He goes through every detail of the escape again in his memory and in his narration; he also draws the escape route on a piece of paper. But Mr. Prawda does not feel liberated today, despite his successful escape, and despite interpreting his life as a "victory over Hitler". He can repeat the story of his rescue, and the rescue of his wife and daughter, again and again, but he still remains trapped in the ghetto. He can draw a map of his escape route from the ghetto – he has a whole sketchbook about it – but he still feels he is in the ghetto, or as the Dutch psychiatrist Jan Bastiaans (1988: 63) puts it: he is out of the ghetto, but the ghetto is in him. "For these victims, life is an unfinished past. Even if they develop an external appearance of adaptation after the war, this does mean they have developed a healthy inner condition. Behind the facade, the person lives with all the fear, all the misery, all the powerlessness of that time" (ibid.; translated from the German).

This feeling of being trapped has led Dr. Prawda to concern himself obsessively with every detail of his survival. Just as he had to think about every move in the situation of escaping, he continues to think about every detail afterwards. As with some other survivors (cf. Tyrangiel 1989: 43), his life narrative gives the impression that nothing significant has happened in his life since his liberation.

In these examples I have discussed various difficulties which people whose biographical coherence has been destroyed can have in presenting their experienced life history as a coherent temporal Gestalt. The experienced life history cannot present itself here as a unified Gestalt without constructive effort, for which the survivor needs help from others (cf. chapter 6.1). The fragmentations, ruptures and speechlessness are the product of specific circumstances in each case. In other words, the fragmented narrative presented today corresponds to a specific experienced life history.

---

23 The phenomenon of hypermnesia, the "over-vivid memory, charged with strong emotion, of traumatic experiences of persecution and the associated mental shock" (Niederland 1980: 230, translated from the German), can be observed in a number of survivors. It is usually accompanied by a disturbance of the ability to remember other events from this period.

On the Gestalt of narrated life stories

And yet, if one reads the literature on the consequences of persecution for the survivors, one tends to get the impression that they are a homogeneous group whose members all suffer from similar psychological and somatic disorders, which are summarized as the survivor syndrome.

4.2 The simple grasping of orderedness[24]

The thematic field of a biographical grand narrative or biographical self-presentation is constituted in the interrelation between how the experienced life history is shaped when remembered in the current interaction with an imagined or physically present listener, and how it is presented. The experienced life history, which is remembered differently depending on the reasons for approaching it, provides a memory frame which – provided it is compatible with the presentation interests of the autobiographer– enables the autobiographer to make a biographical narration without further effort. If the narrated life story coincides with the experienced life history in the interactive process of presentation, and if it is not a "destroyed" and deeply "traumatized" life, we can assume that the grasping of orderedness will not be a problem.

Against this assumption it could be objected that asking an autobiographer to narrate his whole life, or a – thematically limited –area or phase of his life, confronts him with a very difficult task. One could doubt whether such a general request as: "Please tell me the story of your life" can be complied with at all, since the person cannot know what would interest the listener, or what he should select from the great variety of events in his life. Doesn't he look back on a chaos composed of myriad individual, unrelated experiences, a disordered reservoir that can only be pieced together through associations? In order to generate and support these associations, in which the thematization of one experience awakens the memory of another, he would need the help of questions. As social scientists, do we not have to provide an order in our interviews, for otherwise how could the biographer create this order? Based on empirical practice, one can refute this argument: in response to a very general initial narrative question or initial narrative prompt, people are

---

24 The following discussion focuses on Gestalt theory discussions of the ordering structures of theme, thematic field, and margin. See Fritz Schütze (especially 1984) for an elaborated conception of the Gestalt character of biographical narratives.

able to tell their life story, mostly at length and sometimes without hesitation. Moreover, these biographical self-presentations are usually very coherent, the parts are related to each other, and we as listeners do not have the impression of stories strung together through association, but of something ordered by secret principles. Our analyses – if we proceed sequentially and holistically – then make clear how extremely ordered the whole biographical self-presentation is (cf. Schütze 1984). For example, Ms. Stegmann, the daughter of the euthanasia doctor, consistently narrates her biographical experiences as if she were a victim of perpetrators throughout her life, with the main perpetrator being her own father. Each of the stories told has a functional significance for this overall picture and is located in the same thematic field. If, on the other hand, autobiographers leave one thematic field in the course of their biographical narrative and switch to another, the fields do not alternate from story to story. Rather, autobiographers first recount their experiences in one field, and then those in the next. Usually, the change of fields is also manifested linguistically, i.e., the autobiographer either announces it explicitly, as is clear in the example of Mr. Gruen (chapter 4.4.2), or it is expressed implicitly, by making a pause in the interview, or even by the drastic form of breaking off the interview and continuing it at a later time, as in the case of Mr. Jarok (chapter 4.4.4).

One could now think that the biographers intentionally produce this order, that their intention is to convey a certain image of themselves. What incredible concentration this would require! But instead of being exhausted by the effort, our interviewees are still alert, even after hours; only we as listeners slump in our chairs, tired from listening.

We can assume that the experiences described are not randomly chosen, due perhaps to interactive influences or the particular mood of the biographer. The narrated life story does not consist of an atomistic accumulation of experiences whose meaning and structure is produced in the situation of presenting it. Thus, neither the dynamics of the interview (Schütze 1984: 79) nor the work of construction by the narrator can be seen as the decisive factor. Fritz Schütze attributes the structure of the biographical narrative "to the structure of the recollected biographical layering of experiences" (ibid.), although he by no means assumes homology of experience and narrative, as suggested by Heinz Bude (1985).[25] In this context, it is important to take into account the fundamental difference in the temporal structure of the expe-

---

25 Cf. the convincing rejection of this criticism by Gerhard Riemann 1986: 154 f.

rienced life story and the narrated life story, which has been empirically reconstructed in the work of Wolfram Fischer (1982; 1985); otherwise, we would miss the potency of the interaction between noema and noesis as conceived in phenomenology and Gestalt theory. The structural difference between experienced and narrated life story therefore requires a closer look (cf. chapter 4.4).

First of all, it can be assumed that the narration of a life history takes place against the background of a biographically constituted context which determines the selection of experiences to be presented, in the interaction with the listeners or an imagined audience. This context, which is constantly affirmed and transformed by the flow of life, is constituted by the indissoluble network of social rules for the planning and interpretation of one's life, i.e., the biographical course and the given horizons of interpretation for a meaningful life, with biographically significant experiences and their reinterpretation. The order we can observe in a narrated life story arises neither from the subjective performance of the narrator, nor from the objective social rules, neither from ideas nor facts, but – to borrow the words of Edmund Husserl – from the experienced life, the unassailable interrelation between the world and myself (cf. chapter 2.3.1). As we can see from the above considerations, the orderedness of a biographical self-presentation results from the fact that both the person's experienced life and their approach to this life in the present of the narration form in each case a Gestalt. The experienced life history has a coherent character due to the continuous succession of events, and to the coherence of a subject identical with itself. This coherence is given in the immediate experience of the social world without needing a coordinating agency (cf. Gurwitsch 1964/2020: 17). Thus, a relationship between different experiences arises from their integration in the overall context of the subject's life. Even in the case of changes, breaks and discontinuities, the center of the experiences is always the subject and this alone creates coherence.

This is not to say, as Pierre Bourdieu (1986/1990), for instance, wrongly ascribes to biographical research, that the experienced life history is not fragile, contingent and inconsistent. A biographical self-presentation, with its narratives of biographical experiences and theoretical comments on the narrator's own life path, serves, after all, precisely to establish consistency or continuity. Biographers talk about their lives because they want to be sure about their past, however fragile, their present, and their anticipated future. With the narrative they try either to give their life a consistent shape and to explain to themselves the story of their changes, or – as we will see in the case analyses of Mr. Gruen and Mr. Jarok – to avoid or dissolve connections in the narrative, especially if these are threatening and unpleasant for them. The presentation of a fragmentary life, as well as that of an unbroken, smooth, coherent life, can serve to heal problematic experiences. For the biographers, narrating their life story has the function of helping them to live with the changes, the ruptures, the brokenness of their life, or with unpleasant continuities and consistencies.[26]

However, the creation of continuity and consistency in a life that is initially experienced as fragile is not only based on the act of turning one's attention to it. Rather, the life history experienced as fragile presents itself – at least in part – as a coherent structure by showing possible lines of connection between the turning points and the breaks. Even phases that were experienced as very fragile, such as the chaotic years in the trenches, or phases that were incomprehensible and not infrequently traumatizing for the autobiographer, receive orderedness through their integration in the overall life course. In the situation of narration, recalling these phases helps to structure what is still unstructured through the structuring act of speaking. By expressing our experiences in words, we integrate them into the orderedness of the language system. The speech act – at least as Merleau-Ponty (1960) sees it – is itself structuring: "... for the speech act, which declares something and makes it known in a certain sense, is itself a structuring process and constantly draws on existing structures" (Waldenfels 1980: 157, translated from the German). Not only is language itself structured, but it also has a structuring effect beyond the intentions of the speakers.

4.3 Orderedness after biographical turning points

Temporal breaks, i.e., turning points in the life course that separate the time "before" from the time "after," are essential factors in forming the Gestalt of the narrated life story. Therefore, they require detailed consideration. Three types of turning points can be distinguished:

a) turning points relevant from the perspective of development psychology
b) status transitions, i.e., socially typified turning points,

---

26 On the function of biographical narratives, see Alheit 1983, 1985; Fischer 1978; 1989; Kohli 1981; Rosenthal 1987: 132–142.

On the Gestalt of narrated life stories

c) interpretation points, i.e., turning points experienced as significant breaks.

4.3.1 Turning points that affect psychological development

These turning points lead to profound transformations of the individual, but are not necessarily experienced consciously, or remembered, by the subject. Nevertheless, they affect the organized nature of memory and the textual structure of the narrated life story. Three turning points in particular are described in the literature on developmental psychology, with the major psychological changes: the transition from early to middle childhood, the transition to late adolescence and young adulthood, and the transition to middle age from around age 50 (Cohler 1982). However, the transition to old age must also be considered, since this also envolves important psychological changes (cf. Neugarten 1979).

The *first transformation* (approximately between the fifth and seventh year of life) leads in the area of psychodynamic development to the resolution of the Oedipal crisis (Freud 1905), and in the area of cognitive development to operational thinking (Inhelder/Piaget 1958). According to psychoanalytic assessment, this transformation is associated with infantile amnesia (Freud 1905/1960: 75 ff./Anna Freud 1971), since the children no longer want to remember the aggressions associated with the Oedipal conflict, their extreme competitive behavior and their sexual desires: "With childhood amnesia, the remembered past becomes quite different from the past previously recalled. Successive transformations of this personal narrative across adulthood further modify these earlier memories" (Cohler 1982: 216).

Important in the context of the transformation of childhood memories are the "screen memories" discussed by Sigmund Freud (1899): "Screen memories owe their value not to their own content, but to its relation to another repressed content" (ibid. 1960: 551, translated from the German). While the experiences that were significant to the child are repressed, the adult vicariously remembers less significant and, more importantly, less threatening experiences. The screen memories are thus a substitute for other, more significant and threatening, memories. In narrated adult life stories, infantile amnesia manifests itself in that the autobiographer either begins his presentation with experiences from his school years and skips over experiences from the preceding phase, or the text structure of his childhood accounts differs from accounts of later phases. While childhood is presented with fragments of experiences, pictures and compressed episodes (cf. Steinbach 1985: 398), the accounts of the school years, and increasingly those of late adolescence, tend to consist of successive stories.

The following attempt to report on childhood, from an interview with Hans Gruen[27], is typical of the text structure of early memories:

"Then we moved to ... and that's where my first memories of my childhood actually begin. (3 seconds pause) We had our own house there and we had a huge garden with animals, we had a big vegetable garden and (6). Yes somehow yes very nice memory of that time" (translated from the German).

After this, the autobiographer keeps asking himself what else "comes to his mind". Thus, he does not get into a narrative flow in which the recollection of one experience leads to a thematically related one, but he has to search for memories. He does not tell stories, but describes remembered scenes, such as setting mousetraps in the house or going to the cemetery with his father.

During *the transition to late adolescence and early adulthood*, profound processes of identity formation take place (Erikson 1959/1973), in which the adolescent increasingly thinks about himself and designs and plans his future. Making plans for the future is possible only with the development of competence in hypothetico-deductive thinking (Inhelder/Piaget 1958) that begins during middle adolescence, with which the adolescent can detach himself from concrete facts in the real world and think about what is possible and what is to come. While the main task of the Oedipal stage of development is forgetting the past, the central task of adolescence is planning the future (Cohler 1982: 218).

Biographical self-presentations at this age therefore also contain reflections on the future, especially in respect of education and employment. For example, a 17-year-old Israeli girl who was asked[28] to tell her life story begins with the following opening sequence:

"I am 17 years old, I am in the eleventh grade at the Alliance High School. This is a school where they learn 5 points French; all the learning streams here include French. I'm in the biology stream and I'll study this subject after the army."

---

27 The interview is from the project "Biography" (cf. Eulering/Milbradt 1989).

28 The interview is from research carried out by Dan Bar-On at Ben-Gurion University, Beer Sheva. It was conducted in Hebrew and translated into English for my analyses.

Only after introducing herself with information that is relevant to her in the present, going to school and her desire to study biology, does she begin to talk about her past. But after only about 4–5 minutes, she is back in the present and reflects on herself in a way typical for this age:

"My father is a lecturer and my mother writes articles about medical subjects. And all that is an influence. I was always independent. I make my own meals since the fourth grade. I would have preferred it if someone had been home when I came from school, but I never got angry about that. I accepted the fact that my mother was working very hard and until late. My father, who is a professor, also works very hard. All that affected me. I was always the good girl who never protested. I was too much the good girl. I developed my personality in that way. I was always older than my age. I see everything from above".

If we think back to the self-description of the 12-year-old (chapter 4.1.1), a structural difference becomes apparent here: the 17-year-old gives her self-definition a historical dimension; she reflects on it in the context of her biographical development in the parental home.

If a life story is told later in life, it can be assumed – in comparison to childhood – that late adolescence will be the subject of increased thematization and greater narrative density, since this phase of life is associated with biographical plans that are weighed up in the light of their fulfillment or failure in later life.

The turning point to middle age around the age of 50 leads to an increasing awareness of the finiteness of life and the irreversibility of chosen biographical paths. Above all, the time perspective changes: "Time becomes restructured in terms of time left to live instead of time since birth" (Neugarten 1979: 890). Likewise, the perception of the body undergoes change. Not only do physical complaints increase at this age, but bodily sensations and physical abilities that were once expectable and predictable no longer correspond to previous conceptions. One needs less sleep, metabolizing toxins takes longer, certain foods are no longer tolerated, women experience considerable bodily changes during the menopause, and so on. This is accompanied by an increasing awareness and thematization of the body.

This phase of life is associated with mourning: for the death of one's parents, relatives and friends, as well as for the loss of hopes and plans, and, in women, for the loss of fertility (cf. Mitscherlich 1987: 67 ff.). "Grief work makes possible increased reconciliation with life as lived, including resolution of disappointments with the past" (Cohler 1982: 223). Grief work means increased introspection (Neugarten 1973; 1979) and thus creates a need for biographical thematization. While in old age biographical thematizations serve more to prepare for death, here they are still due to the effort to solve present problems (Cohler 1982: 224). Solving current problems means accepting that certain plans will remains unfulfilled, instead of falling into melancholy, and, on the other hand, taking initiatives to change the way one lives (cf. Schütze 1981: 76 f.).

While the range of biographical possibilities narrows in this phase of life, new opportunities open up. Women can take up new activities after their children have left home, and spouses can reshape their relationship. Neugarten's (1979) empirical finding that people in middle adulthood tend to perceive the environment as a challenge, while *older people* tend to experience themselves as adapting to the environment, should be understood in this context: "There seems to be a change from outer world to inner world orientation that we described as increased 'interiority'" (Neugarten 1979: 892). The biographical future horizon is increasingly limited in older people, and with the loss of friends and of husband or wife, there is a stronger inward orientation.

Narrated life stories in middle adulthood thus have different foci than narratives from later years, in which this phase is remembered intensely, especially if it led to revisions. While biographical self-presentation in middle adulthood is more oriented toward solving current problems, it serves older people as a preparation for the end of life. The elderly often feel a strong need to take stock and sum up their lives. As shown by my interviews with veterans of the First World War (born between 1888 and 1900), this retrospection, or reliving of the past, sometimes leads to very detailed narratives about the person's adolescence and early adulthood, and to increased thematization of childhood and family history. When coming to the end of their lives, people need to affirm their wealth of experiences, both happy and sad.

Often, old people want to give an account of themselves and tell posterity something about themselves and their lives before they die. In an interview with an 87-year-old man – I'll call him Mr. Heim – this need is recognizable, for instance, in the following statement:

"We don't want anyone to stand at our grave and say here, look, this is a criminal or anything, I mean (1) we want to die as honest men" (translated from the German).

This autobiographer felt the need for justification and taking stock in three areas of life, which he treated separately. I had invited him for an interview as a veteran of the First World War, but had asked him to tell his entire life story. The thematic field of his biographical grand narrative was in the context of World War II: he wanted to tell me about his time as a member of a Nazi organization, the Reiter-SS (Cavalry Brigade, which was a unit of the SS, the Schutzstaffel, during the Nazi-period), his function as a local, and later district, peasant leader under the Nazis, and his knowledge of the mass murder of the Jews in his homeland, the Memel Territory.[29] He asked me for a second interview, during which he read me his autobiography, which he had written down and addressed to his sons. Here he explained that he had been a successful and wealthy farmer in the Memel Territory before the expulsion in 1945, and why he could not be held responsible for his lack of success as a farmer in West Germany. At the age of 52 he had bought a farm in the state of Hesse (West Germany), which he handed over to his son at the age of 66, who had to give it up eleven years later due to lack of profitability. Furthermore, he had written down the story of his marriage for his sons – of course also for himself – in order to show his innocence in this failed or tense relationship.[30] However, he did not read this story to me, but told me about it whenever his wife was out of earshot. He said that he had married her because of her fortune and the opportunity this offered to expand the farm in the Memel Territory, and for this he had ended a love affair with another woman. Today he thinks he should have married "a poor church mouse" rather than – as he puts it – a rich but cold woman, who avoided physical contact with him.

If Mr. Heim had been between the ages of 50 and 60 when he told his life story, i.e., during the time when he took over a farm and was trying to be as successful as a farmer as he was in the Memel Territory, his presentation would probably have been less summing up and justifying. He probably would have focused more on his hopes as a farmer and reconstructed his past accordingly. His time as a member of the Reiter-SS and as a local and district peasant leader, and the experiences connected with it, would probably also have been less relevant.

An old person who feels the desire to talk about his biography against the background of a life that is not likely to continue much longer is thus working on a problem, just like a young biographer. However, the old person must turn to the past when seeking a solution, i.e., he must reproduce and reinterpret his view of the past, while the young person looks to the future for a solution. Older people use biographical narration to try to heal hitherto un-

---

29 See: https://www.yadvashem.org/odot_pdf/Microsoft%20Word%20-%206479.PDF

30 For a further case analysis, it would be interesting to ask why Mr. Heim treats the three areas of his life separately, or why he tries to avoid a connection.

resolved or withheld memories that have been linked to guilt, or suppressed because of their traumatic content. Likewise, the anticipation of death – and thus loss of the future – can itself become a problem in need of thematization. For example, analysis of the life narrative of a man who was seriously ill in hospital and anticipating death (Rosenthal 1990b) shows how his fear of death evoked memories of his experiences in World War I and World War II, and how he felt a need to talk about them. By verbalizing his fear of death in the trenches during World War I, he biographically processed his current fear of death.

The needs and interests that guide biographical presentations, the functions they fulfill, or the problems they are intended to solve, differ in different phase of life. Although we can assume certain typical tendencies, individual life stories cannot simply be subsumed under these assumptions. My interviews with very old people show that even a 95-year-old man does not necessarily think about death, but can still be focused on planning his future. In other words, life narratives of very old people do not have to show the structural features of a "story about death", i.e., about a life that has reached its end and has no future horizon, but can look to the future. Likewise, biographical self-presentations with a closed future horizon are conceivable in young people, and not only those with a chronic disease. People in a hopeless situation over which they have no influence – as in the extermination camps – can lose their future horizon, in the same way as people planning suicide because they feel they are in a hopeless situation.

4.3.2 Socially typified status transitions

In our culture, the following are considered socially typified turning points at the level of educational and professional careers: starting school, beginning an apprenticeship or a course of study, beginning a career, promotions and retirement. At the family level, these status transitions are caused by marriage, parenthood, divorce, death of a partner, adult children moving out, and the birth of grandchildren. Although these status transitions lead to changes in lifestyle, they do not have to be accompanied by psychological changes, as in the case of developmental turning points. Moreover, with the exception of starting school and college, they do not coincide with the developmental turning points. Status transitions require domain-specific changes in one's concept of oneself and one's practice, but the extent to which they are experienced as intrusions into the general conduct of life, or as biographical crises, depends, among other things, on *when* they occur in the life course (Neugarten 1979: 889). Neugarten gives the example that for most middle-aged mothers, the departure of their children from the parental home does not lead to a crisis, provided that this happens "on time". If, on the other hand, the children leave home too early, i.e., before a process of gradual farewell, or too late, i.e., after the practice of living together with adult children has become established and the parents have not reoriented themselves in new areas of life, a biographical crisis is more likely to occur for the parents. Similarly, the death of relatives and friends is particularly tragic if it occurs too early, and thus unexpectedly.

If, in the presentation of a life story, status transitions function as dividing lines between different phases, or as contours in shaping the Gestalt of thematic fields, this is not because they are social requirements in the sense of socially shared patterns. It is true that in the interview we social scientists – as Joachim Matthes (1985: 318) conjectures – can impose on the narrators the phasing that is typical in our culture complex and which may be absent in other cultures, or "impose" it on the biographies later, during text interpretation, and segment the life narrative according to status transitions. But if we have chosen – according to the premises of the narrative interview – to give autobiographers the space to shape their narrative autonomously and without intervening questions from the interviewer, status transitions will emerge only as data, without being expanded through narratives, so long as they serve the narrator merely as a narrative foil matching social expectations. If status transitions are not experienced as biographically relevant turning points, or if they are not reinterpreted as being biographically significant due to later developments, they will not have a Gestalt-forming effect. If they were not experienced at the time, or after reinterpretation processes, as serious disruptions, not only of everyday routines but also of the routine life course, then they will not have an organizing influence on the presentation of the remembered life story or its narration. They will be a factor in the organization of the life story only if they are not dominated by competing turning points, and thus become obsolete. Thus, the status transition from civilian to soldier in World War II, a life-changing event at the time, will play only a minor role in structuring the narrated life story when the death of a comrade after a year at the front is experienced as a far more significant turning point in the soldier's career, and in his attitude toward the war. This autobiographer will not divide his narrative into "the time before being a soldier" and "the time as a soldier", but into "the time before the friend's death" and "the time after his death".

Although status transitions always mean a certain interruption of the life course, this is not sufficient to distinguish different areas within a thematic field, or even two fields, from each other. The interruption must be experienced by the autobiographer as a change with biographical relevance, or must present itself as such in retrospect. The status transition to being a student, for example, can be seen in retrospect – after failing to obtain a degree – as a turning point marking the beginning of an "unsuccessful life", and thus only gain structural significance with this reinterpretation.

Biographical turning points with retrospective biographical relevance are constituted by biographical processes, in the course of which the autobiographer feels compelled to reinterpret his life story, and past experiences that were previously considered of little relevance present themselves to him as turning points. In view of an unhappy love relationship and threatening separation, the autobiographer may, for example, begin to look for the first traces of this "disaster" in the history of the relationship. A quarrel which until then had been considered rather banal can now present itself as a turning point marking the change from a formerly happy to an increasingly unhappy relationship. This brings us to the concept of interpretation points.

4.3.3 Interpretation points

Biographical turning points which result in reinterpretation of the past, the present and the future horizon, whether consciously by the autobiographer or without any intention on his part, are more dominant for the Gestalt formation of the experienced life history as it presents itself to him than those which do not produce this reinterpretation effect. Let us take the example of "divorce" as a biographical turning point for a woman who subsequently outed herself as a lesbian, and whose self-perception and planning for the future thus changed dramatically. The change of present and future then also demands reinterpretation of her previous life. This experienced break in her life leads to the organization of two figures: the time before her coming-out and the time after, where the turning point, the divorce, loses its structure-forming effect. Wolfram Fischer (1978) discusses these breaks as interpretation points in the life story that temporally structure the past. He calls the final interpretation point that separates the present from the non-present the

On the Gestalt of narrated life stories

"threshold of the present". Life histories are conceivable that present themselves organized according to different interpretation points, as well as those with only one such point, the threshold of the present.

Let us stay with the example of a lesbian woman's coming out, which is based on a case study from our research project "Biography" (Doering/Müller 1989), to demonstrate the impact of interpretation points on life narratives. Simone Hildebrandt[31] divides her life into two phases, as shown by our case analysis: the unhappy past and the happy present. Retrospectively, however, she sees the threshold of the present not in her coming out, but in her divorce. First, she justifies her divorce:

"… it was just that he [the husband] well kept on running up debts" (translated from the German).

She goes on to say that she had taken on a directly enforceable guarantee for her husband, that the man "then vanished into thin air", and that she had had to pay off his debts for years. Only after a few years did she file for divorce:

"So that's how the total change happened with me. That actually only happened when I got divorced at 30, so my life really changed completely. First I sold all the furniture I had and then I somehow found my life the way I wanted it. … And that's also when it started, that I really asked myself yes, did I really have interest in men and why was it always very difficult with men. Then I also remembered that actually in puberty or so … I always found women more interesting, they were actually very attractive to me. Then I said to myself, and even if it puts me in my grave, now I want to know and I want to forget all that with men".

At the time of her divorce, Simone Hildebrandt thought she was leaving her husband because of his financial problems, but her focus today is on her negative physical feelings toward him and toward men in general. She is also convinced today that this discomfort stems from her desire for women, which was not clear to her at the time. The extent to which her problems with men are connected with other difficulties is only hinted at between the lines in the quoted passage. Thus, we wonder what she means by "forget all that" with men. Elsewhere in the interview, she tells us that she was raped by her older brother when she was seven years old. However, she does not connect this sexual abuse to her discomfort during physical contact with men, let alone to her homosexuality.

From her present perspective, Simone Hildebrandt's divorce retrospectively acquires for her the significance of an interpretation point that sep-

---

31 The name is anonymized.

arates her happy present from her unhappy past. Furthermore, it is interesting, and characteristic of life stories with such interpretation points (cf. Fischer 1982), that the narrator assigns all unpleasant bodily experiences to the past before the divorce, while all the positive bodily experiences belong to the time after. For example, when asked to tell the story of her bodily experiences in the course of her life, she answers that everything has changed since her divorce:

"... that from that moment on, actually really from the day I got my divorce, I have simply become more and more aware of all things that concern life. That I began to experience nature more consciously, that I felt the warmth more, felt the cold more. That I felt my own body more, that I lost weight, that I stopped smoking, also that I've been a vegetarian for three years".

4.4 Formal factors for Gestalt connection

After discussing turning points as Gestalt-forming factors in a biographical self-presentation, let us analyze these formal factors in more detail. We can assume that – provided listeners do not repeatedly intervene with questions in a structure-building way – a biographical self-presentation is a sequence of mutually interrelated themes that form a dense network of referential connections (cf. Fischer 1982: 168). But what are the components of a thematic field? How are the contours formed in biographical self-presentations that encompass more than one thematic field? What are the factors that organize the multitude of experiences? We cannot regard the temporal sequence of experiences as the decisive factor for Gestalt formation, since it will not help us to explain the reorganization of groupings and temporal linkages (cf. Fischer 1982), or the mechanisms for selecting certain experiences from memory. Let us first consider the precondition for perceiving a Gestalt: the presentation of an entity that stands out from a background or a theme that stands out in a thematic field and is surrounded by a margin. For the presentation of something that stands out, contours are needed: "In a homogeneous field, certain stimulus differences (inhomogeneities) are needed, so that it is divided in a certain way, so that certain formations appear (stand out)" (Wertheimer 1923: 348, translated from the German).

As already discussed, the formal factors of "division" or contour formation in perceptual processes, according to Wertheimer's analyses, are: proximity, sameness, closure, and good continuation or good Gestalt, with each factor being more dominant than the previously named one.

Below I will try to transfer these regularities to the presentation of an experienced life history. To put it succinctly, my theses in respect of Gestalt formation are:

1. Thematic similarity of experiences is more dominant than their temporal or spatial proximity.
2. Thematic groupings can lead to division into two thematic fields.
3. The belonging of an experience to a thematic field is more dominant than thematic similarity.
4. Interpretation points can lead to division into two thematic fields.
5. A consistent biographical overall view is more dominant than individual thematic fields.

4.4.1 Thematic similarity of experiences is more dominant than their temporal and spatial proximity

The rule that for objects of perception the factor of sameness is more dominant than that of proximity can be demonstrated with the following illustration:

A   o o · · o o · · o o · · o o · · o o

B   o o · · o o · · o o · · o o · · o o

Chart 3
Source: Wertheimer (1923: 312)

While in picture A we perceive pairs or figures due to the factor proximity, in picture B we see pairs due to the factor sameness. Sameness also produces figures or leads to the division of the whole into individual figures: "But again, if some of the individual objects are similar or the same in such properties, while further objects, which in turn are similar or the same, have other shapes or colors, then the whole assembly tends to split, i.e., to appear as a combination of two subgroups" (Köhler 1969: 57).

If we apply this consideration to the presentation of the experienced life history, we can consider the factor of proximity as temporal or even spatial proximity of experiences, and the factor of sameness as thematic similarity of experiences. Proximity in time can sometimes create coherence, because individual situations that follow one another are more likely to form a unit than experiences that are far apart in time – provided that there is no thematic connection between the latter. Similarly, experiences that are spatially close to each other, that take place in the same room, for example, can present themselves as units. For example, if one thinks of one's classroom in the first year of school, experiences from this room will emerge from our memory.

However, links based on temporal and spatial proximity are easily broken by thematic connections. If, for example, I am talking about my school experiences, i.e., if they form a thematic unit, I will probably link an experience from my time at elementary school time with one from my time at high school because it is thematically similar, rather than with a family experience that took place at about the same time but has no thematic connection to what I experienced at school. I will also tend to narrate my school experiences from a particular perspective, such as "my successes at school", and therefore group them, not according to the place where they happened, but according to this perspective. The experience of success in elementary school is thematically similar to the experience of success in high school; this gives rise to the formation of a figure that stands out against the background of "school experiences" and an unthematic margin of "my life at that time".

Temporal shifts

The dominance of thematic similarity over temporal proximity does not mean that narration cannot follow the chronology of experiences. A precondition for chronological narration, however, is that the experiences which the autobiographer wants to report, or which are presented to him by his memory, are congruent with the thematic field of the narration. If an experience or its theme is in contradiction to this thematic field, this causes it to be changed. A new field can then be formed (see below). Forming a Gestalt or a field on the basis of thematic similarity thus means that the selection of experiences to be told is conditioned by this factor and not by their chronological proximity or succession. The thematically linked experiences that are selected are nevertheless often told in a way that suggests they followed one another chronologically and were conditioned, at least in part, by this. Temporal links in a narrated life story can give the appearance of temporal homology with the experienced life history, even if they seriously distort its chronology. If, for example, I form the thematic field "My unhappy childhood", focusing first on the theme "My relationship to my mother", and then changing to the theme "My relationship to my father", it may appear as if the stories succeeded each other chronologically, even though their order in my narrative results from their belonging to the respective theme and does not necessarily correspond to the actual sequence of events.

If the change from one theme to the next, or from one thematic field to the next, corresponds to a biographical turning point, then temporal shifts will bring about even more significant differences between narrated life story and experienced life history. If, for example, the autobiographer speaks about "My life before my divorce" and "My life after my divorce" in the thematic field "Developing my autonomy", the sequence of events can be maintained. But here, too, a closer analysis shows that temporal shifts occur, due to the factor of thematic similarity, so that the narrated life story does not always reflect the chronology of the biographically layered experiences. If the autobiographer feels much more autonomous and independent since her divorce, she can, for example, recount positive experiences from the time before the divorce as if they had occurred after it.

The phenomenon of temporal shifts, as well as the temporal differences between experienced life history and narrated life story in general, are described by Wolfram Fischer (1982; 1982b; 1985) on the basis of life stories told by people who are chronically ill. Using empirical material, Fischer works out how experiences that do not fit the interpretation of certain life phases are narrated as if they had occurred in another phase, to which they thematically "belong". To illustrate this with an example: a patient suffering from chronic kidney failure, for whom the beginning of dialysis meant the opening up of a present which he could enjoy in a considerably improved psychological and physical condition, narrated unpleasant experiences of illness as if they had taken place before this treatment. Since they conflicted with the present perspective that became established with the beginning of the treatment, they were presented as belonging to the past (Fischer 1982: 151).

Our analyses of the life stories of contemporary witnesses of National Socialism (Rosenthal 1989a; 1990c) show how the phenomenon of temporal displacement is used as a repair strategy to detach oneself from entanglements with National Socialism. For example, experiences from the last years of the war which reveal a fascination for Hitler or a still unshaken belief in final victory, are told as if they had taken place in the early years of the so-called "Third Reich", which enables the biographers to restrict their own fascination to the early years. Or by shifting acquaintances with Jewish people from the time before the Nuremberg Race Laws to the time after, they can conceal their subservient adoption of state-imposed anti-Semitism (Rosenthal 1992).

Temporal shifts are usually not the result of conscious reconstruction work on the part of the autobiographer. Rather, they take place implicitly behind their backs with the temporal layering of the narratives. In general, we can assume that the temporal structure of the narration does not correspond to the temporal structure of the experienced life history. Narrated life story and experienced life history differ in their temporal and thematic linkage of experiences, and this means in the organized nature of the experiences. While the experienced life history is organized chronologically, the biographer constructs the overall temporal shape of the text in the present of narration with the aid of his memory.

If the factor of thematic similarity leads to the grouping of themes within a thematic field, its dominance over temporal and spatial proximity is greater in life stories that are split into two thematic fields on the basis of two thematic sectors that are not temporally separated.

4.4.2 Thematic groupings and splitting into thematic fields: "Bourgeois Biography" and "Homosexual Biography"

The biographical self-presentation of Hans Gruen[32], who was born in 1960 (Eulenring/Milbradt 1989), is characterized by the separation of his history as a homosexual from the other biographical strands, or, to put it briefly, from his bourgeois biography. Asked for this interview as a homosexual, and invited to tell his life story, he recounts events in linear sequence, after beginning by announcing that he had "grown up in a middle-class household". He begins with childhood experiences and continues up to the present, but omits all those experiences that for him are related to his life as a homosexual. After a short break, he then starts again from the beginning and tells his homosexual biography.

The first chronological narrative covers his schooldays and professional training, the process of detachment from his mother and her suicide, his

---

32 The name is anonymized. The interview was collected and analyzed in the context of the teaching project "Biography".

work, his marriage and divorce, and even his future prospects. He ends this narrative as follows:

"Yeah and in this part of life I think just to end with that for now I'll say that right now I'm in the process of figuring out how to start learning stuff again ... (5 seconds pause). Yes what I have now actually not mentioned at all is actually so my being gay (16 seconds pause)" (translated from the German).

Here, Hans Gruen explicitly announces a change of approach or a change of thematic fields. With the topic of homosexuality, he comes to something that does not belong "to this part of his life". Hans Gruen thus divides his life into two areas, the homosexual and the non-homosexual. This separation is also clear in the final evaluation at the end of his account of his career as a homosexual that follows a 16-second break:

"so well I will stop this gay life story there anyway, well so I say 'gay to be proud to be gay'"

But which experiences belong to his gay life and which to his bourgeois life? At first glance, there are some parallels between the two biographies: as in the narrative of his "bourgeois career", Hans Gruen tells of situations with his mother or wife when describing his gay biography, which for him begins with the sex education he got from his parents. One might think that there are certain thematic similarities between the two narratives. But themes and thematic fields are not constituted by external, case-independent classification criteria, according to which, for example, experiences with his mother or experiences at work would be considered similar themes. Rather, thematic connections result from their embedding in thematic fields, which are constituted by the autobiographer's attribution of meaning, his biographical overall view (as a latent structure), and his biographical global evaluation (as a manifest meaning). If the biographer sees his life in terms of the overall view "My suffering under my mother", his happy experiences with her will not belong to it, but instead all the experiences where he suffered under her. If, on the other hand, he tells the story of his professional career in terms of the biographical overall view "My success at work", the topic "The support I got from my mother" will belong to it, while the topic "My problems at work" will not be part of this field. Thus, what belongs to the contents of a thematic field cannot be defined case-independently, i.e., independently of the Gestalt of the concrete life story.

These considerations bring us to the second regularity described by Wertheimer: closure is more dominant than sameness and proximity.

4.4.3 The belonging of an experience to a thematic field is more dominant than thematic similarity

First, an illustration to clarify the independence of figures, regardless of their proximity:

Chart 4 and 5 Figure A & B
Source: Wertheimer (1923: 325)

These charts illustrate Wertheimer's observation that we see two figures in both charts, due to the properties of closure, symmetry and inner balance. But can this factor of "closure" be transferred to social phenomena, such as the presentation of thematic fields divided into themes? Does not the criticism of Gestalt theory apply here, that it has not defined its criteria such as that of "closure", or even that of "good continuation", as one can read in textbooks on psychology (cf. Knaurs moderne Psychologie 1972: 79)? In my opinion, this criticism misses the point of Gestalt theory thinking, and results from a positivistic conception of criteria as the sum of a number of elements. Which components belong to figure a, what are its contours, and what belongs to figure b, or why we see figure a as a unit distinguished from b in the first place, cannot be defined by its elements, but by the formation of a characteristic whole that stands out from other wholes.

If we transfer this to Hans Gruen's biographical self-presentation, we can see how he tries to frame his life story as two separate figures. Although thematic "similarity" could exist between individual components of his two thematic fields, were they embedded in other fields, the factor of "closure" of the two thematic fields dominates: "My bourgeois biography" and "My homosexual biography". Thus, although in Hans Gruen's presentation of his bourgeois life the process of detachment from his mother is a central component, he does not link this theme to the theme "My mother warned me about being gay." Rather, this theme belongs to the thematic field "My gayness," which as a closed figure does not lead to any thematic links with the figure "My bourgeois life".

ON THE GESTALT OF NARRATED LIFE STORIES   147

This example shows that the "dividing lines" or contours leading to the division into different figures are based on thematic inhomogeneities resulting from the incompatibility of biographical strands. Fischer (1982b: 10, translated from the German) identifies the five most important biographical strands as follows: "the development of corporeality, the career of gender identity, the family career, the professional career, the group of leisure careers (sports, musical activities, travel, etc.)".

The homosexual career or the biographical strand of gender identity is presented by Hans Gruen as being incongruent with other biographical strands, such as professional career, and thus shows that this is how he experienced it.

However, the contouring of a biographical self-presentation on the basis of assigning biographical strands to different thematic fields does not explain which components belong to which strand for the biographer. Which particular strand a component belongs to is conditioned by the thematic fields in which the biographer views his biographical strands. Thus, in the case of Hans Gruen, it is conceivable that he could embed the painful process of detachment from his mother, or even her suicide when he was 22 years old, in the thematic field of homosexuality. However, since he does not see his homosexuality or his "coming out" after the death of his mother in this context, or avoids seeing it in this context, the result is the creation of two figures that diverge in their biographical overall evaluations. While he evaluates his "bourgeois biography" as a painful, heteronomously produced life, he interprets his "homosexual biography" as a joyful and autonomously constituted life. Linking these two fields would threaten this interpretation of his life. If Hans Gruen wants to maintain his interpretation of a self-determined homosexual life without setbacks, he must avoid connecting it with the life externally determined by his mother. Then the question would force itself on him whether his mother also has a share in his homosexuality. This shows that setting up two thematic fields can have the function of avoiding contact between them, because this is perceived as threatening by the biographer.[33]

---

33 Our analyses of the life stories of supporters and perpetrators of National Socialism (Rosenthal 1990) show how separating the theme of war from the theme of National Socialism can serve as a repair strategy for normalizing the Nazi era. By not placing the war years – and for most of the men this means their time as soldiers – in the context of National Socialism, they remove (both temporally and thematically) its incriminating aspects from this important period of their life

The Gestalt formation of two thematic fields through this thematic – and just not temporal – contouring, however, is not just a construction on the part of the autobiographer, but he will also experience such a separation, which enables maintenance of the perception of separate fields, in his everyday life. In other words, every Gestalt formation is related to everyday life. The determination not to associate all biographical strands with being gay can also be seen as a response to ascription processes in the everyday social environment of the homosexual. It is the attempt to ward off a social identity defined only by the label "gay", i.e., a desire to be identified by other areas of one's life, to be perceived as "the same as" and not "different from" the "others". It corresponds to attempts to avoid "otherness" at work or in other areas of life. This had given Hans Gruen the feeling of being "divided in two". To the interviewer's question whether coming out brought a change for him in his relationship with his body, he answers:

"Before that, I had always seen myself as being divided into two parts. A part of me had to go away, had to be fought. And so my gay feelings and that's an area that had an influence on my physicality, well I put myself together again ... at the beginning of my coming out, I felt like a whole being, like a being with its sexuality" (translated from the German).

Although he now feels like a "unity" in his sexuality, as he argues below, he has not yet succeeded in creating this feeling in other areas of his life.

4.4.4 Interpretation points and splitting into thematic fields: "My life with my parents" and "My life without my parents in Israel"

Besides splitting it into parallel thematic sectors, the life story can also be organized in temporal sectors based on interpretation points. To illustrate this, a biographical self-presentation of this type will be discussed in some detail, since its analysis gives insight into the logic of a consistent Gestalt theory approach, which is more than just a sequential and reconstructive procedure.

The setting up of two separate temporal sectors, as we find in the biographical self-presentation of Abraham Jarok[34], represents an avoidance

---

story. How this separation of themes can be achieved, not only temporally but also thematically or sectorally, is illustrated by the case analysis of a Red Cross nurse (Grote/Rosenthal 1992).

34 Mr. Jarok (pseudonym; Jarok means "green" in Hebrew) Hebrewized his last name when he emigrated to Israel.

strategy by which the life story experienced and narrated after the temporal break is kept away from the threatening past.

My analyses of life stories of German Jews who were able to flee Nazi Germany as teenagers, but who had to leave parents and relatives behind, indicate that this kind of avoidance is typical of this generation.[35] For example, one of my interviewees, who – like the autobiographer presented below – came to Palestine as part of the Youth Aliyah[36], explicitly stated, "The time before my life in Israel is gone and finished forever and has nothing to do with my life here" (translated from German).

Abraham Jarok's biographical self-presentation is characterized by a striking separation of these two phases of life. He broke off the interview after about an hour, abruptly, slightly aggressively and unexpectedly. In telling his life story, he had only reached the year 1944. After an initial refusal to meet me again, he resumed contact with me by telephone after a few weeks and agreed to another interview, on the condition that I should visit him again beforehand and not talk about my interview interests. After the second interview, he again insisted that I should visit him, this time together with my husband.

As the following analysis will show, the case structure reveals itself if we consider a) the breaking off of the first interview as a functional component of Mr. Jarok's biographical self-presentation, and b) *all* meetings between him and myself as significant figures of the overall Gestalt of his biographical self-presentation. Thus, the analysis focuses on parts that we traditionally do not regard as belonging to our data in the narrow sense.

Let us first consider the themes of the four meetings. At the *first meeting*, when I asked him to tell me his life story, Abraham Jarok, who was born in 1921, told me about his life in Germany and his emigration to Erez Israel. He had grown up in a small Westphalian town as the third son of a merchant family. In 1935 he left the middle school because he could no longer bear the humiliations (sitting on the Jewish bench, being attacked by Christian stu-

---

35 While their relatives and friends were murdered by the Nazis, this generation threw itself into the development work in Palestine with great enthusiasm, and now retrospectively feels guilty for leaving their parents behind and for their nonchalance. In order not to let the guilt become overwhelming, they maintain the fragmentation of their life story. For case studies of this generation, as well as their children and grandchildren, see Rosenthal 1998/2010: Part 3).

36 Organized group emigration of 15–17 year olds to Palestine – unaccompanied by their parents – following vocational training. From 1934 to the end of March 1939, 3262 boys and girls were able to flee Germany in this way. Cf. Juliane Wetzel (1988).

dents, assaults on the way to school). With the support of the Zionist Youth Organization, he began preparing for Palestine. His two older siblings had already emigrated there when he followed in 1937 with the Youth Aliyah. His parents remained in Germany with the intention of joining their youngest son. They first wanted to close their business and sell it. The 16-year-old Abraham lived and worked in Palestine in a kibbutz and enjoyed this period of development work. He more or less refused to listen to news of the persecution of Jews in Germany. And even after his parents, as Polish-born Jews, were sent across the German border into Poland with his younger brother in October 1938, and then in September 1939 the German Wehrmacht invaded Poland, the information about the genocide in Europe did not really penetrate Abraham's consciousness. He still believed that his family would come to join him in Palestine. It was not until December 1944, when Abraham Jarok was told of the genocide by a Jewish woman who had escaped from Treblinka, that he suddenly realized what had probably happened to his family in Poland.

The interruption of the presentation of his life story occurs shortly after he has spoken about this painful insight. With a rather aggressive undertone he says:

"I can't go on. I've told you enough now. Turn off the tape" (translated from the German).

The *second meeting*, which lies between the two interviews – and this means between the two biographical narratives – is used by Mr. Jarok to talk about the guilt of the Germans. The conversation is structured by his questions to me, it is about the past of my parents and grandparents, and about my personal guilt. He suggests that I should light a candle on a certain day each year to commemorate the dead of the Shoah. With my answer "that it would probably not be enough to think of it only on one day", I unintentionally question his own "recipe", which he tells me about in one of the next meetings. He remembers the dead on the date he learned about Treblinka and lights a candle. As the case analysis then makes clear, this private annual day of remembrance, which does not coincide with the collective one, relieves him only a little of his feelings of guilt.

At the *third meeting*, the second interview, he then talks about his life in Israel. He talks about his time in the illegal underground organization of the Palmach, his work in the kibbutz, his marriage, leaving the kibbutz, and his new career that began afterwards. In 1977, he suffered a heart attack, stopped working, obtained an upper secondary qualification and went to college. In

1985 he had to undergo heart surgery. This severe physical crisis led him to begin studying the Nazi past of his hometown in Germany. However, his "Holocaust studies", as he calls them, are limited to historical research on what happened in Germany; he still avoids the subject of the genocide in Eastern Europe. For him, his illness represents an interpretation point that led to a renewed interest in the past. While he had refused to speak German all the time since coming to Palestine with the Aliyah, he started teaching German after this turning point and is happy to meet Germans – albeit in all ambivalence and mixed with aggression.

The *fourth meeting* is a visit that my husband and I paid together to Mr. and Ms. Jarok, and which took place at Mr. Jarok's express request. In the course of our conversation, we repeatedly and inevitably come back to National Socialism and its continuities in contemporary Germany. But the couple always changes the subject after a few exchanges and assures us that they had resolved not to bother us with the subject of "Germany and the Nazis" that evening. This is hardly possible, however, since Mr. Jarok in particular repeatedly establishes lines of connection to the Nazis with the topics he introduces. For example, he informs my husband, who has introduced himself as a medical sociologist, about the high rate of heart attacks in his generation, which came to Palestine with the Youth Aliyah, and wants to know his opinion about it. He wants to have it confirmed by the expert and German that such diseases are linked to the Shoah. For him, this link is an issue because since his heart attack he is haunted by a nightmare every second or third night. Again and again he dreams that the earth vibrates, fissures open, people are swallowed up, and he stands by and cannot help them.

Let us first interpret the breaking off of the first interview: Mr. Jarok, in the presentation of his experienced life history, had arrived at the situation in which he realized that his parents had probably been murdered by the Nazis. Here we can now formulate, among other things, the hypothesis that this memory of the "most terrible situation in my life" actualized his grief and the associated feelings of guilt, which then turned into aggression against the Germans and the interviewer. Grief and feelings of guilt led to the statement: "I can't take it anymore," and the aggression was directed against the German non-Jewish woman present, with whom he refused any further cooperation. If we consider his refusal to continue in the overall context of his narrated life story and experienced life history, the following picture emerges: we see a biographical narrative up to the point when the autobiographer realized the death of his parents and brother, then a pause or time gap of a few weeks, then a conversation about the guilt of the Germans, then a continuation of the narrative in which he describes his life without his parents in Israel, and finally a conversation with failed attempts to avoid the Nazi past. We can now formulate the following hypothesis about the connection between these parts considered as a Gestalt: Mr. Jarok has to put a lot of effort into splitting his life into two completely separate parts. He does not do this argumentatively, as we are familiar with from other life stories, for instance in stories of conversion, but tries to draw two independent figures. A gap of several weeks between the interviews helps him to avoid letting too many lines of contact emerge between these two figures. An indication for the plausibility of this assumption is a statement he made at the beginning of the first interview, the meaning of which I did not realize at the time:

"I can offer you different things: my life in Germany, my life in Israel. Take your pick" (translated from the German).

I then asked him to tell me his entire life. He responded, *"Oh, that won't be possible"*.

I ignored this hint and said, *"Why don't you start with your childhood?"*

So I didn't take him seriously with his need to prevent the two halves of his life from getting too close to each other, and perhaps I thus aroused aggression against myself right from the start.

The attempt in the *narrated* life story to keep apart the two phases of his life, namely "my life with my parents" and "my life without my parents," which were brutally separated in his *experienced* life history by the murder of his family, pervades Mr. Jarok's entire biographical self-presentation. This separation is due to the attempt not to link his past in Germany, the abandonment of his family, and their murder, with his life in Israel. In terms of Gestalt theory, we can say he strives not to touch under any circumstances the biographically existing connecting lines between these two figures. Thus, the first interview is characterized by the fact that whenever he touches on the theme "my family stayed in Germany", he immediately leaves this thematic strand and comes close to breaking off the interview. It would be far too superficial to try to explain this "avoidance attitude" exclusively in terms of the unbearable thought of the cruel murder of the family or the concept of "survivor's guilt". Only a reconstruction of the thematic field of the first interview can clarify the case-specific problems of this biography. The more or less manifest thematic field of this interview is "Why I emigrated," but the latent meaning of this field is "I didn't have the courage to stay with my par-

ON THE GESTALT OF NARRATED LIFE STORIES 153

ents." Mr. Jarok feels guilty that he left his parents, that he did not help them and, instead of caring for them, enjoyed his life on the kibbutz. During our third meeting – the interview has already ended, the tape has long since been turned off – he explicitly brings up this feeling of guilt and I turn the tape back on:

"That time from 1938, from the day when the Jews, when my parents went to Poland until the end of the war, until this report – we weren't aware of that whole thing, we were busy struggling to build a life in Palestine, that took 100 percent of our energy – and that whole thing of what was going on with our parents, what was going on with the Jewish people ... that is our feeling of guilt, I can't get rid of that. D'you understand how could I be so indifferent. What about my parents at that time, what my family at that time, but I was indifferent" (translated from the German).

It is this feeling of guilt that constitutes Mr. Jarok's entire biographical self-presentation. In order not to be overwhelmed by it, and in order not to let it overshadow his life story in Israel, he had to break off the first interview. Although he cannot talk about his feelings of guilt, he nevertheless needs to address them and seeks a second meeting with me. During this conversation he can now bring up the subject of "guilt" by reversing the roles and asking me about my personal guilt and the guilt of the Germans. In other words, the second meeting serves to broach the topic he wanted to avoid by breaking off the first interview. At the third meeting, initially without any reference to "my life with my parents", he was then able to speak easily about "my life in Israel" and also about his "Holocaust studies".

The significance of the fourth meeting now becomes understandable, at which we Germans, and thus also Mr. and Ms. Jarok, were to be freed from the subject of "National Socialism". Just as Mr. Jarok tries to separate the two areas for himself, he also wants this to make this possible for us. While he had confronted me with the question of guilt at the second meeting, he now, at the fourth meeting, wants to free me, and himself, from this topic for the evening. But this is not possible without special effort, due to the unavoidable connection of his life with the murder of his parents and his brother, and the theme of the genocide committed by the Germans, which is always co-present in meetings between non-Jewish Germans and Jews.

This also makes clear that the separation of two thematic fields, which stand unconnected next to each other, is always endangered, since each field contains references to the other. The past in Germany cannot be seen independently of the Aliyah, and the present in Israel cannot be seen without the murder of his family in the background. His heart attack triggered a biographical crisis in him, and since then he has been unable to deny the connection between the present and the past. In addition, there is an experience – the encounter with the Treblinka survivor – that separates the two phases and at the same time connects them. This interpretation point – and the altered present that is developing from it – contains a reference to both phases of his life. The biographical self-presentation thus reveals not only a life history experienced as fragile and discontinuous, but also the fragility maintained in the present of the narrative. The fragmentation of this life into two disjointed phases serves to make a threatening past more bearable. Again, it is clear that the structure of the narrated life story emerges both from the experienced life history, and from the act of thinking about it in the present of narration.

Even though in this example each field contains references to the other, no overall picture emerges for us interpreters without further analysis. If, on the other hand, Mr. Jarok succeeded in integrating both phases of his life in a single framework, a biographical overall view, it would be harder for us to recognize the delimiting contours of the two fields.[37] This brings us to my fifth thesis in respect of Gestalt formation:

4.4.5 A consistent biographical overall view is more dominant than individual thematic fields.

The following illustration by Kurt Koffka (1963: 153), among others, shows how two figures become a unit, and how the factor of a good Gestalt thus comes into play (Charts 6 and 7).

In the first picture we see a rectangle with a line in it – i.e., one figure – while in the second picture we see two adjacent hexagons: "The reason is clear: in the first the total figure is a better figure than either of the two part figures, whereas the opposite is true in the second" (ibid). Koffka further discusses the difference between figures that are relatively easy to recognize as unified and coherent entities, while others are identifiable as such only with

---

37 The process of integrating his past into the present began with his illness. However, when I spoke again to Mr. Jarok during the Gulf War, it was clear that this war, with its threat of poison gas supplied by Germany to Iraq, not only stopped this process, but even reversed it. Mr. Jarok handed over all his historical research material to a museum, because "everything became too heavy" for him; this was the end of his "Holocaust studies", at least for the time being.

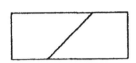

Chart 6 and 7 two part figures
Source: *Koffka (1963: 153)*

some effort. For example, we more easily see a circle as a coherent line than a triangle, since the circle is a perfect good Gestalt. Each part of the circle contains the principle of the whole, while the three sides of the triangle do not bear in themselves the continuation that leads to the triangle.

Applied to a life story, we can assume that with the integration of one figure into another figure, the merging of the figures into a thematic field becomes possible. If the autobiographer succeeds in integrating two initially separate phases or areas of his life into a biographical overall view, the experienced life history will present itself again as a unified and coherent one. We can distinguish between life stories in which there are interconnections between all the phases or thematic areas, and those life stories in which the breaks are so fundamental that they require retrospective integration.

Let us look at an example of the integration of two different figures into one overall figure. The experienced life history of Manfred Sommer[38] (Rosenthal 1987) can be divided into the phase of the convinced Hitler Youth leader and that of the convinced Protestant. As shown by our case analysis, this biographer identified with National Socialism until he had a religious conversion experience in Soviet captivity. Manfred Sommer was born in 1926, joined the Hitler Youth in 1936, rose in the hierarchy of HY leaders, and also became a member of an SS junior organization, the HY patrol service, which was used to control and spy on young people. After his time as an anti-aircraft auxiliary, he applied to study to become a medical officer (a doctor in the Wehrmacht with an officer's rank) and was therefore drafted into the Wehrmacht as an 18-year-old soldier rather than into the SS. Shortly before the end of the war, he was temporarily discharged because of TB, but vol-

---

38 The name is anonymized. The interview conducted by Harald Pilzer and myself is taken from the teaching project "The HY Generation".

unteered for service in the final battle for Berlin. Even after the surrender, he wanted to continue fighting against Bolshevism and make his way to the legendary Wenck's Army, which was supposedly still holding out on the Elbe. But he fell into Soviet captivity, attempted to escape and was sentenced to life imprisonment in Siberia. In his cell – his TB was acute again and he thought he was going to die – he experienced a religious conversion. He recalled his Christian upbringing and his earlier faith in God. This made him lose his belief in National Socialism: "That's when I broke away from my identification with National Socialism and felt free again". Manfred Sommer was released from captivity, returned to Berlin, and studied theology under lecturers from the Confessing Church. Today, Pastor Manfred Sommer sees himself as a determined opponent of National Socialism.

In view of these facts, a biographical self-presentation would be conceivable in which the autobiographer divided his life into two thematic fields, such as "my life as a convinced National Socialist" and "my life as a convinced Protestant". But Manfred Sommer's biographical self-presentation corresponds to the typical shape of a conversion process: the integration of the past into the present. According to his present perspective, he reinterprets his life before conversion as leading toward it. He looks for experiences in his past that demonstrate an early process of detachment from the Nazi regime. He remembers, among other things, that even as a seven-year-old he was upset when the Reich flag was replaced by a swastika flag among his toy soldiers. He presents his HY time, in which he mentions patrol duty only in passing, with the overall evaluation: "We then realized gradually that the Nazi leaders were stupid and that there was a difference between theory and practice". Manfred Sommer, on the other hand, explains his fascination with the skillful educational methods of the National Socialists, and his need to escape the petty-bourgeois narrow atmosphere in his parental home. With this reinterpretation of his time as a convinced HY leader, Manfred Sommer does not get into a narrative flow. He puts forward arguments that he substantiates with individual stories. In the case of experiences that conflict with his present-day perspective, according to which he broke away from his identification with National Socialism early on, and at the latest following the defeat at Stalingrad in the spring of 1943, he tries to tell them as if they had taken place before Stalingrad, or he does not mention them at all.

Manfred Sommer's reinterpretations of his Nazi past, however, are not only due to an attempt to deny his own involvement in National Socialism to himself and others. Rather, this biographer admits to himself – at least in

On the Gestalt of narrated life stories | 157

part – his identification with National Socialism and attempts to explain it. He looks for the reasons for his fascination, and thus reflects on the content of his Nazi socialization far more than many other members of his generation, not to mention older generations. His conversion provided him with a new interpretive framework for his life that was socially shared and affirmed by his new religious environment. This enabled him to integrate his past into this framework and to detach himself from parts of his Nazi identification. His reinterpretations are thus due, on the one hand, to the normalization and partial denial of his involvement in National Socialism, and, on the other hand, they are the product of intensive reflection on is Nazi past.

Manfred Sommer succeeds in creating a meaningful consistency between his life before conversion and his life after conversion. Thus, he does not feel burdened by his past; for him, it is rather a component of his present, with which he identifies. This biographer thus embeds two initially conflicting life phases in one figure. They are so harmoniously fused into one overall figure that the listener or reader has to make some effort to be able to recognize the two partial figures.

Merging a National Socialist past with a present cleansed of National Socialism is not limited to conversions. On the contrary, among non-persecuted Germans, creating the uniform overall Gestalt of a life that has always been apolitical is probably one of the most widespread and successful strategies for freeing oneself from entanglements with the National-Socialist system. In contrast to Manfred Sommer, these biographers, most of whom belong to the older cohorts[39], do not even admit to identifying themselves with the Nazis. They succeed in depoliticizing a former political phase of their lives by excluding from their biographical self-presentation everything that has to do with politics or with proximity to the Nazis (such as membership of a Nazi organization and the experiences associated with it). Everything from the former life that does not fit the present one is left out because it is incriminating, or socially ostracized. Thus the former life inserts itself into the present figure as a figure without contours. This unproblematic and unthematized merging cannot succeed in the case of experienced life histories like that of Manfred Sommer, in which the destruction of the "Third Reich" led to a severe crisis of orientation and his earlier identification could not

---

39 In our study on "Living with the Nazi Past," a generational comparison showed that the HY generation was still the most likely to admit its former identification with the "Third Reich" (Rosenthal 1990c).

simply be denied. Many autobiographers of this type were members of the HY generation and thus still relatively young in 1945; they could not spend the rest of their lives remembering the good old days before 1945, but had to develop new perspectives.

The merging of two figures into one overall figure and, concomitantly, the emergence of a consistent biographical overall view, thus originates either from the continuous flow of life, which changes, but whose changes do not demand any further reflections from the autobiographer, or from the renewed interest of the autobiographer and his or her constructive effort. If those who can see their lives as detached from National Socialism without additional effort could admit their identifications at that time and allow the associated memory of stressful situations, their life would also present itself retrospectively as fractured. Only in a further step could it then be transferred back into a consistent whole.

The formation of a figure from two initially unconnected figures presupposes, in addition to the subject's construction work, a life course that has not been traumatically interrupted. A less dramatically interrupted life course will present itself more easily as "good Gestalt", in which each part refers to the whole, than dramatically interrupted ones like the life course of Mr. Jarok or those of the survivors of concentration and extermination camps. Mr. Jarok's childhood in pre-Nazi Germany did not point to emigration to Palestine, nor could he have foreseen the murder of his family and people in Europe when he emigrated. Such heteronomously produced breaks in the life course, i.e., collective trajectories independent of the biographer's actions and history (cf. Schütze 1982), such as natural disasters, initially draw their lines of connection to the previous life only from the uniformity of the subject experiencing them and not from traces of continuity with the past life. The autobiographers have to learn to see these connections. While in Manfred Sommer's experienced life history there are lines of connection – in the sense of continuities – between his Nazi biography and his Protestant biography, such as the fact that he had been brought up as a Protestant by his parents, and that he had been confirmed as a member of the Hitler Youth, so that his conversion did not mean "losing" his entire past, it would cost Abraham Jarok quite some effort to re-establish this connection or to learn to see it. The integration of one's life before the experience of suffering due to circumstances beyond one's control, into one's life after it, can mean for the autobiographer that he succeeds in *not* considering his earlier life as leading up to this suffering and thus being devalued by it. Abraham Jarok is still able to speak about his childhood and youth, i.e., he has not completely lost them from his life story like other survivors (cf. chapter 4.1.4); however, in retrospect he sees this phase of his life as being devalued by the Nazi genocide, which makes him, like many survivors, feel guilty. Likewise, his present life in Israel, his commitment to the building of this country, is threatened with devaluation by the Shoah. By splitting off the past from the present, he tries to escape this devaluation. Such an attempt, however, cannot succeed in the end. Our biographical past cannot be driven out of our memory any more than the violent death of people close to us. Separating these experiences cannot heal the wounds either; rather, they cost so much in energy that psychosomatic illnesses can be the result. If, on the other hand, Mr. Jarok could give up trying to separate them and allow his past in Germany and his present in Israel to present themselves as two phases of a life that forms a whole, he would gain a new view of his life, and a less stressful biographical processing of his life story could begin. Mr. Jarok's experienced life history – like any other life history – offers other possibilities of presentation, which it might be easier to live with. The healing effect of biographical narration lies in the possibility of reorganizing the way the experienced life history presents itself in the process of narration, due to the ambiguousness of its Gestalt.

5. The healing effect of biographical narration[1]

5.1 The ambiguous Gestalt of the experienced life history

There is always ambiguity in the Gestalt of the narrated life story, as an entity that is constituted in the dialectical interrelationship between the life history as it presents itself to the narrator, the way he approaches it, and the narrative process. There are multiple, though limited, possibilities for shaping its Gestalt, and thus for making different temporal and thematic links. The experienced life history allows for different groupings: what is at one time a theme may be only an unthematized part of the field at another time, or even be pushed to the margin.

In this possibility of different groupings lies the freedom of the subject, or the autobiographer's "possibilities for invention". Let us return to Max Frisch's statement, "Every person invents their own story". We can understand this as meaning that invention lives in the possibilities for grouping our experiences. As Koffka (1915) says in his critique of Benussi, however, this invention is not an intellectual act that is added to perception as a further act of grouping, but rather, depending on the particular interest of the autobiographer, the experienced life history presents itself to him grouped accordingly, and thus is already structured. There is a limit to the ways an experienced life history can present itself: a life cannot be reinvented, and its organization is subject to Gestalt-shaping factors that result from the experienced life history. Painful life-changing events cannot be negated by reinterpretation so that their problematic nature is eliminated once and for all; biographically relevant experiences cannot be pushed to the unthematic margin so easily and without traces, and certain figures resist reorganization. In

---

1 See also a later publication on this topic, Rosenthal 2003.

other words, the experienced life history sets limits for its presentations and imposes a certain organizedness on us (cf. Schütze 1984: 195).

Despite these limits, the experienced life history presents itself in a variety of ways of which the autobiographer is hardly aware. If he does become aware of even a part of this variability, he will discover that he can see his life in a different light, he will learn to see himself as the author of his life, and not just passively exposed to it. Experiencing a reorganization of his view of his biography can gives the narrator a sense of autonomy, and enable him to view the past in a less distressing way. The process of psychoanalytic therapy, and the memory work that is central to it, can also be understood as such a reorganization, as can any form of therapy in which biographical narration, or the acting out of biographical experiences, as in psychodrama, is an essential component. This is in contrast to Sigmund Freud's early view, according to which it was important to uncover the "objective life history". Roy Schafer (1983) and Donald Spence (1982), among others, argue against this and counter that the therapeutic process is effective due to the construction of a "healthier" life story.

I refer here to psychoanalysis and not – as might be expected from my background in Gestalt theory – to Gestalt therapy, although its founder, Fritz Perls, refers to the work of Gestalt theorists, since psychoanalysis is closer to the considerations on healing processes discussed here, both in technique and theory. Gestalt therapy does aim at the awareness of "Gestalts" in the sense of the interplay of feelings, bodily sensations, and thoughts, but its goal is not so much the reorganization as the closure of shapes. In Gestalt therapy, it is important to close unclosed things, since, as figures that conflict with the present, they cause psychological conflicts (cf. Resnick 1975). In the therapeutic process, the acting out of feelings from past situations – and not their interpretation or the reconstruction of the past situation as a whole! – is supposed to help closure and to restore the patient's inner balance.

In psychoanalysis, on the other hand, the task of the interpreting therapist is first to understand the "biographical construction" of the analysand, and then to change it step by step with targeted therapeutic interventions – primarily with the help of transference processes and their transformations (Cremerius 1981; Morgenthaler 1978; Schelling 1985). In contrast to these reorganization effects brought about by the therapist, biographical narration in everyday life, or in a biographical-narrative interview, is a gentler and less invasive method, albeit an effective one, which can lead to reorganization of the biographical overall view and to cathartic effects. Biographical narrative

THE HEALING EFFECT OF BIOGRAPHICAL NARRATION   163

in this case is gentle, in contrast to therapy, because in everyday life, or in a narrative interview, the listener does not use special methods to help the person recall what has been repressed, such as dream interpretation, free association, or body work. The effectiveness of biographical narration does not lie in recalling repressed experiences, but in finding new ways of making sense of one's life. While this can trigger a process of self-healing in everyday life, or even motivate the autobiographer to begin psychotherapy, which I see as a first and very significant step in the therapeutic process, this cannot be equated with the deeper transformative processes in the professional setting of psychoanalytically oriented psychotherapy. Also, telling one's life story over a period of several hours is in structural terms a very different form of intervention from narratives of single experiences and their modification in one-hour therapy sessions. When someone tells his life story, it is not a matter of influencing which experiences present themselves to the autobiographer, but of allowing him to link different experiences and form a narrative chain by focusing on certain themes: this triggers a process in the course of which reorganization of the biographical overall view becomes possible. Although the Gestalt of what the autobiographer presents will be determined by his relevancies and his conscious biographical overall evaluation at the time of narration, his biographical overall view, of which he is not so aware, will have a stronger structure-forming effect. In the course of narration, the autobiographer can become aware of this view of his life. In other words, telling one's life story can create awareness of one's biographical overall view. For example, the autobiographer may start to ask himself, "Why am I talking only about situations in which I was helpless? Do I see myself only as a helpless victim of external circumstances?" He can then resist this tendency and try to remember other experiences, or begin to consider the experiences he has already described against a different background. This process can lead to a change of thematic field, and the experienced life history can now present itself to the autobiographer in the form of an active and autonomous life.

The dynamics of the narrative stream and interaction with the listeners can also provide opportunities for reorganization. Depending on how unstable the thematic field of a biographical self-presentation is – and this is especially the case when the interests of the presenter are not congruent with the experienced life history – it can tip in another direction or take on another Gestalt in the narrative process. Without any conscious intention on the part of the autobiographer, components from the thematic field or margin may present themselves to him, or the narrative constraints (chapter 3.2) may lead to verbalization of previously unconsidered things, or the listener may express interest in further details of marginal items. Even just a frown or a questioning "mm" from the listener can cause the autobiographer to give details of experiences that have not been thematized. Through these processes, individual experiences or entire phases of a person's life can suddenly present themselves from a different perspective, and the change can be so dramatic that the biographical overall view is reorganized as a whole, or that a process of opening up for reorganization is initiated by the narrative situation, which, however, requires further narrative situations in order to bring about lasting changes. The decisive stimulus for reorganization is thematization of hitherto marginalized components of the experienced life history – and this happens inevitably when the autobiographer surrenders himself to a stream of memory and narrative. If this leads to the narration of experiences that have hitherto been withheld with considerable psychic energy, further thematically related memories will emerge: "Because the process of blotting out important biographical experiences has been so intense, repairing the defective narrative presentation will trigger explosive scenic visualizations when recapitulating formerly suppressed climax-like and/or turning-point-like situations involving action, suffering, and interaction" (Schütze 1984: 101 f., translated from the German).

This bringing to mind of previously withheld experiences can make clear to the autobiographer their biographical relevance for his life and cause him to reinterpret them, which leads to a change in his biographical overall view. Fritz Schütze (1984: 108) sees the therapeutic effect of biographical narration precisely in the fact that, by reflecting on "traumatic experiences made explicit through narration", the autobiographer is able to use them for a "consistent conception of identity". The traumatic areas of life that have been excluded from a person's biographical self-perception can be reintegrated into their life story through narration and biographical processing, in the sense of reflecting on the significance of these experiences for their life story.

There is a "risk" inherent in every biographical narrative, and especially in a biographical grand narrative, that existing Gestalts will be reorganized, but here lies the chance of a healing effect, in the sense of finding it easier to live with a threatening past. If one considers this chance as a danger for the mental stability of the biographer, one underestimates, in my opinion, both his defense mechanisms and the threat to his mental stability posed by a defec-

THE HEALING EFFECT OF BIOGRAPHICAL NARRATION   165

tive life story.[2] Biographical narration does not "break into" the unconscious of the autobiographer with radical methods, such as hypnosis. Rather, the autobiographer can only narrate what he or she remembers, however faintly; he or she will continue to keep at bay memories that are too threatening for his mental stability, or will not fully realize the threatening nature of what he or she has put into words. With the narration only those items from memory are translated into stories which haunt the narrator anyway, in dreams, bodily sensations or single images. This is expressed by one of my interviewees in Israel, who survived a concentration camp and suffers from the silence and denial of other survivors:

"It's going to come out at some point anyway. I have experienced that in myself. As much as I wanted to lock the door, as much as I wanted to suppress it, somehow it comes out. Until today. Imagine that, just this week (2) I felt like I'm in a crowded room again and I'm suffocating.... And you know, it comes back again and again, whether you want it to or not, you can suppress it as much as you want, it comes back again. ... So it's better that I talk about it" (translated from the German).

Telling his entire life story also helps the autobiographer regain a sense of continuity. Disruptions in a life story cannot be repaired by not addressing them; this only reinforces the feeling of lost continuity. Telling the story of one's life, on the other hand, can contribute to the necessary reassembling of individual memory fragments, which is also extremely important from a psychoanalytic point of view, and to the integration of the traumatic experience into the overall context of the life story: "For establishing the sense of continuity, the connection between past and present is of central significance in psychological recovery, whether this occurs spontaneously or with the help of psychoanalysis or psychotherapy" (Ornstein 1985: 107). The psychoanalyst Anna Ornstein believes that for survivors of the Holocaust there are chances for healing processes if the traumatic phases of their lives are integrated into their life stories.

What does it mean for people if they cannot talk about a traumatic phase or traumatic experience, such as persecution by the Nazis, being buried under rubble in a bombing raid, or being raped? If experiences are not tellable,

---

2 Jürgen Straub (1991: 60 f., translated from the German), for example, assumes that traumatic experiences "resist, as it were, integration in a narratively constituted biographical context of meaning which creates continuity", and concludes from this that narration leads to the phenomenon of an "irreconcilable rupture and tear in the genetic and temporal development and structure of the self-understanding of the subjects concerned, which prevents continuity and identity".

there is a danger that those affected will remain entrenched in what they have experienced and will not be able to distance themselves from it. It is then hard to distinguish the past from the present: "In narration, the act of reproduction places the past at an objectifying distance from the (narrative-)present and accomplishes a temporal rupture" (Röttgers 1988: 10, translated from the German).

Narration transforms the unfamiliar into the familiar; the unfamiliar is made known and understandable to the narrator himself and to the listener through the act of narrating (Matthes 1985: 313; Schütze 1976a). If, on the other hand, autobiographers cannot communicate, if they cannot talk about what they have experienced, they will receive no empathy from other people who do not share what they have experienced, and have not themselves suffered similar things. We can understand other people's experiences best when they are narrated in detail, as against only brief mentions. In my opinion, not being able to talk about traumatizing experiences or phases of life leads to a second traumatization. If it is not possible to present such experiences in the form of stories, the original traumatization will be further intensified.

5.2 The healing effect of life narratives for survivors of the Shoah[3]

Let us stay with the example of survivors of the Shoah to further elaborate the healing effect of biographical narration, or the dangers of losing a life narrative. The following considerations are based on my interviews with Jewish Israelis, most of whom emigrated to Israel in the years immediately after liberation. All of them lead a more or less normal, i.e., not psychiatrized, life, and the late effects of their experiences – as far as I can judge as a clinical layperson – are limited to somatic and neurotic symptoms. Against the background of these interviews, I can hardly understand the generalized pessimism shared by numerous psychotherapists and psychiatrists regarding the chances of deep psychotherapy for survivors.[4] Paul Chodoff (1975: 944), for example, advocates limiting the goal of therapy to support and symptom relief, and refraining from reconstructive goals. In his view, many survivors'

---

3 The case examples given in this chapter are discussed more fully in later publications. For details of these, see below.

4 For a detailed overview of these assessments, see Klaus Hoppe 1971.

trust in other people has been so deeply destroyed that they can no longer engage in a truly reciprocal relationship with another person, which is a prerequisite for psychoanalysis. It is an open question to what extent therapy with survivors faces fundamental limitations, or whether therapeutic conceptions – especially orthodox psychoanalytic conceptions – need to be corrected. Perhaps other methods than the conventional ones should be used, such as the LSD treatment used by Jan Bastiaans (1988: 71, translated from the German) in the Netherlands, in which "during intoxication there is an immediate psychodramatic re-experiencing of the traumatic experiences of detention and life in the concentration camp". It seems important to me, however, that this generalized image of survivors whose symptoms are all subsumed under the term "survivor syndrome", and the pathologizing tendency – due to the need for reports from expert witnesses to justify the payment of compensation – do not do justice to the survivors. There are survivors who after liberation have been unable to connect to the world outside the extermination camp, and at the same time there are many who show they have the strength to maintain or regain their mental health, human dignity, joie de vivre, and ability to form friendships and love others, despite years of extreme stress or extreme traumatization.

My experience shows that it helps these survivors to be able to talk freely and at length about their experiences of persecution, with the active support of the listener, and that telling their life story can initiate healing processes. This does not exclude the possibility that there may be survivors who need to shield themselves from remembering their experiences, because this would be too great a threat to their mental stability. These survivors will either be unwilling to take part in an interview, or will use conversational techniques that allow them to avoid telling stories. If survivors are capable of successfully living their daily lives and not being completely crushed by their past, we can assume that they have sufficient strength and competence – probably more than other people – to protect themselves in an interview against having to talk about things that are too painful. For example, Wolfram Fischer-Rosenthal (1992) discusses the life story of a man who, instead of talking about how he was persecuted, tells the interviewer he can find everything about this phase in his written autobiography, which his wife wrote down on the basis of documents from his psychotherapy. In the interview, he only wants to talk about the time after his liberation.

If biographers who hitherto have not spoken about the traumatic phases of their lives try to narrate their experiences, or if biographers who have talked obsessively about their persecution try to address experiences about which they have not spoken[5], and if they are helped by supportive and active listening, this can have several positive effects.[6] First of all, it has the cathartic effect of being able to "give up" a burden. It is also a relief to find that, contrary to their fears, their terrible and inexpressible experiences can be put into words, and thus become communicable, and, above all, real. Quite a few survivors ask themselves again and again, "Did I really experience that, isn't it just a dream?" or "Am I just imagining all that?" The time of their persecution belongs to another world. While the survivors were initially convinced that there was no possibility of translation between the world of extermination and their world today, a bridge between the two worlds is revealed to them as they tell their stories. Several of my interviewees were very surprised that they had succeeded – at least partially – in narrating their experiences of persecution. For example, one person said after the interview, "I never thought that storytelling could be so easy." Some asked me at the next meeting, "What did you do to me that I told so much? You hardly asked any questions!" They had suffered from their previous speechlessness, and believed they could not tell these stories.[7] By telling me their life story, they have discovered that they can tell it with almost no help, needing only a listener – and no special tricks! Following their experience in the interview, some of the survivors then plucked up the courage to talk to others about their past suffering, and began to break the silence in their families. During further interview appointments with me, it became apparent how, as a result of the first interview, further memories returned to consciousness like an explosion, and how much the biographers now felt a need, which they had hitherto suppressed, to talk about their memories. The experience of producing a biographical grand narrative leads here to awareness of a need to communicate, and is thus a precondition for telling more stories. If survivors who had previously limited themselves to making general assessments of their time as prisoners in the camp are motivated

---

5 Obsessive speaking, like non-speaking, can be a defensive mechanism, where the survivor talks in order to avoid having to address the experiences that burden him or her.

6 Likewise, it helps the children and grandchildren of victims to put into words the fantasies that oppress them about the cruelties suffered by their relatives, or about their deaths. On the effect on the second and third generations of non-narrated stories, and their fantasies, see Rosenthal, Dasberg, Moore 1998/2010; Rosenthal 2002).

7 The Yad Vashem National Memorial in Jerusalem offers seminars specifically for survivors to help them to talk about their persecution.

by an interview to tell their stories, a further process of opening up is set in motion. Kurt E. Eissler (1968: 459, translated from the German), on the other hand, reports that it takes a long time and "a special skillful technique of psychiatric interrogation" to get these survivors to tell their stories. In my opinion, asking someone to tell their *whole* life story is one of the particularly skillful techniques in everyday life, i.e., outside of psychiatric practice.

In our interviews, the narrators also discovered that their fears of being crushed and overwhelmed by the memories that were now being brought up were unfounded. Even though the survivors often had difficulty sleeping in the nights following the interviews, with renewed dreams of the time of their persecution, they nevertheless had the feeling – as they repeatedly confirmed to me in follow-up contacts – that speaking had freed them from the oppression of silence. They were relieved to learn that someone could listen to them with interest and empathy, that they could make themselves understood, even by a listener who had never experienced any of this, and who would not condemn them for the actions, thoughts and feelings that caused them so many feelings of guilt and embarrassment.[8]

At this point it is important to reflect on the fact that I conducted these interviews as a non-Jewish German. I am well aware that the positive feedback I repeatedly received from my interviewees – for instance in letters written after the interviews – contains, besides the manifest content, a latent dynamic that is connected with my being German. Nevertheless, the positive feedbacks are not only due to this dynamic, but are expressions of feelings. As a result of these contacts with my interviewees, which have lasted many years, and above all through interviews conducted with their children and grandchildren since 1993 in the context of a new research project (Rosenthal 1998/2010), it has become clear that the initial interviews led to the opening of a familial dialogue.

It seems likely that my being German is what helped some survivors to speak, although it made others refuse to take part in an interview with me.[9]

---

8 However, this requires listeners who do not signal non-verbal thoughts such as "How can you expect me to listen to such terrible things?" or who feel sorry for themselves because of their own feelings of guilt.

9 I experienced this in very few cases. In the context of our current research project (funded by the German Research Foundation, DFG), in which Israelis and non-Jewish Germans are conducting interviews in three-generation families, we Germans tend to find that members of the second generation refuse to talk to us, while the parents' generation sometimes prefers us as interviewers. See, for instance, our analysis of the Arads family (Rosenthal/Völter/Gilad 1998/2010).

While survivors do not want to burden their children and other members of the second generation with their traumatic experiences, this concern does not apply to a non-Jewish German interviewer. With me, the survivors tend to adopt the attitude that I, as a German, should tell other Germans about their experiences of persecution. The comparative analyses of interviews conducted by German or Israeli colleagues in the context of the project "The Holocaust in Three Generations" (e.g. Rosenthal 1998/2010) offer further indications that socially taboo extreme experiences, such as sexual abuse during the time of persecution, are more likely to be told or hinted at to a non-Jewish German than to a Jew.

Let us now consider the statements of a survivor about the effects of an interview. Hannah Zweig[10], who survived the concentration camp at Theresienstadt, answers my question whether she had been haunted again by her nightmares – which she had told me about – after our first interview:

"I had the dreams once, twice, but then it subsided. I want to tell you something, it is not so bad to talk about it, maybe it is better to talk about it. Memories always come out that you haven't thought about for years, something new always comes out. But I find it helps to talk. It doesn't have to be that you can understand me one hundred percent, but I have the feeling that you definitely try to understand what I want to pass on to you" (translated from the German).

For Ms. Zweig, it was especially important that she believed I understood her feelings of survivor's guilt. After I had motivated her to tell me about the selection for transports to Auschwitz that took place in Theresienstadt, she admitted her feelings of relief at that time that the others, and not she, were transported: "And again I thought: 'Thank God it's not me'". The way she continues after this admission makes it clear that saying this does not burden her – as we might assume – but rather relieves her:

"Yes, you know, what is hard for me, I can't talk to my daughter to my son I can't talk about all this (2). I can't express myself to the children, for example like I can tell you this, they would never be able to understand if I told them feel guilty and ashamed about the people who left and I'm still alive".

Behind this statement lies more than we might assume from the manifest content. On the one hand, Hannah Zweig is afraid of the lack of understanding of her children, to whom she cannot even hint at many of the things

---

10 The name is anonymized. For a case analysis of Hannah Zweig and her family, see Rosenthal (2001).

THE HEALING EFFECT OF BIOGRAPHICAL NARRATION 171

connected with her concrete feelings of guilt – such as the fact that prostitution helped her to survive in Theresienstadt. On the other hand, for the children, the question of their parents' right to live, and thus also their own right to live, which is connected with the guilt of survival, is beyond their understanding. Thus, as a rule, parents and children are at pains to maintain silence. Parents tend to conceal their experiences of degradation and dehumanization from their children. The children tend to make this their own secret, which they in turn pass on to the grandchildren (Kestenberg 1991: 113).

Ms. Zweig is one of those who have tried to talk to other survivors about the time of persecution, her nightmares and her anxiety. But except for an acquaintance who has since died, she has found no listeners. She feels misunderstood and lonely: "You feel like you're shut out of everything and you have to get over it on your own" (translated from the German).

This experience of being excluded, of being different, means that the interview must be conducted in a way that does not further intensify this feeling. This means, among other things, that when asking about very stressful memories we must be careful to respect the fears and defenses of the interviewee. Rather, we should use narrative-generating questions to help construct stories about the threatening experiences.

In order to initiate detailed narratives about experiences associated with feelings of guilt and embarrassment, detailed follow-up questions on the part of the interviewer were often necessary. Most of the time, the narrators only hinted between the lines at what particularly burdened them in the main narration, in which they were not interrupted with questions. Very attentive listening was necessary in order to be able to detect these stressful topics and ask about them in the questioning part of the interview. From interview to interview, the reactions of my interviewees to these questions confirmed the notion that they find it helpful to recount experiences that are consciously accessible to them and which haunt their memories, but which they would rather not address. The experiences are not yet available to them as stories but only as single images, or they reckon with incomprehension on the part of the listener. Often autobiographers – and this does not only apply to survivors of the Holocaust –unconsciously signal a need to communicate when approaching certain experiences about which they have never spoken and – manifestly – do not want to speak about.[11] As interviewers, we must learn to

---

11 This ambivalence between wanting to speak and wanting to remain silent was evident in all of our research contexts. Many of the interviewees had offered to take part precisely because of their

perceive these signals. With questions such as "Would you like to talk about it?" or "Would you like me to help you remember it again?" we can find out whether the autobiographers want to respond or not.[12]

A request to say more about certain situations and detailed questions related to them – for instance, in the case of Ms. Zweig, the question about selection for the transports and her feelings about it – can show autobiographers that one is trying to understand them, not condemning them, and accepting the normality of their actions and feelings in this extreme situation. In the narration of very traumatic experiences, it is palpable for both the narrator and the listener how the narration and ending the speechlessness of repeatedly revived feelings and bodily sensations make the experiences lose their horror, and enable the narrator to put a certain distance between himself and what he had experienced. While the revival of feelings and weeping is liberating, narration is the key to distancing oneself from the past and to "telling oneself out" with stories, following the linearity of one's experiences during the time of persecution. This allows the narrators to leave the past behind, and feel how the present differs from the past, but without losing the past as a component of their own lives. Rather, through narration, the past is reclaimed as a real and accessible part of one's life story. The past should not be closed, in the sense of being inaccessible: it should be made understandable as a past life that differs from the present, but nevertheless reaches into it. One should not try to eliminate all traces of the past in the present, but learn to accept them, if one can integrate them into one's everyday life.

For us social scientists, too, it would make much more sense not to subsume the long-term effects of persecution under categories of psychopathology, but to regard them as normal consequences of an abnormal past, as biographical achievements in dealing with traumatization.[13] As biographical researchers, we assume "that deviation from the norm is an active biographical achievement which is in itself a *solution* and has a specific function in

---

experiences and burdens. Their attempts to "get rid of it" and break the silence they had practiced for years were not always wholly successful.

12 In the "warming-up" phase of an interview, I ask my interviewees to signal to me which phases of their persecution they do not want to talk about. Likewise, I usually formulate my later questions, which initially refer only to things they have already mentioned (cf. chapter 6.1.), very tentatively, for instance "Perhaps you could talk about ... in more detail?" or "May I ask you about the time when you ...?"

13 The psychiatrist and psychoanalyst Hillel Klein (1968) comes to a similar view in the context of survivor's guilt. He understands it as a positive force in the healing process.

THE HEALING EFFECT OF BIOGRAPHICAL NARRATION

the person's life story" (Fischer-Rosenthal 1992: 20, translated from the German). Fischer-Rosenthal (1992) uses the case study of a man who survived the Warsaw Ghetto as a child and who, as mentioned above, is unable to talk about the time of persecution, to show how a physical symptom, a speech anomaly, maintains the link to the past: "The bodily realization of a traumatized life, the production of 'symptoms', if you will, must be seen directly as a positive biographical function, between the two extreme poles of destructive repression or total detachment, on the one hand, and the broadest possible emotional and cognitive working through of the past as the best possibility, on the other" (ibid: 26).

For the survivors, a cognitive restructuring of their "deviations from the norm" as "solutions" means learning to accept these deviations and themselves. Why should one go to the hairdresser if one is afraid of having one's hair cut and feels reminded of Auschwitz? Why should one be worried about needing such a large supply of food in the house to reduce one's fear of starvation? Why should one declare oneself crazy for buying and hoarding so many shoes, when shoes mean survival? This shoe tic can be seen as a successful way of dealing with past persecution, as an effective way of coping with the fear and torment of that time in the camp, when a lost shoe meant working barefoot for a day, with a bleeding and swollen foot, and not knowing whether one could organize a new shoe in the evening, or whether one would be the next to be selected for the gas chamber.

I was able to learn about one of these biographical achievements for dealing with anxiety from past situations in the present, in an interview with Ms. Steinberg.[14] Her way of dealing with specific fears, which she talked about for the first time in the interview, but the memory of which she tries to avoid in her present everyday life, was shown in an indirect way in the first minutes of our encounter. On a chilly winter's morning in Haifa, I came straight from the hotel to Ms. Steinberg. Obviously very relieved to find how young I was, she greeted me warmly and invited me to take a shower in her newly installed shower unit, speaking enthusiastically about its frosted glass and its privacy. After establishing that the year of my birth (1954) meant I was far removed from the generation of the perpetrators, she was able to invite me to use the shower, which for her, as we shall see, meant protection from cruelty and humiliation.

---

14 For a detailed case presentation of this interview, as well as the interview with Ms. Steinberg's daughter and grandson, see Rosenthal (1999).

Although such invitations to shower were not unusual in Israel in the summer, for me in this context, and also because of the enthusiasm with which she explained the advantages of the shower cubicle, the was the first hint of a memory trace. There were initially no further such hints in Ms. Steinberg's life narrative. However, when I asked her about situations in her present everyday life that for her were connected with the concentration camp, she said that she could not shower in public, such as on the beach or in shared showers in the kibbutz. Without saying anything more about her associations, she then quickly abandoned this topic and talked about something else for a long time. Anyone who did not understand this as a case-specific feature, and perhaps associated with it the gas chambers disguised as showers, would probably leave it at that. However, we can assume that the specific consequences of persecution in the past – or traces of the past in general – are based on experiences linked to specific situations. Also, the same symptoms in different people (such as fear of the hairdresser, a constantly overflowing refrigerator, or a cleaning tic) are always based on different case-specific biographical experiences. Therefore, at a later point in the interview, I asked Ms. Steinberg, "Was there a bad situation in the shower room that you experienced?" In response, she recounted how, in the concentration camp, while the women prisoners were showering, SS men were running around, repeatedly beating their breasts, and selecting women for a brothel for SS men and soldiers. The threatening nature of this memory for Ms. Steinberg is intensified by other experiences in the thematic field of undergoing sexual abuse while being called a "Jewish whore". Ms. Steinberg was presumably aware before this interview that her refusal to shower in public was due to her experiences in the camp, but she had not previously admitted this to others, or explained it pro-actively to anyone. As long as she lived on the kibbutz, for example, she had showered only secretly at night.

Some of my interviewees, on the other hand, realized the connection between their "symptoms" and certain concrete experiences only through my questions. For example, a woman who said she had a shoe tic and therefore declared herself to be "meshugge". When I asked her what had happened to her shoes in the concentration camp, she told the story given above. So far she had seen her "shoe tic" as a consequence of the past in general, but not in connection with that day when shoes were necessary for her survival. If a connection between the symptom and the experience is made, this may be a first step for the survivor to learn to accept the traces of the past as "legitimate" and "in line with reality".

By recounting situations associated with feelings of guilt and embarrassment, it then becomes possible for those affected to see them in a different light, to understand their behavior at the time, and to forgive themselves for thinking only of their own shoes, for example, or for being glad to be spared when women were being selected for the brothel – as with all other selections. Also, linking these memories with others, embedding them in a thematic context, offers a chance to become aware of previously hidden experiences and their threatening aspects. This is true, for example, in the case of Ms. Steinberg, for whom public showers are located in the thematic field of sexual abuse, which she had to endure from SS men in other situations during her time in the camp.

Another important effect of talking about the time of persecution is that the autobiographer again becomes an actor in a story in which he was deprived of autonomy of action for such a long time. By recounting situations in which he acted in one way or another, he regains a sense of agency and is no longer in the position of a puppet helplessly at the mercy of the persecutors.

The survivors of the Shoah survived because they did not allow themselves to drift into the condition of prisoners who were referred to as "Muselmann" in the camp language, those who had given up and who in a psychological sense were already dead. Telling their life story gives the survivors a sense of power by raising awareness of their active struggle for survival, which demanded enormous strength and continued in the equally painful time after liberation. However, the struggle for survival is also linked to actions which cause them feelings of guilt. I believe that these feelings are not reinforced by recounting the situations around which they are centered. Rather, those affected are enabled to see that the desperate nature of their situation made their survival depend on actions that would be considered morally reprehensible outside the world of extermination.

Just as the biographical narration of persecution in the past can have a healing effect, the regaining of one's life story *before* and *after* persecution, and the embedding of these phases in thematic fields that are not related to the persecution, is of crucial importance for being able to live with this past (cf. chapter 4.1.4). A precondition for this integration process in interviews with survivors of the Shoah, but also with traumatized people in general (see Rosenthal 2003), is that they should be asked to tell their *entire* life story, and that they are supported in this narrative process. If they are only asked to tell the story of their persecution, this will reinforce their focus on "having survived" and their inability to tell stories from other phases of their life.[15]

Biographical storytelling about the time before persecution helps survivors uncover buried continuities and reclaim experiences unrelated to their persecution. To support this in the interview, we must repeatedly try to motivate them to tell stories about the time before their persecution by asking detailed narrative-generating and memory-promoting questions. With the gradual regaining of a narratable past before the Shoah, the life of that time can be revived, and the biographer can become aware that this past was not destroyed by the persecution. Even if family and friends have been murdered, the shared experiences with them do not have to be lost; rather, they can be seen as part of one's own life story. While the emigrants who were driven out of Europe have lost their homeland, and many of them in Israel, for example, long for the "green" of Europe, remembering excursions to the forest and the lakes does not cause a lapse into melancholy, but to a regaining of this time as part of one's own life. Thus, in my opinion, the gradually decreasing pressure in Israel on European emigrants to assimilate – for instance, by allowing another main language besides Hebrew and bilingual education for the children or grandchildren, which was frowned upon for a long time in many kibbutzim – can help to give a sense of continuity not only to the survivors of the Shoah, but also to those expelled from Europe whose parents and relatives were murdered.

While memories of positive experiences have a relieving effect, it is also necessary to remember and address unpleasant and stressful experiences. For example, it is much more difficult for survivors to admit the feelings of jealousy or hatred they harbored toward their siblings before their persecution, when these siblings were murdered in Auschwitz. However, these feelings are not extinguished by their death, but have an effect on the survivor's attitude to life and against himself. Thus, it can be seen that feelings of guilt are particularly strong when there was a bad relationship between the survivor and the dead before their separation (cf. Trautman 1961: 547).

Grieving for the murdered and for the loss of one's own life worlds and life plans means remembering both the unpleasant and pleasant experiences.

---

15 If the autobiographers can be motivated to tell stories from their life before their persecution, this has the effect that they get into a narrative flow before beginning to talk about it, which results in far more detailed stories about their persecution than if one begins the interview with this (cf. chapter 6.1).

Mourning is easier for the survivors if they do not have to view their experiences with the people and the life worlds they have lost exclusively in the frame of reference of the Shoah, and can thus protect them – as well as themselves – from being devalued by their persecution. If they succeed in seeing their life after persecution in thematic fields other than that of persecution, and in finding traces of lived continuities through the regaining of a life story before persecution, then they have taken the first important steps toward making it easier to live with their experience of persecution in the past.

6. Methodological implications

6.1 Principles of interviewing to obtain a biographical narrative[1]

If we ask someone to tell his life history, or phases of his life, and want to support him in such a way that he can surrender to a flow of memory and narration without great effort, we should have at our disposal specific techniques and competencies of interviewing. The frequently heard view – especially from scholars who use qualitative methods – that everyday competence[2] is sufficient for conducting an open or narrative interview, is based on failure to appreciate the difficulty of restrained and at the same time attentive listening, on the one hand, and, on the other hand, underestimation of the need to formulate sensitive and narrative-generating questions – a skill which is unfortunately rarely learned and practiced in everyday life, or which is easily forgotten.

In addition to the principles discussed by Christa Hoffmann-Riem (1980), which claim general validity for interpretative social research, the "principle of openness", by which is meant renouncing hypothesis-guided data generation, and the "principle of communication", which means being guided by the rule system of everyday communication, further principles can be formulated for conducting a biographical interview:

1. allowing enough space for the development of a Gestalt, for instance through long sequences of storytelling,
2. supporting the process of remembering,
3. encouraging verbalization of sensitive topics,

---

1 See also a later publication on this topic: Rosenthal 2018: chapter 5.4.
2 Cf. also Christel Hopf's criticism of this attitude and her detailed remarks on interviewer errors (1991: 181 f).

4. a temporally and thematically wide enough initial narrative prompt,
5. attentive and active listening,
6. sensitive and narrative-generating questions,
7. assistance with scenic remembering.

The *narrative interview* as developed by Fritz Schütze (1976a; 1977; 1987) is – if applied according to the rules[3] – not only the most consistent, but the only effective method to meet these methodological requirements. The decisive factor in a biographical narrative interview is that the autobiographer is first asked to tell their life history or certain phases and areas of their life, with no specific restrictions, and is not interrupted with detailed questions during their subsequent presentation, the *main narration*. Only in the second phase of the interview, the *questioning period*, is the person encouraged to tell more stories with the help of narrative-generating follow-up questions. The most open form of invitation, which avoids any thematic restriction, goes something like this:

"I would like to ask you to tell me your life history, all the experiences that were personally important to you. You can take as much time as you like. I won't interrupt you. I will just note questions that I will ask later".

If we follow the conception of a dialectical relationship between experienced life history and narrated life story, as in Gestalt theory and phenomenology, the structure of the interview does not depend on the topics in which we are interested. This conception implies an interest in how people experienced their world in the past, and how they experience it today, and how their biographical experiences present themselves to them. In order to do justice to this interest, we must not set the themes, we must not define what belongs to a theme and what does not, in which thematic field a theme is embedded, and what its contents are. The principles for evoking and sustaining a biographical narrative are the same, whether we want to learn something from the life of our interviewee out of sociological or everyday interest, or whether we want to help the narrator to deal with a difficult past history, or to find a biographical solution to a present crisis. If we are interested, for

---

3 The term "narrative interview" is used in an inflationary manner in social science debates today. Even when narratives are only asked for in individual sequences of a guided interview, such interviews tend to be referred to as "narrative". For the technique of the narrative interview in the sense meant here, in addition to the work of Schütze, see Hermanns 1987; Kraimers 1983; Rosenthal 1987: 119–132; 2003; 2019, 2018: chapter 5).

example, in learning something about the long-term course of a chronic disease such as multiple sclerosis, or about the life courses of so-called career women, we cannot guess in advance, a) which areas of life belong to this biographical strand for the autobiographers, b) in which thematic fields, and in what way, their themes are embedded, and how this manifests itself in the sequential order of their presentation, or c) when the story of this thematic area begins for them. The "beginning" of the story will differ from autobiographer to autobiographer, not only in the case of a disease that is difficult to diagnose, such as MS, where the first symptoms may disappear after an initial episode and the affected person does not have to define himself as "ill"[4]. In the same way, in the case of the manager's career, we cannot foresee whether she thinks her career began with an intensive relationship with her father and his support during her childhood, or only when she was promoted within the company where she worked. And, independently of how much we know about the course of illness or career[5], we cannot know beforehand which areas of life are seen by these people as belonging to these biographical strands: whether, for example, the biographer sees a deep marital crisis or dependence on her mother as having something to do with her illness or her career. Generally speaking, if we want to conduct an everyday conversation or an academic interview with the goal of evoking a biographical narrative, we must leave the shaping of the narrative to the biographer, regardless of which particular topics interest us and from which perspective.

Apart from the questions asked in the questioning period of the interview, the way the interview is conducted is always the same. It does not matter whether we are more interested in the present or in the past, i.e., whether as oral historians or as family members, we want to learn something about the autobiographers' past under National Socialism, or whether, as sociologists and psychologists, we want to reconstruct how they deal with it today. As I have tried to show, the narrated stories are based on a reciprocal relationship between what was experienced then and how it presents itself today in the act of turning one's attention to it. In order to learn something

---

4 See the case study of the life story of a woman who developed MS by Christiane Grote (1987).

5 Too much knowledge about a subject area can stand in the way of good interviewing more than it supports it. The moment we take on the expert role as interviewer or interlocutor, we believe we know what belongs to the theme and what does not. This leads us, on the one hand, to be less attentive and restrained during the main narration and, on the other hand, to inquire too little into certain points later, the meaning of which we think we know. In other word, we miss the particular features of this specific case.

about the past, we have to take into account the present of the narration, and, vice versa, we have to get to know the past, if we want to understand how the autobiographers live with it today. Only when we have reconstructed the experienced life history in its layering of experiences (cf. chapter 6.2) will the biographer's present attitude, his present processing and interpretation of the experiences become interpretable: "Without knowing the biographical framework of events and experiences which determines the biographer's own theoretical knowledge production, it is impossible to determine the significance for the life course of autobiographical theory production" (Schütze 1983: 286, translated from the German). And conversely, we can say: if we know nothing about the perspectivity of the narrated life stories, i.e., about the structure of the narrator's present view of his memories, which co-constitutes the thematic fields of his presentation, we cannot reconstruct the past experiences of the autobiographer.

The unavoidable link between the past and the present, as well as the fundamental difference between the experienced life history and the narrated life story, must therefore be taken into account, not only during the analysis of the text (see below), but already during the interview. Let us assume that we are interested in someone's experiences during the Second World War, but our interviewee, who was informed about this concern when contact was made, begins with long explanations about his arthritis. We might think this is not part of the theme, and try to get him to recount his war experiences. But his present physical disabilities, his fears of the next attack of pain, may decisively determine his biographical overall view, i.e., the way he regards his war experiences. The content of his thematic field could be all experiences relating to illness, injury and death, or all those experiences in which he felt physically fit and active – and which to us may seem unrelated to arthritis. Every single theme of his narrative would then present itself to him against the background of his present physical impairment. If, on the other hand, we do not understand his remarks about arthritis as belonging to the interview (and do not transcribe them later), and if we prevent the autobiographer from giving further explanations, we not only signal to him a lack of interest in his difficult situation – and thus fail to create a confidential and dense conversational atmosphere – but also reduce our chances of being able to reconstruct the rules that structure his war narrative. We would fail to see that his many stories about wounded soldiers are an expression of his present bodily infirmity, and that this gives them a special biographical relevance. Furthermore, it is possible that the autobiographer begins the interview with the theme of "Late effects of the war" because he knows what our interest is and sees a connection between his arthritis and his deployment as a soldier in Russia, the frostbite he had on his hands and feet, and his years of malnutrition in French captivity. In an interpretative procedure, in which we understand our interviewees as experts for their lives and their everyday situation, the basic methodological rule for the interviewer, and later for the interpreter of the text, is to assume there is a thematic connection between each individual sequence and the main theme, even if the autobiographer is not always aware of this.

Our example can now also be constructed in reverse for a sociologist who is interested in the history of arthritis and not in war experiences. If the biographer began the interview by talking about his war experiences and the interviewer intervened, she could miss an opportunity to get to know his implicit theory of illness. She would also prevent the autobiographer from becoming aware of this connection through his narration. He could develop this view of his illness in the act of narration, because for him it is not part of a theory detached from his narrative, and thus cannot be asked about with questions such as, "How do you think it came about that you got arthritis?". Analyzing interviews, and contrasting the narrators' theoretical comments with their narratives, also repeatedly shows "that people 'know' and can tell much more about their lives than they include in their theories about themselves and their lives. This knowledge is available to the informants on the level of storytelling, but not on the level of theorizing" (Hermanns 1991: 185, translated from the German).

If we curtail the themes chosen by the autobiographer too early, i.e., before we as listeners can understand the meaning of certain themes for the autobiographer, this can result in communication and comprehension difficulties. The autobiographer may respond rudimentarily to the theme given by the interviewer and yet stick to his own themes. These two figures, the figure of his thematic field and the figure of our thematic field can then merge in a way that is hardly noticeable to us, as listeners, and during the analysis of the interview text we can only reconstruct with difficulty what belongs to which figure. Not only do we not know which themes have biographical relevance for the autobiographer, the entanglements can be much more far-reaching. Let us illustrate this with an example: Gerhard Heim, who had agreed to take part in an interview as a veteran of the First World War, began his life story with the end of the Second World War and his flight from the Memel Territory. Still believing at the time that it would be better for the autobiographer to narrate his experiences in chronological order, I interrupted him by saying, "Could you perhaps begin with your childhood and then tell me what happened to you in World War I?" Mr. Heim responded to this request very briefly, including mention of an escape he experienced during the First World War, and then – at first without my noticing – returned to his escape in 1945. At some points I could not understand what he was talking about, because for me the stories were embedded in a completely different historical and biographical context. When it became clear to me that Mr. Heim had been talking about the flight in 1945 for some time, I could no longer reconstruct in the interview situation which of the experiences he had described belonged to which period.

If we do not assume that a theme has an invariant core of meaning independent of its embedding in thematic fields, then embedding a theme in another framework would mean destroying its meaning in the context of origin. The destructive potential of interventions which impose themes, and, in general, of questions that interrupt the formation of a Gestalt in the main narration, is measured by whether they refer to, a) the theme, b) other contents of the thematic field, or c) marginal matters. Such disturbances during the setting of themes and formation of fields can lead to irreversible destruction of the figures that the autobiographer would have drawn without our interventions. While these products of interaction, i.e., the joint construction of a thematic field by interviewer and autobiographer, may reveal interesting and significant phenomena concerning their interactional behavior, they run counter to the intention of evoking a biographical narrative and to the subsequent biographical analysis. If we are interested not only in the communication behavior of our interviewees, but also in their biographical experiences, and how these present themselves to them today, we are dependent on autonomously shaped narratives. In the questioning period of the interview we still have enough opportunity to initiate interaction processes with our interviewees, in the sense of jointly creating a biographical view of their lives. What would we gain if we used the misunderstanding between Mr. Heim and me to show that his escape in the Second World War has a greater biographical relevance for him than his escape in the First World War, and that he can assert himself and his interests in the interview? This could be clarified in the questioning part of the interview. If we intervene during the main narration, we miss the opportunity to see whether and how the autobiographer himself makes the connection with the topic that interests us, i.e., what thematic links with the First World War exist for him.

Now, this does not mean that interventions are to be rejected in general, they should just not start too early and rashly. For example, I conducted an interview with a man who was most likely a train driver on the trains that transported Jews to the death camps during World War II. The autobiographer spent about an hour telling his life history up to the time when, instead of being drafted into the Wehrmacht, he accompanied transports to Poland as a train driver. Then he started talking about the health benefits of bee pollen. I waited about ten minutes for him to return to his life story of his own accord. I was fully aware that his remarks had a distracting function, but I feared that he would not tell me anything more about his time as a train driver, and I asked him several times to tell me more about the war years. Significantly, in this case I did not succeed. My interventions were nevertheless important for the case analysis, since they revealed the case-specific nature of this autobiographer. Although he had agreed to be interviewed, he did not want to talk about his distressing memories of the years under National Socialism, and he knew how to avoid questions about this time.

Based on the above considerations, the first and most important principle for initiating the narration of a life history can now be formulated: we must give the autobiographer *space for Gestalt development*. If we follow the assumption that individual sequences of a biographical self-presentation, whether the narration of a story or an argumentative sequence, can be grasped in their manifest and latent meaning for the biographer only through their relationship to the thematic field surrounding them, then it is important that we give the autobiographer freedom to shape this space. The meaning of an individual episode in a life history and a life story, both the experience at the time and its presentation today, can only be reconstructed in the way it is positioned within the biographical self-presentation. How the autobiographer arranges his presentation, what he talks about, what he leaves out, and in which thematic fields he embeds which biographical experiences, gives us information about the structure of his biographical self-perception and the meaning of his past experiences. In all the case studies discussed in the previous chapters, our analysis of the current biographical strategies with which the autobiographers try to repair their fragile life histories, and of the biographical meaning of their experiences, was only possible on the basis of their autonomously shaped narratives. Whether in the self-presentation of Hans Gruen, who splits his homosexual life story from his bourgeois one (chapter 4.4.2), or that of Abraham Jarok, who tries to separate his life in Germany from his life in Israel (chapter 4.4.4), these mechanisms of biographical self-presentation only became clear because the interviewers did not intervene prematurely. Hans Gruen could have been asked during his first narration about his "bourgeois biography": "And when was your coming out?" or Abraham Jarok during the narration about his parents: "Did your parents survive?" Apart from the fact that these questions do not evoke narratives but rather argumentation, there is nothing wrong with them; what matters is *when* they are asked in the course of an interview. If we do not refrain from asking them during the autobiographer's main narration, we not only decisively structure his account, but also forfeit the chance to see if, when, and how he himself introduces these details. Let us take the example of Abraham Jarok, who in his narrative about his life in Palestine after his expulsion from Germany, in 1938, initially does not mention his parents who stayed behind. He speaks instead about his happy life in the kibbutz. His parents, and his assumption that they were murdered, do not reappear in his account until he tells about his encounter with the Jewish woman who escaped from Treblinka in 1944. This structure of his biographical self-presentation corresponds to his unconcern at the time about the family's descendants and his resistance to all information about the genocide in Europe. If, on the other hand, we had asked during his narration about his departure from Germany: "And were your parents able to follow you?", we would have missed the chance to let this structure become manifest. Mr. Jarok would have come under pressure to legitimize himself, his feelings of guilt would have found expression here, he probably would not have said anything more about his happy and optimistic time in the kibbutz – for which he feels retrospectively guilty – and perhaps he would have broken off the interview at this point.

If we do not want to succumb to the danger of subsuming sequences under our system of relevance and categories during the interview, which increases during the subsequent analysis, we have to leave the shaping of the biographical self-presentation to the autobiographer. Many interviewers tend to interrupt the narrative flow by asking for further details or by requesting the interviewee to speak about other areas of their life history, but this is usually based on an inability to listen and the arrogant idea that the interviewer knows better than the interviewee what belongs to the theme. It means ultimately that the interviewer takes over the shaping of the biographical self-presentation. If we intervene by asking questions, we influence the development of the themes and define relevancies which do not necessarily coincide with those of the autobiographer. Even minor interventions, such as asking about the time of an experience ("In which year was that?"), can have far-reaching consequences. An autobiographer who finds it hard to reconstruct his life, and who now assumes that the interviewer is interested in the "objective" framework and tries to take this into account, is wrenched out of the narrative flow. Instead of being able to abandon himself to the flow of his memories, he now keeps stopping and tries to reconstruct the date of each experience.

If we intervene by asking questions instead of exercising restraint, we hinder the process of remembering which depends on the interviewee being allowed to *shape his narrative autonomously*. Each question interrupts the flow of memories and obliges the narrator to follow the interviewer's relevancies. This makes the memory process laborious for the narrator: he cannot just talk about what comes to his mind, but has to search for memories that he thinks will interest the interviewer. If the interviewer's expectation does not correspond to the memory units that come to mind, the autobiographer will abandon the narrative scheme. Narratives are replaced by reports and argumentations that reflect his present-day reflections on the experiences of that time. The more he responds to the interviewer's questions, the less he can let himself glide from experience unit to experience unit in his memory stream, and tell story upon story, because he is not sure whether they correspond to the interviewer's interests. We can see here a negative correlation between the length of the narrative and the number of questions or interventions. In interviews that begin with an invitation to speak freely, but in which the informant is repeatedly interrupted with questions about details of what has already been told ("When was that?", "Where was that?", "How did you feel when that happened?" etc.), or even with questions about other experiences, we can observe how the narrative sequences become shorter from question to question, and how the autobiographer switches from the level of storytelling to that of concise reporting and argumentation. He responds increasingly to the interviewer's questions, until at some point the question-answer scheme becomes established. If, on the other hand, the interviewee is not interrupted, the reverse phenomenon occurs: from story to story, the narrative become more complex, as more and more details and experiences emerge from the narrator's memory. If the narrator senses that we are listening to him with interest, attention and understanding, he can increasingly abandon himself to his stream of memory. He begins to create a thematic field, a memory frame, which allows him to present more and more stories. While at the beginning of the interview, the narrator may have to consciously decide what to select from his memories, what is relevant to the theme, or what could be interesting for the interviewer, this self-control gradually decreases as the narrative flow begins. Sometimes he will check himself and explicitly ask the interviewer: "Is that of any interest to you?" or "That's not relevant to the theme". If the interviewer then encourages him: "I'm interested in everything that is important to you" or "The experiences that were important to you belong to the theme", the narrator can abandon himself to his relevancies. Similarly, the narrator uses pauses and eye contact to make sure that the listener is still interested in the line of narration he or she has followed. If the interviewer then asks a question that ignores the interviewee's thematic focus, or even his thematic field – and this is not unlikely – instead of prompting him to continue the narrative with encouraging paralinguistic signals, the narrator will begin to modify his focus accordingly, or even switch to another thematic field.

Attentive listening supports storytelling far more than any question. It also creates more trust and mutual closeness than a question-answer dialog. By listening, we become involved in the individuality of our interviewee. The more we learn about someone, the closer they come to us and the more we can understand them in their being-as-they-are. By listening attentively, we convey to the narrator that we take him and his experiences seriously, that we are interested in his life and that we are not just using him to provide information about certain phenomena. Even interviewees who are initially rather suspicious, and who do not know whether they can confide in the interviewer, are more likely to be convinced by supportive listening than by any explanations about the interviewer and the research project in the warming-up phase of the interview. Besides being open about his or her own biographical motives for the research, the interviewer can establish trust mainly by being able to listen, and, connected to this, by getting involved with the biographer. The interaction that takes place during the main narration, and the closeness that develops between the narrator and the listener, encourage the narrator to be open, and lead to *the verbalization of sensitive subject areas*. The narrator feels accepted and not condemned for his experiences; this helps him to address sensitive issues.

The feeling of being accepted is based on a reciprocal process between narrator and listener, and not just on the impression gained by the narrator. Indeed, attentive listening makes the interviewer able to accept and understand the autobiographer and his experiences, his individual life path. When we get to know a person's life history, we can put ourselves in their place and have far more empathy for them than if we only know about particular actions that are problematic or even condemnable for us. The interpersonal closeness that arises during a biographical narrative is not produced instrumentally, based only on technique, and does not, as some critics suggest, tempt the autobiographer to make unintended revelations. This closeness arises on both sides in the process of interaction. Given that we social scientists are not sensation-hungry neurotics who feast on the suffering of other people, a sensitive approach to an autobiographer's traumatic, embarrassing or guilt-laden experiences serves less our academic interests than to accept him with these experiences, and to help him verbalize them. As mentioned elsewhere (cf. chapter 5.2), it is often precisely these sensitive areas that latently motivate biographers to agree to be interviewed. And – provided that the listener shows a sympathetic attitude – it is often a relief for them to be able to speak about such delicate matters. In my opinion, we owe a person whom we motivate to tell his life history or phases of his life this support, and cannot adopt the attitude of wanting to hear only about pleasant and less stressful experiences.

In order to do justice to the above requirements of developing a Gestalt, encouraging processes of remembering, and dealing with sensitive subject areas, it is important to offer a *thematically and temporally open initial narrative prompt*. Because the main narration, which is autonomously shaped by the autobiographer, becomes increasingly dense in the course of time and is oriented more and more to the biographer's own relevancies, we should, in the case of an initial narrative prompt that sets a starting point, choose it in such a way that it lies *before* the phase of life that mainly interests us. Likewise, we should keep in mind that we should not specify an end point that is temporally anchored in a stressful phase of life in the past. Rather, it is important for autobiographers to be able to "narrate" their way out of this period (cf. chapter 5.2). If, for example, we intend to conduct a medico-sociological study on the topic "Biographical processing of the diagnosis of a chronic illness", a narrative invitation such as the following is not very helpful: "I am interested in the history of your illness. Maybe you could start with the time when your disease was diagnosed and continue up to the first severe episodes of the disease and your blindness". If the autobiographer adhered to this guideline, he would hardly say anything about earlier events which perhaps influenced the way he experienced the situation in which the doctor informed him of the diagnosis[6]. And yet, like any other experience, this was co-constituted by his specific biographical past. If we want to understand an experience from the perspective of the experiencer, we must also know the history leading up to it. This insight ultimately excludes an analysis that is restricted to individual episodes, and requires us to make a biographical analysis. Setting a beginning for the narrative such as "Perhaps you could begin by telling me how you first noticed symptoms" would allow the person to explain what led up to the diagnosis. Also, setting an end point, such as "and perhaps you could continue the story up to the present day, and tell me how you have learned to live with your condition", would be more likely to help someone to leave a sensitive subject area such as going blind – even if their present situation is still very problematic – than the more restricted suggestion in the previous example. Likewise, I would not ask autobiographers to tell me their story up to the end of the war in 1945, since this period was not easy for those persecuted by the Nazis, nor for Nazi followers and perpetrators.

However, we can make the initial narrative prompt more open if we consider that concentrating on a single biographical strand (such as an illness, or a professional career), or on one phase (such as the war years, or adolescence) denies biographers the possibility of embedding this part of their life in their entire life story, and thus of understanding it better themselves and making it more comprehensible to us. Thus, inviting the person to tell their life history without any thematic restriction is the most fruitful for a biographical-interpretive analysis. For example, we could ask a biographer suffering from multiple sclerosis to narrate their biography using the following formulation: "We are interested in the life history of people with a chronic illness. We would like you to tell us your life history, that is, to tell us not only about your illness, but also about any other experiences that were important to you". In this way, we would specify the topic in which we are interested and thus ensure that the narrator will talk about it, while leaving enough room for other biographical strands. The narrative that follows would clarify the importance of the illness in the autobiographer's life, through the way it is linked it to other biographical strands, and through attempts to locate the beginning of the illness that was diagnosed only later.

---

6 Not infrequently, however, structurally similar initial narrative prompts were ignored to some extent by our interviewees, for instance by explicitly saying, *"But first I have to tell you what led up to this"*.

It would be even better if we did not mention our interest in the chronic disease at all. This is not easy because we usually give the reason for our interest when first making contact, or the interviewee makes assumptions about our reason. A certain thematic interest is obvious if the contact comes about via a self-help group of MS patients, for instance. We can hardly ask a Holocaust survivor for an interview with the explanation that we are interested in the life histories of people in general. However, we can assure him in the interview that we are not only interested in his experiences of persecution, but in his entire life history.

Why is it necessary to impose our topic on the interviewee in the main narration, instead of asking about it later if the interviewee does not address it? For a biographical analysis in which we want to reconstruct how the autobiographers live with their illness, it would be particularly interesting if they hardly mentioned anything about it in their main narration. In our analysis of this narrative, we could then pursue the question of the biographical function of this dethematization. If we want to learn how someone experienced a certain part of his life, whether a chronic illness or war experiences, and how he lives with it today, the way it is embedded in his overall biography – and in extreme cases in the unthematic margin – opens a way for us to reconstruct its meaning for the autobiographer. The methodological consequence of viewing experience, memory and narrative from the perspective of Gestalt theory and phenomenology is that we can reconstruct the references inherent in single narrative units, as well as the way they are connected and embedded in the whole in the particular context, without forcing them into our frameworks. This applies both to the analysis of how "inner processes", such as an illness, are experienced, and "outer processes", such as collective historical events. If we assume an indissoluble interrelation between event and experience (cf. chapter 2.3.1), such a dualistic view of inside and outside becomes obsolete anyway. Whether we want to know about a person's illness or about what happened to them at the end of the war, we will only learn how these experiences present themselves to the experiencer – for other sources are not available to us, since experience is bound to subjects – and not how it "really" was. Neither the course of an illness nor the surrender of the German Wehrmacht are social realities outside of experience (Rosenthal 1993a). I feel obliged to underline this, since we, as scientists, are also at the mercy of our everyday mind, according to which "external things" are more real than "internal" ones, and we tend to overlook that the external world is also a social construction (cf. Bertalanffy 1966).

Attentive and active listening

During the main narration, in addition to attentive listening, which is necessary for later questions, we should not underestimate the importance of nonverbal support. In addition to paralinguistic noises such as "mm" or "aha", we as listeners can use facial expression, eye contact and body posture to show that we are listening attentively and that we accept and are trying to understand the narrator and his experiences. By contrast, expressions of disinterest or rejection, such as shaking one's head or looking around the room, however minimal, will inhibit the narrative. Nothing is easier than breaking off the process of opening up – especially when it comes to guilt-ridden or traumatic experiences – with a wrong look or remark.

If there are pauses in the narrative, the autobiographer should be encouraged to continue by prompts that do not introduce new themes but merely motivate him or her to continue, such as the following questions: "What happened next?" or "What else can you remember?".

In addition to passive listening, we can also use *active listening* techniques from client-centered interviewing (Gordon 1977; Rogers 1951; Schwäbisch/Siems 1974: chapter 6) to support the narrator in his narrative. Thus, an occasional paraphrasing of what has been said, i.e., a concise repetition of the content in one's own words, has the effect of encouraging the speaker. In this way, the interviewer shows that he or she is trying to understand what has been said. In order not to interrupt the autonomous narrative flow, we should use this technique very sparingly during the main narration, or only during passages that are particularly hard for the autobiographer. In difficult passages, in which the autobiographer describes depressing or painful experiences, in which feelings are re-actualized, the person cries, or shows signs of distress or anger, it will take more than just an encouraging "mm" or a paraphrase to signal understanding and help the person to continue with their story. By "verbalizing the content of an emotional experience", the listener attempts to respond to the feelings he or she "hears" in the narration and reflect them back to the narrator. Instead of comforting the narrator with remarks like, "It's over now" or even distracting him with a question, verbalizing his feelings with remarks like, "You were very angry at the time" or, "This still affects you very much today" opens the door to further thematization. With these "door openers", the listener shows his or her willingness to engage with what is difficult and not to reject it as embarrassing, unpleasant, or burdensome. This helps the

METHODOLOGICAL IMPLICATIONS   193

autobiographer to talk about his or her stressful experiences and thus make them more bearable. If, on the other hand, we as listeners do not respond to stressful memories in a way that invites narration, but prevent further discussion with "roadblocks" (Gordon 1977: 51 ff.), with well-intentioned consolation, appeasement, advice or a change of topic, we do not accept the autobiographer with his difficulties; instead we signal to him that it would be better not to say anything more about them, and to forget such problems.

If the narrator signals to us that his narrative or his autobiographical self-presentation is finished, we can move on to the questioning period of the interview. The notes we have made[7] during the narrative on points that were unclear to us or about which we would like to know more, or on biographical experiences and phases of life that the autobiographer only hinted at or left unmentioned, now serve us to develop *sensitive and narrative-generating follow-up questions*. These questions, based on what we heard during the main narration, can be regarded as an interview guide designed especially for this individual case. Just like the need for restraint during the main narration, developing these questions is quite a challenging task for the interviewer.

In a certain way, the follow-up questions have the function of "testing" assumptions that impose themselves on us during the main narration. Thus, while listening, we already begin to make assumptions about why the autobiographer leaves certain subject areas and experiences unmentioned, why he speaks so unemotionally about the death of his parents, why he shows such a high pressure to legitimize an area of his life, or why he talks so much about the first years of his marriage. Our questions serve to extract further stories which we deem important for a case analysis. In asking these case-specific questions, therefore, no guideline developed in advance, no matter how clever and well thought-out, can help us, since it could only be formulated according to categories chosen by us. While it could be helpful to consider before the interview how we might evoke certain narratives, and which thematic areas and life phases we would like to address, prepared questions, however open, and even if we have not pre-formulated them, would be counterproductive for an interview based on the relevance system and the biographical experiences and memories of the narrator. Even if we do not understand our preconceived questions as questions that have to be

---

7 Short notes for later questions are absolutely necessary during long narrative sequences, which sometimes last for hours, since one may easily forget things that are interesting, especially during attentive listening, which focuses on meaning rather than on content.

asked, there is the danger that they will prevent us from engaging with the relevance system and the structure of our interviewee[8]. On the one hand, a guide tempts us to ask preconceived questions instead of developing new ones on the basis of this particular person's narrative. On the other hand, it tends to subsume the narrated sequences under our preconceived ideas, i.e., to listen to them according to the criterion "assignable or not", instead of trying to understand their theme and the thematic field surrounding them, and to explore this with our questions.

Another advantage of asking follow-up questions is that after the main narration we can better gauge the significance of certain questions and not rashly intervene in traumatic or embarrassing areas of life. Let us recall the life story of Abraham Jarok, who lost his parents in the Holocaust while living and working enthusiastically on the kibbutz in Palestine. After his account of the night when he learned about Treblinka, and which – according to him – changed his life, the listener can understand that he feels guilty about death of his family, and any questions about it can be correspondingly sensitive. Suppose we were conducting the interview as part of a research project on migration processes, and were particularly interested in how the first years in the new country were experienced. After hearing his life story, we could then ask Mr. Jarok to tell us something about his first years on the kibbutz, instead of asking a general question such as, *How did you fare after emigrating from Germany?* After the main narration, we would also know that we should initially avoid any reference to the Shoah with our questions. We would be aware, for example, that a question such as, "In the kibbutz, did you talk about the persecution of Jews in Europe during World War II?" would elicit arguments from Mr. Jarok legitimating his lack of concern, and thus he would probably not tell us more about his life during that time. So before asking this question, it would be advisable to first ask Mr. Jarok, "Can you tell me a little more about your life on the kibbutz in the early years when you first came to this country?" This open invitation to tell us more will also allow Mr. Jarok to perhaps address spontaneously some of the questions that we are interested in. In general, the more openly we formulate an initial narrative question, the more questions will become superfluous. Therefore, it also makes sense to ask the questions in the order of our notes, i.e., according to the sequence of the main narration. Not infrequently, and especially when the narrative scheme has become established, the narrator will return to the

---

8 Cf. the discussion on the bureaucratization of interviews by Christel Hopf (1978).

sequential shape of his biographical narrative when answering the question, will describe in detail some other experiences and phases of his life which we had intended to ask about.

To further illustrate the technique of asking sensitive and narrative-generating questions, which can only be developed in the context of concrete interviews, let us consider another project, namely "Anti-Semitism in Germany in the 1930s", using the example of Mr. Jarok, who lived in Germany until he was sixteen and left the country before the November pogrom. Let us assume that Mr. Jarok had told us nothing about anti-Semitism in his main narration. Probably the most common question that could be introduced at this point would be, "Did you experience anti-Semitism in your childhood and youth in Germany?" The following answer to such a question would not be atypical for a Jew expelled from Germany:

"You know, in relation to what happened later, when I was already in Palestine, that's not worth mentioning. I wasn't there when the Reichskristallnacht happened. Apart from the few Nazi teachers at school and the graffiti on shop windows, there wasn't much. If we had known then what was coming, my parents would have emigrated immediately".

Apart from the fact that this question refers to a sensitive area of Abraham Jarok's life, it poses two further structural problems: a) it targets experiences that the autobiographer himself has already classified or typified as anti-Semitic in his store of knowledge, and b) it does not invite any narrative. If, on the other hand, Mr. Jarok were asked, for example, to tell a story about his schooldays, he might recount experiences that he had not previously classified as anti-Semitic, but as humiliating in his store of experience, such as the fact that he had to sit on the so-called Jews' bench at school, separated from the other students, as early as 1933.

With questions that are formulated relatively openly, we give the autobiographer an opportunity to autonomously shape a thematic field, because the open formulation means that, in accordance with his memory framework, the narrator is presented with experiences from his memory that would probably not otherwise occur to him. The more open and the more guided by the biographer's main narration our question is, the more experiences will come to the autobiographer's mind which he can tell in the form of stories – this being the linguistic and communicable translation of a memory noema. A specific question about a certain experience, on the other hand, can have the consequence that a) the narrator only tells what has already become an anecdote through frequent repetition and thus is not based on a memory noema, or b) he answers with general assessments and arguments from his present perspective, which are very remote from what he experienced at that time, and which do not tell us anything about what actually happened. This does not mean that we cannot ask questions about specific areas, such as anti-Semitism in schools. But we should try to start with relatively open questions and only then focus on special areas or situations. If, after being asked to tell us about his schooldays, Mr. Jarok were to report no situations that could be seen in the context of anti-Semitism, we could then ask him, "Can you recall any situations at school in which you were disadvantaged or antagonized as a Jew?" This introduces the second typical narrative-generating question structure. In a narrative interview, we can either ask the person to tell us more about a certain phase of their life or an experience that has already been mentioned, or we can ask whether the narrator remembers any situations relating to a certain theme.

But why do we prefer narratives? Even though the rationale of the narrative approach must be evident from the above discussion of the dialectical relationship between experience, memory and narrative, I would like to go into this point again because the criticism expressed by Heinz Bude (1985), who fails to see the importance of the narrative approach, is eagerly taken up by those who have always been against narrative interviews. As Fritz Schütze (1976a; 1976b; 1977) has made very clear, narratives of one's own lived experiences, in contrast to descriptions and argumentations, are "those linguistic texts which are separate from the factual action that is of thematic interest, are closest to it, and reconstruct to a considerable extent the orientation structures of the factual action from the perspective of recapitulating experience" (Schütze 1977: 1, translated from the German). If we do not want to be satisfied with learning something about the everyday theories of members of society that are detached from their experiences and memories – without case-specific possibilities of interpretation – and thus again fall prey to the dualism of thought and action so prevalent in the social sciences, but want to reconstruct what people have experienced in the course of their lives and how this experience shapes their present-day biographical overall view, or their present handling of their past, and their present actions, we have to evoke memory processes and their linguistic translation into narratives. Besides playfully re-enacting past situations, only the narration of a story makes the holistic reproduction of a course of action or of the Gestalt of events at that time possible, in contrast to today's cognitive, but also emotional and bodily view of this event. If, on the other hand, we evoke only parts such as single

METHODOLOGICAL IMPLICATIONS 197

images or arguments about the present meaning of experiences, we cannot reconstruct the experiences of the autobiographer and the history of his "patterns of interpretation". With questions asking for opinions and justification ("Why did you ...?"; "Why did you emigrate at that time...?"; "Why did you not ....?"), we do not encourage holistic reproduction. Rather, we will elicit arguments that are valid in the here and now and in the relationship with the interviewer. These arguments, as shown by Fritz Schütze, are on the secondary level of legitimation and tell us nothing about the motives that guided the action in the past. Involved as we are in the production of remoteness from the action by the way we conduct the interview, we can then join in the lament that people act differently from the way they talk. As long as we focus only on cognition, even if we reconstruct so-called everyday theories or patterns of interpretation instead of querying attitudes, but do not consider how these theories and patterns have been constituted in the life history of the person concerned, through and in action, we are still far removed from an understanding of everyday practices.

Assistance with scenic remembering

If we want to help the autobiographer, who signals a need to communicate, to translate difficult and traumatic experiences that are hard to remember and form into stories which make them comprehensible to himself and to others, further techniques are needed that go beyond narrative-generating questions. Sometimes it is not enough to ask, "Can you tell me a little more about your time in the trenches?", and even questions about specific situations such as, "Can you tell me how you arrived at the ramp in Auschwitz?" do not necessarily help. When we talk to an autobiographer who, until the interview, has hardly ever spoken about that time or about situations that are hard to present as narratives (cf. chapter 4.1.4), and when only single images or sensations are present to him, narrator and listener need to work together to construct stories. As listeners, we can help the narrator to put himself back into the situation at the time and to remember individual components, which we then put together to form a story.

Similar to the various therapy approaches that turn to the past in a reconstructive way – such as psychodrama, in which scenes are playfully reconstructed – the technique of "scenic remembering" supports the autobiographers in putting themselves back into the past scenes and then translating them into stories. Starting with sensory and bodily memory fragments, we can gradually flesh out those scenes by asking questions about individual details, first by recalling the "external" setting – the place, the climate, the sounds, the smells, the people present, etc. Rather than asking for thoughts or feelings, which are usually very difficult to remember, as Maurice Halbwachs (1985: 81 ff.) has pointed out, it helps to gradually fill out the spatial frame of the scene, and, following on from this, gradually reproduce sequences of actions. Let us consider the example of an Auschwitz survivor whom we would like to assist in her attempt to put herself back in the situation upon arrival at the ramp in Auschwitz. We can first ask her, "Try to put yourself in the situation at the ramp ... the wagon is opened ... You hear the screaming ... You are pushed out of the wagon". So we don't ask the biographer if she can remember it, but ask her to put herself back into the situation and begin to picture the scene, phrasing the questions in the historical present tense. We can then move forward from detail to detail: "What do you see?"; "Who are you standing with?"; "What do you hear?"; "Is it dark?"; "Is it cold?". With this, the autobiographer gradually reimagines this scene from memory, gaining shape as she names individual details. Less and less does she need our questions, and can gradually recall sequences of action and begin to translate them into a story.

6.2 Principles of a reconstructive case analysis

The "principle of openness", which prevents us from *conducting the interview* on the basis of preconceived hypotheses, applies equally to the *data analysis*, in which we analyze the text neither with categories developed in advance nor with categories developed on the basis of the text, to which we then assign individual parts. Thus, we avoid subsuming the text under our everyday and scientific systems of relevance and theory; instead, our aim is to reconstruct its structural rules. The principle of giving the autobiographer "space for Gestalt development", which we observe when conducting the interview, can be used to derive another principle: *"the Gestalt must not be destroyed"*, which is important during the analysis of the interview. This is because the autonomously shaped biographical self-presentation only makes sense for a sociological analysis if we do not chop it up into individual parts and place them in a context different from that of the context of origin. If we give up the idea of the identity of individual parts, on the other hand, we can make a consistent analysis of their functional significance for the overall structure and its rules. Therefore, *reconstruction of the Gestalt* of both the experienced and the narrated life story is the highest principle of a Gestalt-theory oriented analysis, affecting all analytical steps. When considering a part of the main narration – such as a story, or, as in the case of Mr. Jarok, the abrupt end of the interview (cf. chapter 4.4.4) – the question arises in each case: what is the functional significance of this sequence for the overall Gestalt of the biographical self-presentation? If, on the other hand, we interpret a biographical experience in terms of its significance in the person's life, the question arises: What is the functional significance of this experience for the overall Gestalt of the experienced life history?

In order to be able to grasp the sequential Gestalt and the development of the thematic fields of a biographical narrative and its interrelationship with the experienced life history, and in order to be able to understand the individual sequences both in their latent and in their manifest meaning in the context of the *narrated*, but also of the *experienced* life history, the following principles must be observed:

1. the principle of *reconstructing* the *experienced* life history and *narrated* life story based on the method of *abduction*;
2. the principle of *sequentiality*, i.e., sequential analysis of both the temporal and the thematic structure of the life history and life story;
3. the principle of *contrasting* the Gestalt of the life history and the life story.

In contrast to methods based on subsumption, a *reconstructive analysis* avoids looking at the text with predefined classification and variable systems. Instead, in a hermeneutic reconstruction, "by explicating the structuredness of a concretely given social event one can reconstruct the general structural type... of which the concrete event is an exemplar" (Oevermann 1983: 246, translated from the German). Categories developed from the text – as the "principle of openness" may be understood – will also not help us to penetrate the case structure of a narrated life story, or to reconstruct the rules governing the constitution of the narrative, the constituting moments of the Gestalt-forming process and its thematic fields. Nor can we do justice to the Gestalt of the experienced life history and grasp the functional significance of the biographical experiences if we remove these experiences from the overall context of the life history and subsume them – in order to be able to understand them – under a different framework. What biographical relevance, for example, a marriage or a divorce had for the life history of an autobiographer can only be reconstructed if we see how it is embedded in this concrete life, in the preceding and subsequent biographical experiences.

Structurally, there is no difference whether we proceed inductively and develop our classification systems on the basis of our interviews, as required by so-called qualitative content analysis (cf. Lisch/Kriz 1978; Mayring 1983), or whether we derive our categories deductively from theories. In both cases, the Gestalt of the text is destroyed: the individual elements are grouped across cases with the help of categories formed on the basis of their outward phenomenal similarity, and not on the basis of their similar structural and functional significance in the overall context of a particular case. Subsuming text parts under categories means assigning individual parts to a certain logical class and checking them for their "regularity", in the sense of frequently occurring together. In contrast to this Aristotelian conception, reconstructive analysis – in accordance with Galileo's conception – refrains from dividing parts into classes with the concomitant characterization (cf. Lewin 1930/31). Instead, the full concreteness of a case is considered, and its constitutive moments are determined in distinction from the situation-specific residual factors. This procedure is based on the assumption that social entities, like a biographical self-presentation, are unitary entities which are generated by *a single* underlying system of rules and cannot be broken down into individual groupings for which separate rules apply in each case. The meaning of parts of a Gestalt can only be determined on the basis of the structuring rules of this one concrete Gestalt, of which they are a part. In the reconstruction of a Gestalt, therefore, the isolation of individual elements must literally be avoided.

When seeking to determine the typicality of a case – in the sense meant here – the frequency of its occurrence is of no importance: "The frequency with which examples of a specific type are realized in unique world events remains 'accidental' for the characterization of the type, for which the only relevant dimension is its essence (Sosein). From the standpoint of systematics, i.e., of characterization as a type, this is tantamount to saying: a matter of historico-geographical 'constellations'." (Lewin 1927/1992: 394). Thus, a reconstructive analysis does not have to consider as many cases as possible: "It must, on the contrary, become important to comprehend "the whole situation involved, with all its characteristics, as precisely as possible" (Lewin 1930/1931: 166).

The typicality of a case is determined by the rules which generate it and which organize its manifold parts. In contrast to a notion of elements and their and-connection (cf. Wertheimer 1922), according to which the summation of equal elements leads to equal totals and, vice versa, equal totals are based on equal elements, in the understanding of a genetic and structural – not descriptive – type there need not be any correspondence between the constituents of two totals in order to belong to one and the same type. Likewise, very different cause-and-effect relationships can underlie the same actualities at the phenomenal level (cf. Lewin 1927/1992: 390). It follows that the assignment of a case to a type is possible only after a reconstructive case analysis, since its structure can be derived neither from the same elements nor from the same external circumstances. This is also the reason for the failure of the well-intentioned offers by practitioners of quantitative social research to test the frequency of occurrence of types with their quantitative methods after their interpretative colleagues have reconstructed them. While there is nothing wrong with the question of how frequently a type occurs in a given population, numerical frequency can only be determined on the basis of reconstructive analyses of all the cases required for this purpose – and this is probably an undertaking that can rarely be accomplished because it would be too costly. On the other hand, a reconstructive analysis of a few cases – if they represent distinct types – and a modeling of the interaction between the types based on this analysis can certainly make statements about the social effectiveness of a type, which cannot be derived from the frequency of its occurrence.

Now, what place do our prior knowledge and our scientific theories take in a reconstructive analysis, and how can we interpret texts at all if we reject both a deductive and an inductive procedure? In a reconstructive analysis, everyday and theoretical knowledge does not serve to develop hypotheses and categories under which the empirical phenomena are subsumed, but rather takes on a heuristic status in the sense of the abductive procedure discussed by Charles Sanders Peirce. In contrast to deductive analysis, abduction begins with empirical phenomena, with facts, "without, at the outset, having any particular theory in view, though it is motivated by the feeling that a theory is needed to explain the surprising facts" (Peirce 1933/1980: 7.218). An inductive procedure, on the other hand, begins with a hypothesis. As we can read in Sherlock Holmes[9] and as empirically shown by Ulrich Oev-

---

9 As an entertaining introduction to abduction, we recommend reading the Sherlock Holmes detective stories, in which Holmes repeatedly explains his method to his colleague Watson – in distinction to the inductive procedure of the police. See, among others, "The Sign of the Four" (Doyle

ermann and his colleagues (1985), induction is a popular procedure with the police. Starting, for example, from the hypothesis "The brother was the murderer", the detective would look for circumstantial evidence confirming this hypothesis, such as the brother's lack of an alibi, the violent quarrel between the brothers two days ago, the conflict over an inheritance, and so on. In abduction, on the other hand, starting from the observable facts, for example, that the murdered man's room is locked and the window is smashed, the detective – and that is what we are in a reconstructive case analysis – would consider all possible interpretations of their meaning. The broken window can mean a feigned entry, only entry or only exit, or even both. In the second step of the abduction process, these possible readings are used to infer consequential phenomena, in this case, for example, signs in the flowerbed under the window or in the broken pane of glass that would confirm the plausibility of the readings entry or exit. If footprints are found during the empirical examination, and if they are such that entry and exit appear to be plausible, the detective can then, in view of the enormous height of the window, make various deductions about the physical constitution of the person entering and exiting (but not about whether he is the murderer) or about what help he had. Thus, it may be possible that the murdered person himself helped the perpetrator to enter through the window and locked the door of the room because they both wanted to keep their meeting secret. But in this case why was the window broken? Again, we can posit possible readings and infer consequential phenomena. Moving from one empirical fact to the next, more and more readings would prove improbable and others increasingly plausible. To avoid proving one hypothesis over and over again, however, we must strive not to lose sight of the other hypothetical lines of argument. Rather, we must continue to pursue them until they are finally shown to be improbable. The reading that remains at the end is then considered as the most probable. Unlike the policeman who proceeds inductively, seeking circumstantial evidence to confirm his hypothesis, "in abduction the consideration of the facts suggests the hypothesis", while "in induction the study of hypothesis suggests the experiments which bring to light the very facts to which the hypothesis had pointed" (Peirce 1980 : 7.218). Thus, in contrast to induction and deduction, in which hypotheses are derived from a general assumption or theory, abduction is the only method involving the reflection of hypothesis generation,

---

1975: 41–50). For a comparison between Holmes and Peirce, see Sebeok/Umiker-Sebeok (1983). Umberto Eco's novel "The Name of the Rose" also makes this procedure clear.

METHODOLOGICAL IMPLICATIONS

and not only of hypothesis testing. Here, the generation of hypotheses is not due to the personal intuition of the researcher, but to his interaction in the social world, to his socially constituted experiences (cf. Fann 1970).

The assignment of a certain phenomenon to a theoretical concept in a reconstructive analysis based on abduction does not mean, however, that we can dispense with showing a connection in the concrete individual case. Rather, reconstructive analysis aims at detecting a connection in each individual case for which we carry out both hypothesis generation and hypothesis testing.

Let us summarize the procedure of abduction, which, like inductive and deductive procedures, consists of three stages of inquiry, each of which represents a type of inference:

1. *From an empirical phenomenon to all possible hypotheses.*
   Starting from an empirical phenomenon in a given unit of empirical data, a general rule is inferred with respect "to the supposition of a general principle to account for the facts" (Fann 1970: 10). This step is the actual abductive inference. The important thing is to formulate not only one hypothesis, but all the hypotheses that are possible at the time of consideration and might explain the phenomenon.
2. *From hypothesis to follow-up hypothesis or follow-up phenomenon*
   Follow-up phenomena are deduced from the formulated hypotheses, i.e. from this rule other phenomena are inferred that confirm this rule. Or put differently: for each hypothesis a follow-up hypothesis is considered according to what comes next in the text, if this reading proves to be plausible.
3. *The empirical test*
   This is where empirical testing is carried out in the sense of inductive inference. The concrete case is investigated for indices to match the deduced follow-up phenomenon. In a sequential procedure this means that the follow-up hypotheses are now contrasted with the text sequences or the empirical data that follow. Some of them gain plausibility whereas others are falsified. The interpretations that cannot be falsified in the process of sequential analysis – that are left over after hypothesis testing has excluded the improbable readings – are then regarded as the most probable.

With the *principle of sequentiality*, the processual character of social action is taken into account in the analysis of both the experienced life history and the narrated life story. Each action – whether in the concrete biographical situation or in the way it is thematized in the interview – represents a choice between different possible alternatives in the respective situation. In our experienced life history, every action represents a selection from given possibilities and – as a consequence – a resulting determination of our further course of development. Whether we marry the man we primarily need as a father substitute or relegate him to the role of a fatherly friend, whether we raise our children alone after divorce or place them in a boarding school, we choose from various possibilities, of which we are not necessarily aware, and thus open up specific further developments while closing off others. Likewise, when we tell the story of our life, we have different possible ways of presenting it. The horizon of possibilities is wide open at the beginning of our presentation, and becomes narrower with each sequence. The way we choose to begin starts to shape a possible thematic field; certain thematic foci thus become more likely than others. Each subsequent narrative, as well as each argument or description, influences the process of creating a Gestalt. Each selection we make from the range of memories accessible to us, and from the different forms of presentation open to us, means, on the one hand, opening up certain paths of action, while, on the other hand, excluding other thematic fields and actions. Concrete actions, which in texts take on the form of records of actions, are thus processes of selection, leading in each case – whatever the perspective of the person acting – to certain subsequent actions and excluding others.

This conception calls for an analytical method that asks which horizon of possibilities is open for a certain sequence, which choice the actor makes, which he disregards, and what follows from this for the future. Sequential analysis is a result of these considerations. "Interpreting is thus reconstructing of the meaning of the text 'following the line of events'" writes Hans-Georg Soeffner (1982: 13, translated from the German), following Wilhelm Dilthey. In accordance with the abductive method, all possible readings of the meaning of a sequence in the person's life, or of a text sequence in their biographical self-presentation, are used in order to reach conclusions as to what might come next. Only then are these hypotheses compared with the relevant facts. Thus, before we get caught up in the interpretive system of the autobiographer and in the logic of the concrete situation, we are able to grasp the multiplicity of possibilities that were open to the autobiographer in the actual situation in the past, and in the interview situation. Explicating the contexts in which a biographical action or a biographical thematization appear to be pragmatically meaningful and appropriate to the situation serves, as pointed out by Oevermann (1988: 248, translated from the German), as a "foil to the 'objective possibilities'...that were open in respect of the case structure and constitute its specific character by not having been chosen". Only against the background of this negative foil will the special nature of this case, the structure of the case of a life story to be interpreted, be able to reveal itself. In the course of the sequential analysis it will become clear whether the autobiographer systematically excludes possible interpretations or actions, i.e., whether rules can be detected which determine his choice.

In the biographical analysis of life stories, sequential analysis always means two things: sequential analysis of the experienced life history and sequential analysis of the narrated life story. The sequential analysis of the experienced life history, the genetic analysis, serves to reconstruct the chronological sedimentation of biographical experiences, the biographical meaning of the experiences at that time, as well as the structures that have been formed in the course of socialization, their reproductions and transformations during the person's life. In our analysis of the narrated life story, on the other hand, we reconstruct its temporal and thematic design, that is, the temporal and thematic links that the autobiographer makes in designing the thematic fields, or that impose themselves on him as a result of his experiential history. Here we focus on the biographical meaning of the experiences for the interviewee in the present, their biographical overall view and overall evaluation which constitute the process of creation of a Gestalt. Thus, in the genetic analysis, the chronological sequence of the biographical experiences (what happened first and what happened at a later time) is reconstructed as far as this is possible, as well as the meaning that these experiences had for the autobiographer at that time. Here, we filter out the Gestalt of the experienced life history and the functional significance of its parts. Our analysis of the biographical narrative, on the other hand, is concerned with the sequences that make up the biographical self-presentation, and what meaning the narrated experiences have for the autobiographer today. Here, we are concerned with the Gestalt of the narrated life story and the functional significance of its parts.

Procedure[10]

The analysis of a biographical self-presentation that is selected for individual case analysis, following a global analysis of all conducted interviews according to the criteria for a theoretical sample (Glaser/Strauss 1967: 45–78), is based on a complete transcription of the tape recording in its audible Gestalt (Rosenthal 1990a: 246 f.). The following steps should be carried out in this order:

1. analysis of the biographical data
2. textual and thematic field analysis
3. reconstruction of the experienced life history
4. microanalysis of individual text segments
5. Contrastive comparison of the narrated life story with the experienced life history.

1. In the sequential analysis of *biographical data* (cf. Oevermann et al. 1980), we begin by analyzing data that are not subject to interpretation by the biographer, such as birth, number of siblings, education, marriage, or entry into the armed forces, in the chronological sequence of the life course. The context of events with which the autobiographer was confronted is reconstructed, and in thought experiments we consider what problems these might have resulted in, and what alternatives for action were available in the situation. We ask what initial problems characterize the case and what possibilities for action the biographer had in the respective situation, i.e., what he "reasonably" (according to the assumed rule system) "could or should do in a specified context when confronted with a specified problem" (Oevermann et al. 1980: 23, translated from the German). In this step of the analysis, the biographical event is interpreted independently of the knowledge that the interpreters have from the narrated life story, in other words regardless of what we know about the further biographical course. In accordance with the abductive method, we make prognoses about possible consequences, meaning we deduce follow-up hypotheses concerning what comes next. These prognoses refer not only to possible reproductions of the case structure, but also to constellations of events in which transformations would be possible. In this way, the danger of a premature deterministic in-

---

10 I have discussed these steps, first in my doctoral thesis (Rosenthal 1987: 143–244), and later in much more detail in the English edition of my methods handbook (Rosenthal 2018: chapter 6).

terpretation can be avoided. The interpretation of one sequence is followed by interpretation of the next sequence which tells the interpreters which path the biographers actually have taken – initially disregarding their self-interpretations and narratives. Again, the possible consequences of this "new" biographical information are imagined in thought experiments. For each piece of information, several structural hypotheses can be developed, with the sequential analysis excluding more and more readings as it progresses, so that by the conclusion of the analysis only certain structural hypotheses remain as probable, which then present case-specific questions for further interpretation of the individual case.

This analytical step serves to prepare our reconstruction of the experienced life history, in which our analysis is contrasted with the autobiographer's narratives in respect of the various biographical "data". It also provides us with a foil for the textual and thematic field analysis, in which we can then see which biographical data are narratively developed by the autobiographer and in which order they are presented.

In order to make the procedure more comprehensible, examples from the case analysis of Hiltrud Stegmann, the daughter of the euthanasia doctor (cf. chapter 2.3.5), are given here and in the following steps. When analyzing the biographical data of this case history, one can start with the data concerning the parents, their involvement in Nazi crimes, especially in euthanasia, and with the information that an older brother of Hiltrud was born with a clubfoot before her birth and died after a few weeks. Among others, the following assumption can be formulated here, for example: this initial constellation in the family suggests the possibility that Hiltrud might develop a fantasy that her parents murdered her brother. With the later information that Hiltrud attended an SS boarding school, which was housed in a building in which mentally handicapped children had previously lived, we can then conjecture that here she remembered her brother (supported by the compulsory lessons on racial ideology in such a school), and became aware that according to Nazi doctrine his handicap was a "hereditary disease", the further inheritance of which was to be prevented by sterilization. Perhaps she now began to develop the fantasy suspected above and to ask herself whether she fulfilled the criteria for being considered "worthy of life". In the textual and thematic field analysis, we can then see in which context and how Hiltrud Stegmann speaks about this brother. In our reconstruction of the life history, we need to ask when and in what context she learned of his death, and in the microanalysis, our hypotheses would have to be further examined.

It should be emphasized at this point that our analysis of the biographical data can by no means cover all possible meanings. Rather, analysis of the text always opens up new horizons of meaning that were previously not accessible to us. In the course of a case reconstruction we constantly discover something new, which helps us to reformulate previous concepts. Only this makes the effort of such a procedure worthwhile.

2. In the *text and thematic field analysis* (the second step of data analysis) – I make use of Fritz Schütze's (1983) methodological procedure for narrative and text analysis, as well as Wolfram Fischer's (1982) suggestions for thematic field analysis, which are based on the theoretical work of Aron Gurwitsch. This step, which is central to the analysis of a narrated life story, is an attempt to implement methodologically the structuralist variant of Aron Gurwitsch's phenomenological sociology of knowledge, his conception based on Gestalt theory and phenomenology. It is about reconstructing the knowledge and relevance systems of the subjects, about their interpretation of their lives, their classification of experiences in thematic fields, but not with the intention of reconstructing the subjective meaning. Rather, our aim is to reconstruct the overall Gestalt of the biography as it is presented in the act of turning to it, the interactively constituted meaning of the experiences and actions of the subject, which goes partly beyond their intention. Thus, we can analyze not only how the biographers experience the social world, but also how the social world constitutes their experience.

Therefore, in the text and thematic field analysis the sequential Gestalt of the biographical self-presentation is not analyzed only with the aim of tracing the autobiographer's conscious evaluation of their overall biography, but also in order to contrast this with the biographical overall view as a latently acting control mechanism of Gestalt formation. The general goal of the analysis is to find out which mechanisms control the selection and the temporal and thematic linking of the stories.

To prepare the analysis, the interview text is divided into chronological sequences using keywords, i.e., into units of analysis. Criteria for sequencing[11] are: speech changes, text type (argumentation, description, or narration and their subcategories), and thematic modifications based on an initial assessment of the themes. The points in the interview at which the biographer argues, describes, or narrates, in which thematic areas, and at which

---

11 Cf. the definition of the criteria in the appendix.

biographical points in time, are noted. The analytical procedure for interpreting sequencing is the same as the sequential analysis of objective data: sequence by sequence is interpreted according to the structure of the text. The different possible meanings of each sequence to be interpreted are formulated without knowing what comes next. What we need to interpret in this step of analysis is the nature and function of the presentation in the interview, and not the biographical experience *per se*. For example, at the beginning of the analysis, the question might arise why an autobiographer begins her life story with a very detailed argument about her divorce at the age of 23. Unlike our analysis of the biographical data and the way they contrast with the narratives of the autobiographer, when reconstructing the case history we do not ask what it meant for the biographer at that time that she was divorced after only one year of marriage. Rather, we are interested in the function that this way of beginning her presentation has for her today, why she uses argumentation rather than a narration in talking of this experience, why the sequence is so detailed, and what theme it represents in what thematic field. For each sequence, the aim is to identify inherent references to possible thematic fields (cf. chapter 2.3.4) and to form hypotheses concerning possible subsequent sequences. In the course of the analysis, it becomes clear which thematic fields are created by the biographer, which potential contents of these fields are not developed or only hinted at, and which fields are avoided (cf. chapter 2.3.5). Thus, it becomes clear, a) which topics are not thematized although they are co-present – independently of the autobiographers' self-interpretations, and b) how the autobiographer systematically embeds his experiences only in specific fields and avoids possible other framings inherent to the experiences.

Let us return to Hiltrud Stegmann's autobiography. As shown by the text and thematic field analysis, this woman presents her life story in the thematic field: "My suffering under my Nazi parents". She mentions her deceased brother only in the questioning period of the interview in connection with the theme that asking questions was not allowed in her parental home. She tells the story of how she discovered her brother's grave in the cemetery when she was eight years old. Before this time, she had heard that he had a club foot and had died of pneumonia, but she now has more questions. She goes home and asks her mother, among other things, whether she was sad about this brother's death. Her mother becomes angry and answers that she must not speak about it. In the present, this narrative serves the autobiographer to justify why she stopped asking questions in the family. But at the time, this was probably an experience that led to her fear of annihilation.

3. In the next step of reconstructing the experienced life history, all further biographical experiences are recorded and reconstructed following the chronology of the experienced life history, in accordance with the interpretative logic of the analysis of the biographical data. At this point, the biographical data or experiences are contrasted with the biographer's narratives and self-interpretations. The preceding text and thematic field analysis gives us important clues as to the present perspective of the autobiographers and the functional significance of the stories they tell for today's presentation of their life story. Now, however, it is a matter of reconstructing their perspective in the past, the biographical meaning that the experiences had for the biographers at the time.

While in the text and thematic field analysis, individual sequences are analyzed in order to determine their functional significance for the overall Gestalt of the biographical self-presentation, the reconstruction of the life history enables us to decipher its Gestalt. Here we are concerned with reconstructing the functional significance of a biographical experience for the overall Gestalt of the experienced life history, and with consistently avoiding the atomization of single biographical experiences. While in the text and thematic field analysis we reconstruct, for example, at which point in the biographical self-presentation the autobiographer reports her chronic sleep disorder, and in which thematic field these sequences are embedded, here we consider the embedding of this "symptom" in her experienced life history, i.e., when and in which biographical constellation it appeared for the first time, in which life phases it became intensified, and in which it disappeared. We thus try to trace the Gestalt-shaping process of both the narrated life story and the experienced life history, without losing sight of their mutual interpenetration. The separate analytical steps simply focus more strongly on one or the other side.

In this step of the analysis, we can now embed Ms. Stegmann's story about how she discovered her deceased brother's grave in the cemetery into her experienced life history. Here we can see that her chronic sleep disorder began in that year. At this point we can now develop hypotheses about the connection between her brother's death, the angry rejection of Hiltrud's questions by her mother, her possible fantasies and her sleeping disorder.

METHODOLOGICAL IMPLICATIONS

4. The *microanalysis* of individual text passages is based on the procedure of structural hermeneutics (cf. Oevermann 1983). Here, we test the hypotheses set up in the previous steps, in respect of both the biographical meaning of experiences within the experienced life history, and the biographical overall view and overall evaluation of the biographer. Furthermore, microanalysis enables the "discovery" of previously unexplained mechanisms and rules of the case structure.

The selection of text passages for the microanalysis is based, on the one hand, on the structural hypotheses obtained so far and, on the other hand, on text passages whose meaning has so far remained elusive to us. Text passages are selected which, due to their content, seem particularly suitable for the verification or falsification of these hypotheses; previous interpretations are set aside (bracketed) for the time being. If, for example, one of our structural hypotheses in the analysis of the experienced life history– as in the case of Hiltrud Stegmann – relates to her identification with National Socialism, we might select a text passage in which she speaks about her rejection of Hitler, which could falsify this hypothesis. If we have reconstructed the thematic field "My suffering under my Nazi parents" in the text and thematic field analysis, we would also look here for text passages – such as a narrative about the loving care of her parents – that refer to other possible thematic fields and thus also to other possible biographical overall evaluations produced by the biographer.

Previous interpretations are already set aside in the process of decontextualizing the text passage to be analyzed or the individual meaning units, which are interpreted sequentially. All possible contexts in which the utterance could be regarded as "meaningful" according to our expectations of normality are sketched out in a thought experiment. Progressing from sequence to sequence – or from meaning unit to meaning unit – the inner context gradually unfolds. After the analysis of a text passage has been completed, it is then possible, based on the previous analytical steps, to compare the contexts which have been sketched out in a thought experiment and which become increasingly concrete in the course of the analysis, with the overall Gestalt of the biographical self-presentation, as well as with the overall Gestalt of the experienced life history.

This process of decontextualization will be briefly explained here with a condensed and result-oriented presentation of the microanalysis of a text passage (translated from the German) from the interview with Hiltrud Stegmann. We begin with the utterance:

"But I wanted to see in order to live"

The peculiarity or particularity of this sentence is revealed precisely when we take it out of its context of origin and design thought experiments in which it makes sense according to our normal expectations. Two structurally different contexts can be imagined: one in which the emphasis is on *Seeing* or one in which it is on seeing *Something*. In the first case, we may think of incipient blindness. In this reading, the speaker would be referring to the time when she began to fear she was becoming blind and believed that she could only live as a sighted person. If we think of this in the context of National Socialism, we can paraphrase this fear as follows: I wanted to see so that I, as a blind person, would not be committed to an asylum for the handicapped and possibly sterilized or even killed.

In the second case, we may imagine there is a danger that the person wants to see or realize. This danger could be:

a) a person from whom one can protect oneself only if one sees him or recognizes who he is;
b) a situation which one must recognize in order to be able to protect oneself;
c) information that is important for survival.

Further, in the phrase "but still I wanted to see" we must note that it also contains the meaning of not wanting to see. We can formulate the following hypothesis: There is an ambivalence between wanting to see and not wanting to see or not wanting to perceive.

Following our sequential methodological procedure, let us now consider how Ms. Stegmann continues:

"and then I probably always pushed myself to the front where the board was so that I could see what was on it"

Thus, the speaker wanted to "see what" was written on the blackboard. To shorten the account, here is the corresponding contextual information: Ms. Stegmann is speaking about lessons in the Napola (National-Socialist boarding school) she attended, and that she had "probably" sat close to the blackboard because she was short-sighted. This context, in which the first statement "but I wanted to see in order to live" is embedded, is surprising in its harmlessness. There is nothing here to confirm our idea of a life-threatening danger. Even in the historical context of National Socialism, myopia was not a threat to life. So we have to look for other, so-called inner conditions of the case, which make this utterance understandable. Perhaps Hiltrud Stegmann feared at that time that her myopia could lead to blindness,

a) because she had blind family members, or
b) because she was socialized in a milieu in which people were divided into those worthy of life and those not worthy of life, and developed fears of herself being regarded as not worthy of life.

If we look further at the word "probably", ambivalence is also apparent here. The narrator is not even sure that she has pushed herself to the front. The phrase "so that I could see what was on it" contains the meaning that it is not just about seeing *per se*, but about seeing something. Thus, the reference is to a context in which something necessary for survival was on the blackboard. Perhaps on that blackboard were the criteria for being worthy of life. Maybe Hiltrud was afraid of seeing these criteria at that time, because she herself, or persons with whom she identified herself, were threatened by them.

If we combine these two possible contexts, seeing as perceptual ability and seeing something, and include the ambivalence hypothesis, we can now formulate this hypothesis: The speaker developed vision difficulties because she did not want to see what was on the blackboard, as this threatened her life.

The next meaning unit:

"but I don't – I could not – saying I can't see it"

Here we can formulate the hypothesis that the speaker wanted to hide her myopia. Thus, the reading that she was afraid of going blind, since this would have threatened her life, gains plausibility. This meaning unit also points to the plausibility of the ambivalence hypothesis.

The next meaning unit:

"that came after the war (3 sec. pause)"

After the war, the threat was over. The speaker could now freely admit that she had poor vision. Her life was no longer threatened by myopia, and what she did not want to see was over. So "seeing" as well as "seeing something" are related to National Socialism.

The speaker continues:

"This is typical because doctors' children are not examined and this was an infirmity, don't forget"

The narrator informs us that she was not examined because she was a doctor's daughter, and therefore her myopia was not discovered. She speaks of an infirmity; this formulation sounds unusual in the context of myopia. Here we can again formulate the hypothesis that the autobiographer places her myopia in the frame of reference of the criteria for being worthy of life.

"So he as a father- but what he- but for heaven's sake his children didn't have it (1 sec. pause) and they really didn't have it, the three oldest, only I was the one who had inherited his mother's absolute shortsightedness, but no one paid attention to it, my grandmother was blind when she died"

Here, the speaker's *intention* becomes apparent: she wants to say that because her father did not accept physical infirmities in his family, her myopia was not noticed. If we had started by reading the whole story, including the one preceding the first unit analyzed here, we would probably have missed the latent content. The latent content of the story, which is also manifested in the lines preceding the text analyzed here, is: until the end of the war, the narrator was afraid that her myopia would be discovered, because she feared that this could be life threatening for her.

5. By comparing the two levels we do justice to the principle of *contrasting* the Gestalts of the *experienced life history and the narrated life story*. This enables us to gain information about the mechanisms of remembering and selecting experiences from memory and how they are presented, about the differences between past and present perspectives, and about the related difference in the temporality of narrated life story and experienced life history. For example, while our text and thematic field analysis showed that a biographer presented his life story with the biographical global evaluation "I was against the NS after Stalingrad", thus recounting converging experiences as if they had all taken place before Stalingrad, our microanalysis of text passages, on the other hand, led to the interpretation that he still identified with the NS after the surrender of the German Wehrmacht, and our reconstruction of the case history revealed that the biographical turning point of rejecting the NS took place only during his captivity. Now, in contrasting the narrated life story and experienced life history, we can ask ourselves what function this presentation has for the autobiographer and, conversely, what biographical experiences led to this presentation.

Our analysis of the case of Hiltrud Stegmann reveals a difference in her past and present perspectives regarding her relationship to her parents.

While in the present she presents herself as a victim of these Nazi parents, the reconstruction of her experienced life history shows that during National Socialism she identified with these parents, she enjoyed the status of the daughter of a respected Nazi family, was proud of her admission to the Napola and was quite happy there. However, because she cannot admit this part of her past, as she feels very guilty because of her own fascination for the "Third Reich", because of having taken the place of children at the Napola who were presumably murdered, and especially on account of her father's crimes, she focuses on her own suffering under these parents when looking back on her life. The consequence of this biographical overall view is that her fears of being not worthy of life, which she had already developed during National Socialism, escalated into fears of annihilation, and she finds it hard to fall asleep at night because she has to be on her guard against these imagined parents.

If we want to avoid interpretative fallacies, we are compelled to reconstruct both levels, the experienced and the narrated life story, regardless of whether we are primarily interested in the history of a life path, in the experience of specific historical epochs, or in the present perspective of the biographer. The analysis of the experienced life history, based on a text that is constituted in the present of speaking or writing and that refers to a lived past, presupposes an analysis of the Gestalt and structure of the present production and reproduction of this text. The first question that must be asked of the *text* is not "What was experienced at that time, and how close is the memory noema, as translated in the narrative, to the experience at that time?", but first the present narrative situation must be reconstructed, the present perspective of the biographer, and thus the mechanisms that control the selection of the stories told and the presentation of the memories presented. The reverse is correspondingly true: if I want to make statements about the biographical overall view, about the construct "biography", this presupposes knowledge of this life. We cannot, for example, speak of temporal shifts if we have not reconstructed the chronological sequence of experiences – in a separate analytical step. It is not possible to determine how people live with their past today if we, as interpreters, do not try to trace this past. The question arises how we, as social scientists, can infer the meaning of a social action, or its thematization in its context of origin, if we do not know the history of the individual or of the social system leading up to it. If we start from the basic theoretical assumption that social action can only be understood and explained by analyzing the conditions of its origin, this implies that we need to make a diachronic biographical analysis.

7. Biographies – Discourses – Figurations: Social-constructivist and figurational biographical research[1]

Artur Bogner & Gabriele Rosenthal

Preliminary remark. The purpose of this concluding chapter is to show how the work of the authors in recent decades – not least as a result of participating in joint projects with Artur Bogner – has developed into an approach that can be described as social-constructivist and figurational biographical research. This approach grew mainly out of a desire to counter more effectively the dangerous tendency to consider social processes from an ahistorical perspective, with an excessive focus on single individuals (often conceived as isolated), while neglecting (usually reciprocal but often asymmetrical) dependencies and resulting power inequalities. Despite all well-meant declarations of intention, we constantly face this temptation ourselves in the daily practice of doing biographical research. In order to meet this challenge, our proposal is to combine social-constructivist biographical research with the basic principles of figurational sociology. This makes it possible to study the mutual constitution of individuals and societies[2] and the interdependencies between different groupings (including what may be called we-groups), as well as changing power inequalities or power balances within different figurations – whether of individuals or of we-groups or other groupings – in very different "social", historical and geographical contexts.

---

1 This chapter is a slightly modified version of Bogner/Rosenthal 2017b.
2 An indispensable and very basic step in this direction is to think and speak of individuals or societies only in the plural (see Goudsblom 1979: 140; 144).

7.1 Introduction

Social-constructivist biographical research, the sociology-of-knowledge approach to discourse analysis, and figurational sociology are fields of inquiry which have recently become established in different academic communities, mostly independently of each other, although they are relatively close in terms of various characteristics, and, at least partly, share important historical roots. In this chapter we want to show the possible benefits of bringing their key concepts together in one integrated theoretical and methodological approach, and of combining them in research practice. It seems to us, as proponents of biographical research and figurational sociology, that the concept of discourse, as used for example by Michel Foucault or by the sociology-of-knowledge approach to discourse analysis (see Keller 2005; 2011; 2012), may serve as an intermediary concept that can be used to elucidate and explain some of the most fundamental links between figurations of human beings and the biographies of the individuals who form these figurations. This idea is discussed in detail below. By "intermediary" we mean that this concept can help us to recognize, describe, understand and explain the *mutual constitution* of societies and individuals. In biographical research, a synthesis of these three theoretical and research perspectives can open up possibilities for more rigorous investigations of the diverse ways human beings interrelate with other human beings, amongst others in the context of we-groups or organized groups, other social groupings, organizations or "institutions". Such a synthesis also makes it possible to study, for example, the role of "cultural" images, patterns, concepts and practices in the interrelations between human beings. In figurational sociology, linking these three research and theoretical perspectives could assist a more thorough understanding of the activities, lived experiences and sentiments of individuals in their particular historical, biographical and situational contexts, and help to take into account their "subjective" perspectives. By this we do not mean that social-constructivist biographical research, with its focus on case reconstructions, fails to show how biographies form social figurations. Rather, this has been the declared aim from the beginning of biographical research in sociology, which is bound up with the large-scale study by William I. Thomas and Florian Znaniecki of peasants who emigrated from Poland to the US. With their analysis of the "experiences and attitudes of an individual", Thomas and Znaniecki claimed to be able to identify the "laws of social becoming" (1958 [1918–1922], 1831–1832). Figurational sociology also looks at the "actors" and their personal histories and individual developmental processes. This can be seen, for instance, in the study of Mozart by Norbert Elias, in which he makes clear that the life course of this musician becomes more understandable, "if it is seen as a micro-process within the central transformation period of (the) macro-process" that Elias describes, in both the world of artists and wider society (Elias 2010b: 91; our amendment, A.B./G.R.). In both research traditions, societies and organizations cannot be conceived without individuals. Both are based on a conception of societies, or the social world, as a dynamic reality that is constantly generated and created anew, constantly reproduced and altered through the interplay of individuals, in other words on a processual (and strictly relational) conception of the existence of this field of "objects". But why do we want to bring these two traditions of research, and even a version of discourse analysis, together? It is our belief that if biographical research, which concentrates on individual and familial (hi)stories, were to be combined with figurational sociology, which has a stronger focus on *collective and long-term* processes, this would make it much easier to overcome the fruitless segregation of micro-, meso- and macro-perspectives which dominates theory and methodology in the social and cultural sciences (chapter 7.2). Furthermore, we have found that research into collective *discourses* can assume a significant role in this context, and that a social-science analysis of discourses (as proposed for example by Keller 2005; 2012) can help biographical research to more clearly see the effect, or lack of effect, for example of conflicting or dominant discourses on individual or collective self-presentations and self-interpretations. Such an analysis also helps to investigate the interrelations between dominant discourses and power inequalities within and between social groupings and figurations –not least figurations of "established" and "outsiders" in the sense proposed by Elias and John Scotson (chapter 7.3). We also believe that discourse analysis and the concepts used in it can be of benefit, and the meanings of these concepts can be made more transparent (and precise), when articulated using sociological terminology. In order to make these ideas clearer, and to show their empirical grounding, we will briefly present *two empirical studies* (chapter 7.4), followed by a résumé of our methodological conclusions (chapter 7.5).

7.2 Commonalities and differences between biographical research and figurational sociology

Biographical research

Despite various differences between authors, the biographical research that has been practiced in sociology in Germany since the 1970s is generally based on social constructivism as formulated by Peter L. Berger and Thomas Luckmann (1966).[3] From a methodological and practical point of view, it involves reconstructing the *genesis* of the "subjective" perspectives and experiences and everyday knowledge of one or various individuals, which are usually considered the requisite starting point of empirical enquiry and analysis. Revealing, and taking account of, the mutual constitution or interplay of individuals and society has always been a central concern of social-constructivist biographical research. Contrary to prevalent stereotypes, biographical research in sociology has never been concerned with the individual conceived in isolation, but has always been devoted to the empirical study of *individual and collective* processes in their entwinedness, their inescapable interconnectedness. Thus, "biography" is understood not as something purely individual or "subjective", but as a social construct that refers to collective discourses and collective processes. A biography, both in its lived course and as it is remembered and (re-)interpreted, is always an individual and collective product. As Bettina Dausien (2010: 113) puts it, biographies are both "a medium for the construction of identity and subjectivity, and [...] the result of social construction processes" (our translation, A.B./G.R.). Besides attempting to do justice to these "interrelationships" (in the sense proposed by Georg Simmel and George H. Mead) by taking the biographies and life courses of individuals as a starting point, two other methodological requirements are bound up with a biographical approach in this research tradition. It is important, on the one hand, to understand and explain the meaning of experiences not in isolation, but in the overall context of the life history, and, on the other hand, to carry out a processual analysis, a reconstruction of the emergence, persistence and modification of social phenomena in the context of studying life courses, taking into account *the permanent intertwining of life courses*

---

3 See for example Alheit and Dausien (2000), Dausien (1996); Fischer and Kohli (1987); Rosenthal (1995; 2004); Schütze (1992; 2007 a; b).

and biographical (self-)interpretations. And the reconstruction of biographical processes, in their indissoluble interconnection with collective processes, is not simply a matter of answering "why" questions, like "Why did this person behave or act this way and not another way?" Questions of this type are generally avoided. Using a processual and transgenerational perspective – as proposed and discussed in particular by Elias (e.g. 2009b: 108: n.1, passim; 2007: 90–103) – means asking: What was the long or protracted individual and collective history that led to this biographical constellation of a person, to his or her current situation in relation to others, to this particular activity, decision, view, sentiment, experience or perception? For example, it is not adequate to simply ask why someone made a decision to join a particular political party. Instead, one needs to enquire into the collective *and* individual situation in which the person joined the party – including the long collective *and* individual courses of events that formed the "background" to, or were part of, the "set of circumstances" for this conduct. In stringent social-constructivist biographical research, an individual life course and self-interpretation are always reconstructed in their interconnectedness with the life courses and self-interpretations of other individuals, organized groups, we-groups, or "institutions", and in their entwinement with the discourses that prevailed during different phases of an individual and collective history. This also applies to the interconnectedness of generations that communicate with each other, or are linked in other ways – and this does not just apply to the interdependencies and interactions between different "generations" (both in the genealogical and in the socio-historical sense) within a certain family or household. In order to analyze a life course in which someone joins a party and becomes politically active, it is necessary to ask about the webs of interdependencies in which the biographer was, and still is, involved, the institutional, organizational and informal networks of relationships in which she/he was socialized, and the historical constellations, including the discourses, she/he was influenced by.

In order to analyze life courses and life stories in this way, and to get away from static or mechanical "why" accounts which point to only one direction of influence, and from explanations that are reduced to motives or intentions, Fritz Schütze (1977; 1983) introduced the method known as the biographical-narrative interview. Asking people to tell their whole life story provides opportunities to gain insights into their present perspectives and sets of circumstances, into the way they orientate themselves towards, or are influenced by, current discourses, and into the various ways their life courses have been shaped by discourses, relationships and biographical constellations in the past. In contrast to other interview methods, it is thus possible to uncover not only the interpretations of the interviewees in the *present* of the interview or the text production, but also the genesis of these interpretations and the *sequential* gestalt of the *lived* life history, and to reconstruct courses of action and conduct in the past and how they were experienced at the time. In order to avoid drawing hasty conclusions from the biographical self-presentation of interviewees when talking about their past, we try to reconstruct both their present *and* their past perspectives in the light of their "four-dimensional" contexts,[4] or of the relevant "historical" (individual and collective) processes, and to trace the processes of their production, entwinement, interplay and change. This is done in several distinct steps, in accordance with the *analytical method* developed by Gabriele Rosenthal – initially in the context of her research into the life courses of former members of the Hitler Youth movement (Rosenthal 1987: 143–244; see also 1993b; 2018: chapter 6).

In biographical-narrative interviews, the interviewees may argue and describe, but most importantly they narrate and remember their own experiences, or at least this is what they are invited to do by the interviewer. Here, it is important to take into account that memory practices – to borrow from Maurice Halbwachs – are framed by the *collective* memories of different *social* groupings. The relevant frames that are pertinent here, usually because they are connected with these groupings and their collective self-interpretation may, depending on the interview's setting or context, be selected and understood or "defined" in various ways – and in ways which may change more than once during the course of a single conversation or interview (Rosenthal 2016a). *Memory practices* are always interrelated with the experienced past that people remember and talk about, and the stocks of collective knowledge that have been established and internalized over various generations (ibid.). Depending on the historical and cultural context, memory practices are subject to collective rules which become consolidated and change over time. They will thus show traces of rules which were valid in the past or in other social or situational contexts, and at the same time traces of social rules which apply in current interactive memory practices or collective discourses.

---

4 Following a suggestion by Elias (2009a; 2011) it would be even more fitting to talk here of *five-dimensional contexts*, with the dimension of time as the familiar "fourth" dimension, and the dimension of meaning (or symbols) as a "fifth" dimension.

The memory process cannot be considered independently of the present situation, nor independently of past experiences or the handed-down past. It is interrelated with the collective memory – or collective memories, to put it more correctly – of different societal groupings, organized groups or organizations. These memories are part of the cultural practices which (amongst others) determine which memories and constructions of the past are excluded or marginalized, and which become dominant in the discourse of each grouping or we-group (such as the family, the historical generation, or political, religious or ethnic we-groups), and in public and mass media discourses. We argue that the question whether this leads to conflicts between different worldviews (Mannheim 1980: 307–308) and the corresponding collective memories, or rather to the parallel co-existence of divergent and maybe incompatible collective memories that are mutually tolerated or ignored by various groupings, or to a kind of creolization of collective memories,[5] is an *empirical question*. It is important in every case to make a precise and detailed empirical reconstruction, showing which form of memory has dominated in which historical and social context and in which phases of the lengthier or shorter processes under investigation.

Any analysis thus requires us to reconstruct the dominant discourses in the present and in the past, and how they have changed. In addition to the empirical reconstruction of contemporary memory practices, a broad diachronic perspective is necessary in order to show empirically which *groupings*, in which figurations with other groupings and under which historical boundary conditions, assert which *versions of the collective history* with the aid of which *rules*, and how *counter-discourses* have nevertheless been able to develop. We plead here in favor of an empirical approach, i.e. an empirically exact reconstruction of the historical and social contexts in which certain cultural practices have become dominant while others have been marginalized, and how their interaction has changed.

Sociologists who undertake biographical research have recognized the importance of extending case studies across several generations (Bertaux and Bertaux-Wiame 1991; Hildenbrand 1999; Rosenthal 2012), because this can reveal how social phenomena such as cultural memory practices emerge

---

5 With regard to culture and postcolonial studies, Hubert Knoblauch (2007, 24) discusses processes of creolization in the sense of a "subdivision into an unfathomable patchwork of cultures belonging to very different milieus, groupings and lifestyles, in which local and supralocal tradition become blurred" (our translation, A.B./G.R.).

and develop over a long period. The approach recommended here is aimed at reconstructing the intertwining and interplay between the individual's history of experiences and the short- and long-term transformations of the collective, social and cultural, circumstances of these experiences. Meticulous reconstructions based on thick descriptions make it possible to overcome the dualism of macro- and micro-perspectives. As suggested by Elias, the objects on the micro level are to be understood as *concrete parts* of (or a different organizational level of) larger objects which appear to be separate units on the macro level – and not (or not primarily) as *instances* of generalized laws or generalized features (e.g. Elias 2009a; 2007: 205–224 and passim; 2012a, 125–127). The dualist conception of individual and society can be overcome by adopting a processual and figurational perspective, where individuals and their memory practices are considered in the historical context of concrete groupings in their particular figurations with other groupings.

Figurational sociology

It should be clear that our formulation of a social-constructivist biographical approach (see also Rosenthal 2012; 2016a; Bogner and Rosenthal 2014; 2022) has been inspired to a considerable extent by figurational sociology. However, conceptions of a "dialectical" relationship between society and individual that are compatible with, if not closely related to, Elias's figurational sociology have existed for a long time in different strands within the sociology of knowledge, as well as in the Chicago school of sociology (perhaps partly due to the early contact between Karl Mannheim and Louis Wirth[6]). Before discussing the similarities and important differences between these two theoretical (and empirical) research traditions, first a few remarks on the central concepts and basic assumptions of figurational sociology.

---

6 See Smith (2001: 176–177). Louis Wirth, then at the Chicago Department of Sociology, later first president of the International Sociological Association, translated (with Edward Shils) Mannheim's first book, "Ideology and Utopia" and wrote the preface for the English and American edition of 1936, which also included a translation of Mannheim's essay on the sociology of knowledge published in 1931. See the Wikipedia articles on "Louis Wirth" and "International Sociological Association" (details in the list of references). Elias was Mannheim's student in Heidelberg in the 1920s and became his assistant when Mannheim became Professor of Sociology at the University of Frankfurt. On the close relationship and affinities between Mannheim's and Elias's thought, see foremost Kilminster (2007: chapter 3).

By *figuration* Elias understands a dynamic web of interdependences in flux, a continuously changing network of *mutual* dependencies between people. People have relationships with each other and are dependent on each other, usually in respect of several different dimensions or aspects of the relationship at the same time. For example, pupils usually receive from their teachers not only information or knowledge, but also "attention" in the sense of recognition, appreciation, disapproval or challenges. Among other things, teachers often offer their students models of conduct, activity and experience – models which the latter may accept or reject, copy, modify, ignore or deviate from. An essential element of Elias' conception is that changing, and often asymmetric, power balances (i.e., power inequalities) are an integral part of all relationships between people. Meanwhile these power relations are constantly subject to modification, just like the relationships themselves. For example, teachers are also dependent on their students, at least to some extent. They will usually have a very difficult time if they do not receive a certain degree of cooperation and respect from their pupils. Elias uses the term "power balance" to refer to the proportionate ratio between these mutual dependencies. Their interplay results (potentially) in varying degrees of power inequality or equality. All these are *features of the whole figuration* (i.e., of the whole network of mutual dependencies) and not just of parts of it.

"At the core of changing figurations – indeed the very hub of the figuration process – is a fluctuating, tensile equilibrium, a balance of power moving to and fro [...]. This kind of fluctuating balance of power is a structural characteristic of the flow of every figuration" (Elias 2012a: 126).

Because of this processuality, human figurations, as well as their inherent power balances and power inequalities, can be adequately conceived only as "dynamic", changeable facts that are *tied to certain periods of time* (and thus "historical" in this specific meaning of the word). To describe and explain their dynamic and historical nature satisfactorily, it is essential to adopt a *long-term*, sometimes extremely long, time perspective (Elias 2009b; 2009a; 2012a: 140–152, 135–140). Informative examples of this are Elias' studies of civilizational processes, the socio-historical roots of, and changes in, the collective habitus and nationalism of the Germans, or the genesis of "sport" in the modern sense (Elias 2012b; 2013; Elias and Dunning 1986). Elias applies the three terms *figuration*, *interdependence* and *power* not only to small units like a school class or a married couple, but also to big units like megacities and other large-scale organizations, and even, for instance, to the webs of mutual dependencies or "figurations" that may nowadays be formed by several megacities, or by several societies which are organized for example in the form of nation-states (Elias 2012a, 126; Elias and Scotson 1965).

The concept of figuration is a reference to the *gestalt-like* nature of the "interrelationships" between individuals on the one hand, and between them and social structures and collectivities on the other (Elias and Scotson 1965: 8–12; esp. 10). At the same time it emphasizes the dynamic, restless nature, and the generally non-intentional, altogether uncontrollable structuredness or unplanned directionality of social processes and formations. This is expressed in a condensed form in two passages from his first and most renowned book on the "process of civilization":

"[...] plans and actions, the emotional and rational impulses of individual people, constantly interweave in a friendly or hostile way. This continuous interweaving of people's plans and actions, can give rise to changes and patterns that no individual person has planned or created. From this [...] arises an order sui generis, an order more compelling and stronger than the will and reason of the individual people composing it. It is this order of interweaving human impulses and strivings, this social order, which determines the course of historical change [...]" (Elias 2012b: 404; original emphasis).

"But this intertwining of the actions and plans of many people, which, moreover, goes on continuously from generation to generation, is itself not planned. It cannot be understood in terms of the plans and purposeful intentions of individuals, nor in terms which, though not directly purposive, are modeled on teleological modes of thinking. [...] And only an awareness of the relative autonomy of the intertwining of individual plans and actions [...] permits a better understanding of the very fact of individuality itself. The coexistence of people, [...] the bonds they place on each other [...] provide the medium in which it can develop" (Elias 2012b: 591).

These two quotations from Elias' magnum opus of 1939 contain several central motifs of *figurational sociology* or *process sociology*. Human beings exist and live with each other in configurations or constellations of mutual, and often asymmetric, dependencies. They exist only as parts of such "figurations", of *gestalt-like* and dynamic webs of interdependencies that are characterized by relatively close links between *the parts and the whole* (Elias 2010a: 13–23). In other words, the relationship between human individuals and the "social" figurations which they form can be described as one of *mutual constitution*. The one cannot exist without the other (see for instance Elias and Scotson 1965: 10; Elias 2009a). As Elias put it in the 1930s, in terms which reveal his closeness to George Herbert Mead's theory of the social genesis of the self:

"Without the assimilation of preformed social models [...] the child remains [...] little more than an animal. [...] the individuality of the adult can only be understood in terms of the trajectory of his or her relationships, only in connection with the structure of the society in which he or she has grown up. However certain it may be that each person is a totality unto himself [...] it is no less certain that the whole structure of his self-control, both conscious and unconscious, is a product of interweaving formed in a continuous interplay of relationships with other people, and that the individual gestalt of the adult is a society-specific gestalt" (Elias 2010a: 29; the English translation has been corrected by us, A.B./ G.R.).

Only in figurations with other people is individualization in the narrow sense possible, including both the typically human acquisition and use of language, and the acquisition of other kinds of collective knowledge and "cultural" competence (see Elias 2010a 58–59, 29; 2009a). Therefore individuals and societies belong to the same "social" level of reality and spring *simultaneously from the same origin.* Thus, for Elias "society not only produces the similar and typical, but also the individuality" (Elias 2010a: 58; original emphasis).

For biographical research, this means that individuality must always be understood as "social" or collective at the same time; it always has collective roots and is a part of webs of interpersonal relationships and of long-term, transgenerational processes – even when a particular, "individual" form has developed that is different from all others, such as a particular person or a particular city. The webs of interdependencies which Elias calls "figurations" must be regarded as *long-term, trans- and intergenerational and (by the same token) collective processes,* that are, to borrow Elias' term, "unplanned" – and ultimately "beginningless". This must be underlined here because in his studies Elias lays much greater emphasis on this long-term ("historical" or "diachronic") perspective, and on the corresponding qualities of the field of enquiry, than is the case in the social-constructivist sociology of knowledge.[7] This means that from the perspective of a plurality of individuals, and when considered over a longer period of time, these processes themselves (at

---

7 And in sociology generally since the Second World War. Due to their common emphasis on the need for long-term diachronic ("historical") studies, especially in combination with a *microscopic analysis of power*, there is a degree of similarity between Elias's and Foucault's works in methodological (not only thematic) terms, which is striking for social theorists, especially when one is a sociologist and the other a philosopher. See especially Landweer (1997). On the noticeable thematic convergences between Elias's work and Foucault's (and Weber's) writings, see also the highly instructive commentaries by Breuer (2006a; 2006b; 1988); Van Krieken (1990); Lemke (2001) and Smith (2001: chapter 5).

least "as a whole") are the *unplanned consequences* of the intertwining of the activities and impulses of many people and many generations. At the same time, however, these unplanned, or at least not completely planned, "consequences" also form the "circumstances", the preconditions or boundary conditions, of all human activities. Elias argues that other sociologists have not grasped the full importance of this dialectic of non-intended results and unrecognized or unknown conditions of human activity, if they only speak of unintentional or "paradoxical" consequences. They do not thoroughly recognize that this kind of phenomenon is omnipresent due to the ordinary involvement of *many* people and *several*, often many, generations, and that in the case of social formations or processes it requires a kind of Copernican turn from actions and actors to the big, long-term, "unplanned", generally or largely unintended, processes in which every activity and every experience is embedded.

This is true regardless of whether the activities are knowingly or consciously directed or oriented towards other people. It is a specific reformulation of Marx's observation that people make their own history, but under pre-existing conditions, not conditions they have created themselves. These conditions are "made" by individuals, but not created, since they result from the desired *and* undesired interweaving of the activities of *many* individuals in specific historical constellations. The long-term unplanned entanglement of the activities and impulses of many people, including the interactions and interrelationships between different generations, is a process that usually develops a powerful endogenous dynamic or momentum of its own, and which very often cannot be treated (methodologically) in the same way as events that are planned and controlled *by a single actor*. Elias thus sets up a theory of social processes (or more precisely *collective* processes) in opposition to the hitherto dominant theoretical and methodological conceptions of sociology as a theory of intentional action. Not least, his formulations are directed against the idea that the realm of sociology can be adequately defined as the actions of individuals that are (consciously) oriented towards other people. This basic rule of sociological methodology, which was inherited from economic theory, is not superfluous, but it is not sufficient, because collective processes (and *spontaneous* forms of order, or structures) develop from the interweaving of many people. These are processes which nobody intended and which are relatively independent of individuals and the ideas or plans bound up with their activities. While biographical research is focused on individuals, it often reveals the enormous (though varying) extent to which they are dependent on others by showing how the activities and experiences of one person are influenced by their entanglement in familial and transgenerational dependencies – dependencies which often stretch back into the past beyond their lifetime.

The processual and long-term character of these phenomena was concretized by Elias, and before him by Mannheim, by referring amongst others to the *involvement of several generations*, especially with regard to the transfer, genesis and transformation of stocks of collective knowledge (Elias 2009a; Mannheim 1952a [1928]). This is an aspect which has played a peripheral role to date in figurational sociology. Linkages and interactions between generations mostly tend to be treated as a theoretical background assumption and are not usually made the focus of concrete studies in their own right. Therefore this remains a desideratum for future research.

Such a "dialectical" conception of the relations between individuals and society as a *structured plurality* of individuals may sound relatively familiar to social scientists; but this cannot be said of the *methodological* conclusion drawn by Elias in the 1930s, in *The Society of Individuals* (later published as Part I of the book with the same title). He argued that the balance between the determination of individuals by collective phenomena, on the one hand, and the determination of collective phenomena by individuals, on the other hand, is *variable*, and that describing and explaining this balance is a matter for *empirical research* and not – as sociologists usually assume – a "theoretical" or "methodological" question that can, or must, be answered before any empirical research activity is embarked upon.

"Individual scope for decision is always limited, but it is *also very variable* in nature and extent, *depending on the instruments of power which a person controls*. A glance at the nature of human integration is enough to make *this variability of individual bonds* comprehensible. What binds and limits individuals is, seen from the other side, the exact opposite of this confinement: their individual activity, their ability to take decisions in very diverse and individual ways. The individual activity of some is the social limitation of others. And it depends only on the power of the interdependent functions concerned, the degree of reciprocal dependence, who is more able to limit whom by his activity" (Elias 2010a: 54; our emphases, A.B./G.R.; see also Elias 2006: 33–35).

It is a simple and observable fact that a person's freedom of action depends on other people's freedom of action, and is thus limited by the latter in a variable way (and vice versa). Both therefore vary *empirically* (Elias 2010a: 51–54). The logical conclusion to this has to be that it is impossible without empirical research to answer questions in respect of "free will" or "autonomy" or the determination by social structures. It shows that questions which are almost always formulated in the context of an "epistemological" or "philosophical" discourse should far more often be made the subject of *empirical* research in the social and cultural sciences (see Elias 2006: 32–36; Elias 2002 [1969], 56–62; 2010a: 51–55).

The arguments presented above from the point of view of figurational sociology with regard to the relationship between figurations and individuals can also be applied to collective and individual self-descriptions. Just as in the case of *individuals* and social *figurations*, this relationship can be described as one of mutual constitution: the self-descriptions of individuals are inseparably bound up with and dependent on collective self-descriptions (or "discourses") *and vice versa*. Collective self-descriptions are produced and received, or understood, by no one other than individuals, who in turn are always parts of bigger collectivities and figurations *and their intrinsic collective discourses*. Collective self-descriptions exist only as components of individual self-descriptions, but at the same time they lend them their means, materials, models and methods. Individual self-descriptions are therefore also self-descriptions of the groupings, we-groups or collectivities (or the respective figurations of various groupings) to which the individuals belong. Their collective stocks of knowledge, conceptions and imaginary worlds are realized and documented in the self-descriptions of individuals. Only in these do they become real or readable.

7.3 Discourses as an intermediary element?

Before proceeding to discuss the mutual constitution of biographies, discourses, individuals and figurations, let us first take a look at the concept of discourse as used by Foucault, a concept which has been over-emphasized and used in contradictory ways in the reception of his work. In the social and cultural sciences, Foucault was one of the most important and inspiring scholars in the second half of the 20th century. Nevertheless, it is our opinion that his work and his originality have been overestimated to some extent. This is partly because Foucault rediscovered in his own way a number of important motifs and ideas which were not new in sociology and social philosophy (at least in the German-speaking countries), but which had been marginalized in the decades following the Second World War. Moreover, the perception of Foucault's work was filtered to a notable degree by a reception that was influenced and distorted by fashionable keywords. Not a few of Foucault's intentions and impulses, including the clear tendencies in his (late) work, were either reversed or marginalized. This applies, for instance, to his striving – which became evident after *L'ordre du discours* (Foucault 1971, Engl. Foucault 1972), but was tangible already in *The Archaeology of Knowledge* (Foucault 1969, Engl. Foucault 1972) – to get away from a form of linguistic structuralism which presented itself as radical, both politically and philosophically, and his later emphasis on "power". This was a concept of power which set itself apart from the early modern concept of sovereignty (or "rule"), and had more in common with the dynamic and voluntaristic connotations of the term "struggle" than with the normative, deterministic and static connotations of the terms "structure" and "language" (Sarasin 2010: 118–121). It is well known that this *decentralized and dynamized* concept of power, which was closely related to the concept of struggle, gained increasing importance in his work from circa 1970 onwards – at the cost of the central position of the concept of "discourse" (Sarasin 2010, 124; Keller 2008, 81–89; Ruoff 2009, 99–100). His readers frequently failed to appreciate this important change in Foucault's terminology and approach and method, and interpreted Foucault's concept of discourse as a rediscovery of the independent variable, of the deepest truth of "cultural science", once again liberated from the irrelevancies of classical sociology and economic history. This shift was often treated as a mere exchange of synonymous words (from "structure" to "discourse" and from there to a concept of power that was identical to "knowledge"), instead of as a significant change in his strategy of research and his terminological tools. Recent secondary literature refutes this widespread view of Foucault's complex and often difficult work, and of his concept of discourse. Foucault, who used to be considered as a leading structuralist, said in later years: "One can agree that structuralism formed the most systematic effort to evacuate the concept of the event [...] from history. In that sense, I don't see who could be more of an anti-structuralist than myself" (Foucault 1980: 114). At the latest in *Discipline and Punish* (Foucault 1977), Foucault set up another model in opposition to the structuralist paradigm of language:

"Here I believe one's point of reference should not be to the great model of language (*langue*) and signs, but to that of war and battle. The history which bears and determines us has the form of a war *rather than that of a language: relations of power, not relations of meaning*. History [...] is intelligible – but this in accordance with the intelligibility of struggles, of strategies and tactics" (Foucault 1980: 114; our emphasis, A.B./G.R.).

This understanding of a "historicity" which is not determined by big "centralist" structures finds expression in his late work in the *decentralized* concept of power and the *microscopic* analysis of power. What has been said about distortions in Foucault's popular reception in respect of the relationship between discourse and power, also applies to the relationship between so-called knowledge-power complexes and the "autonomy" of individuals. In particular it applies to the techniques or strategies of *self-guidance*, which came into the focus of his unfinished "history of sexuality". It can therefore be described as an example of the irony of history that Foucault's reception has contributed much to the recent linguistic "turn" in the social and cultural sciences. For Foucault himself, and especially the developmental tendencies in his late work, it would be more accurate to speak of a *sociological* or a *historical-sociological-empirical* turn (see Keller 2008: 15, 37).

The corresponding transformation of his problem definition was already implied in the earlier change in Foucault's concept of discourse, which began to include what is traditionally seen as the Outside of a discourse (including the so-called "non-discursive practices"), and which became increasingly *decentralized and fluid*. The later Foucault referred to this Outside or Beyond using more rather sociological concepts – concepts which are attuned to the analysis of power relations, such as the concept *dispositive* (see for example Bührmann and Schneider 2008: 52–62; Sarasin 2010: 114–124). Roughly speaking, at this point of our discussion we refer to the undecided, oscillating concept of discourse from Foucault's middle period (Sarasin 2010: 124), and prefer to express in more clearly sociological terms what before Foucault was considered as the Beyond or Outside of "discourses".

Foucault's concept of discourse is anti-idealistic and "anti-hermeneutic" (Sarasin), in the sense that it is directed against the goal of fusing the "subject" and "object" of knowledge in the medium of an over- or intersubjective spirit (Sarasin 2010: 104–105). This aspect is formulated pointedly by Philipp Sarasin as follows:[8]

"From a discourse analysis perspective, the idea that history is always 'our' history, that 'we' make it, fails to recognize the degree of otherness which is indelibly inscribed right from the beginning in our 'own' history and in the results of our 'own' production of meaning by *patterns of order which cannot be attributed to the activity of consciousness*. The order of the discourse is not suspended in a higher order of history, but is contingent, discontinuous and

---

8 Sarasin's formulations here mainly concern the middle stage in the development of Foucault's concept of discourse, around 1970/71.

BIOGRAPHIES – DISCOURSES – FIGURATIONS 233

antecedent and external to all meaning" (Sarasin 2010: 105; our translation and emphasis, A.B./G.R.).

We should perhaps underline that our aim at this point is only to contribute to a better understanding of Foucault's concept of discourse and its embedment in a work that remained always changing and unfinished during his lifetime. In the modifications of terminology and perspective that we have mentioned, Sarasin sees the reason why the concepts *power* and *dispositive* occupy in his late work the central position which had previously been occupied by the concepts *discourse* and *episteme* (Sarasin 2010: 114–124; Ruoff 2009: 99, 126). The "great process" of the transfiguration of sex into discourse means not only a subjection of bodies to discourses, but also a subjection of discourses to the emerging dispositive[9] of sexuality (Foucault 1978b: 22, 20 and passim). Obviously, the "discourse" here increasingly takes on the role of an *explanandum* or dependent variable – and, which is more important, becomes an object of empirical (and historical) research.

We believe that this should be seen as a movement away from a primarily linguistic or "philosophical" definition of Foucault's research work, and towards what should be regarded primarily as a *sociology-of-knowledge* definition. Thus, it is not only playful and ironic but also highly instructive and precise when Foucault describes his method in this context as a "joyful positivism"[10] and refers at the same time to Nietzsche's concept of "genealogy", which was directed against the ahistorical and transcendental concepts of established philosophy (Foucault 1972: 234, 125–128; see also Sarasin 2010: 120–121, 118–119; Keller 2008: 46–48; Ruoff 2009: 126–129). The provocative character of Foucault's "philosophy" is due not least to this antiphilosophical feature of his research strategy, to his call for an *empirical* study of discourses, cultures, history and society.

This is not particularly new, but it needs to be expressly underlined because it is vital to an understanding of the main trend of Foucault's thought (see Keller 2008: chapter V). Our reading of his ideas and concepts may be at times unorthodox, but, as we believe, it offers a legitimate interpretation and use of his notion of discourse. More important than differences over the question whether methodological primacy in research strategies (and per-

---

9 But see the comparable statements concerning the relationships between "doctrine" and discourse, or between education system and discourse, in *L'ordre du discours* (Foucault 1972: 226–227).

10 Our translation, A.B./G.R. For an ideal-typical philosophical critique of this self-interpretation by Foucault, see Habermas (1988: 322–333, especially 325–331).

haps the role of a determinant in the last instance) should be accorded to discourses or dispositives, meaning or power, structures or individuals, continuities or discontinuities, or whether we should take "war" or "language" as our model[11] for understanding the intelligible forms of order of the historical, is for us the fact that the "philosopher" Foucault lifted these questions out of the eternal sphere of pre- or extra-empirical (and static) entities and made them the subject matter of an *empirical and diachronic* study of cultural and social processes (as proposed for instance in the last section of *The Archaeology of Knowledge*: Foucault 1972, *Conclusion*: 125–128). Our reception is therefore concentrated on the term discourse and its use in empirical or historical research, in the sense once defined by Foucault as "practices" of speaking and writing, which "systematically form the objects of which they speak" – and not, or not only, "as groups of signs (signifying elements referring to contents or representations)" (Foucault 1972: 49).

Although a discourse is always concerned with a "group of statements that belong to a single system of formation" (Foucault 1972: 107), yet this "system of formation" is by no means only of a linguistic nature. Rather, it encompasses what is said and what is unsaid, discursive and "non-discursive practices" or realms, as well as *spatial and temporal* orders (Foucault 1972: 53–54). This applies (not only) to those discourses which belong to what Foucault calls "institutions", and to their specialized and relatively canonized, in other words socially stereotyped or standardized, and in this sense institutionalized forms of knowledge. Medical discourse, for example, is to be understood

"as the establishment of a relation [...] between a number of distinct elements, some of which concerned the status of doctors, others the institutional and technical site from which they spoke, others their position as subjects perceiving, observing, describing, teaching, etc. It can be said that [the establishing of] this relation between different [heterogeneous] elements (some of which are new, while others were already in existence) is effected by [the] clinical discourse: it is this [the discourse], *as a practice*, that establishes between them all a system of relations that is not 'really' given or constituted a priori" (Foucault 1972: 53–54; our emphasis and clarifications, A.B./G.R.).

---

11 In our opinion, the model of war is in itself an indication that multiple – divergent and polycentric – perspectives, goals, activities and actors are recognized, while the model of "language" (in the singular) assumes from the outset a non-empirical, pre-, supra- or extra-empirical level of discourse or interpretation of the world, because language in the singular does not exist in the empirical world.

As we understand the history of his work, it is precisely this *establishing of relations* between very heterogeneous elements that Foucault at first tries to describe conceptually, at first by using a peculiar and ambiguous, only rudimentarily *sociologized* concept of discourse, but later more frequently with the help of more clearly sociological terms – and especially of terms which are suitable to the description of fluctuating power relations (see Sarasin 2010: 105–106). Above all the term "dispositive" is used to mean not exactly the same thing as, but something very similar to, what Elias means by his concept of "figuration", namely a "web of combined discourse and power structures" (Sarasin 2010: 103).The concept of figuration, which Elias has defined in detail, and illustrated in a graphic manner, for instance[12] in *The Court Society* (Elias 2002, e.g. 451–460), also seeks to bring together *spatial and temporal* arrangements with power relations and power inequalities, body relations, and non-intended mutual dependencies, *as well as* meaningful relationships, multiple "perspectives" and "multipolar tensions" in the sense of struggle or competition (Elias 2002 [1969]: 451–460; see also Chartier 1989; Bogner 1992: 42–47). Besides the striking thematic similarities and overlaps between these two scholars, and the historical method practiced by both in different ways,[13] it is our opinion that these ideas should inspire a quasi experimental attempt to combine the concepts of discourse and figuration; among other things, they raise questions that are important in biographical research concerning the (not only) discursive relationships between individuals and discourse

---

12 But compare the similar use of the terms *social configuration* and *configurational analysis* in Elias and Scotson (1965) (see index of this first edition).

13 We will note here just two more arguments for such an apparently perplexing "connection": 1. In the first chapter of On the Process of Civilisation (Elias 2012b: 13–57), Elias offers a sociology-of-knowledge analysis and explanation for the specific differences between the German terms for "civilization" and "culture" that is connected to the differing long-term paths of socio-political and socio-cultural development in Germany, on the one hand, and in France and England on the other, and can be read as an investigation in the spirit of Foucault's and Nietzsche's "genealogy" – or alternatively as an implementation of the methodological conclusions of Mannheim's famous essay on competition in the intellectual sphere (Mannheim 1952b [1929]). In the classical sociology of knowledge, this text is probably the one to which Foucault's later linking of discourse analysis and analysis of power and its methodological principles shows the greatest closeness. 2. Reiner Keller has shrewdly described the whole of Foucault's work as a "historical sociology-of-knowledge analysis of subjectivizations" or "manners of subjectivization" (Keller 2008: chapter V; see also Lemke 2001: 85–90, 83–84). Probably the best candidate for another shorthand that applies equally to both Elias and Foucault is the well-known label "microphysics of power" (Foucault 1976). On the relationship between Elias's and Foucault's works, see, besides the aforementioned sources (see note 7), also Arnason (2003: 201–202, 206, 340–342); Bührmann and Ernst (2010).

communities.[14] It should also be said that we do not expect that such a combination would leave the two concepts unchanged.

Discourses in Foucault's sense are practices by means of which "subjects make their world, at the same time as being guided, restricted and decentered by the rules of the discourses" (Sarasin 2010: 105; our translation, A.B./G.R.). They are understood by Foucault as *volatile processes*. They begin, they change and they come to an end. With this processual orientation, and above all with the attempt to investigate the decentral, empirical interdependences and entanglement of proposition systems and "discursive events" with power *relations* and with "non-discursive practices", this understanding of the concept of discourse is compatible with an empirical sociology of knowledge like that of Elias or Mannheim – and with biographical research in sociology.

Discourses include (empirically reconstructable) rules in respect of the empowerment, exclusion or marginalization of speakers, in other words in respect of who is empowered or legitimated to speak about what in which context: they are subject to rules in respect of what and in which context may or may not be said or written. In our analysis of interviews, and during participant observation of discourses in diverse contexts (especially everyday contexts), we discover and reconstruct the existence of such rules for the discourse dominance of speakers and topics, and thus of interrelated complexes of certain discursive and non-discursive practices. Power must be understood here not as something, as a force or object, that influences the so-called subject or discourses from the "outside", but, foremost, as a part of the empirical constellation that is immanent in other objects or relations – not least as the power of definition, as a part or structural aspect that participates in the production or constitution of the *collective and individual* reality in the historical and social world but is an integral part of all its components. "Relations of power are not in a position of exteriority with respect to other types of relationships (economic processes, knowledge relationships, sexual relations), but are immanent in the latter" (Foucault 1978b: 94). Foucault underlines several times "the strictly relational character of power relationships" (Foucault 1978b: 95) and – in an important, but obscure, formulation – that power relations are "both intentional and nonsubjective" (1978b: 94).

The question remains as to who or what could be the actor or bearer of the "subjectless" *purposefulness* ("intentionality", "strategies") described here.

---

14 On combining discourse research and biographical research, see Alber (2016); Pohn-Lauggas (2016); Tuider (2007); Schäfer and Völter (2005); Spies (2009).

This is possibly the most important unsolved problem in Foucault's work: the anonymous purposefulness of the historical-social processes which he tries to capture by speaking of authorless strategies, tactics, techniques and *dispositives* (a term with denotations such as "battle order, line-up, arrangement"). In the context of the collective disciplining of wage laborers, Foucault speaks of "strategies with no subject": diverse part-processes coalesce in such a way "that you get a coherent, rational strategy", "but without it being necessary to attribute to it a subject" (Foucault 1980: 203, 204–205). At these points and in this respect, several of the ideas formulated during the phase of his work in which Foucault focused on the analysis of power come critically close to the argumentation figures and weaknesses of classical functionalism, even though a dynamized and decentralized functionalism.[15]

According to Foucault, "subjects" are always subjected to discursive rules; they are permeated by discourses, and so are their biographical (and all other) self-presentations (see for instance Tuider 2007). In our understanding, the question as to *how far* this permeation goes, *to what degree* subjects are restricted and shaped by it in their active involvement with social reality, in their own creative activity, can only be answered empirically. Here, we agree with Schäfer and Völter (2005: 182: n. 2) that *complete* permeation of individuals by discourses, where subjects "think and act in accordance with (discourses) wholly automatically and without reflection", must be seen as an extreme case in empirical terms. "Subjects" are "both producers and recipients of discourses" (Pohn-Weidinger 2014: 31; our translations, A.B./G.R.). To which we would like to add: neither of these functions or roles is mechanically determined and it is therefore impossible to describe the relationship between them by purely "deductive" means.

We present below some examples from our own research which show that it is always required to empirically examine the concrete historical-biographical constellations and concrete social figurations in which people attempt (sometimes successfully) to resist the hegemonic discourses in their local environment, contribute to the transformation of older discourses, or engage in a conscious, critical discussion of the potent discourses to which

---

15 Compare the critical questions put by the participants in a long discussion with members of the Department of Psychoanalysis at the University of Paris/Vincennes (Foucault 1978a: 118–175, here: 138–142; see also Foucault 2003: 405–408). This is true, although Foucault's military or mechanical metaphors from the fields of the "correlation of forces" and "battle" throw doubt on the applicability of analogies with organism-like functional integration.

they are exposed (see for example Pohn-Lauggas 2016; Tuider 2007; Wundrak 2010). And conversely, it is necessary to ask in which social constellations or phases of historical change do certain discourses exercise a particularly strong, or particularly direct, effect on individuals, often without their being aware of it. Moreover, compliance with discourses such as those dominant in the speaker's we-group does not always mean disempowerment of the individual. Rather, concrete discourses can *empower* or strengthen not only individuals but also the inner coherence of an organized group or we-group. They can be used as a means of empowering or enhancing their *individual and collective capacity for action*, in other words serve as an element of "agency".

As a consequence of these theoretical considerations, we must assume that self-interpretations and self-representations of individuals (and groups) are determined and "permeated" not only by collective patterns of interpretation or discourses, but also by non-intended interdependencies and interrelationships within collective ("social") processes and figurations, of which the fluctuating empirical discourse formations themselves are an inseparable part.

By analyzing biographical we- and self-presentations[16] it is possible to gain insights into the effectiveness of discourses and the unequal, asymmetric power balances in the particular historical-social and physical space in which the biographers live, or have lived. Such analysis makes it possible to reconstruct which groups or groupings have more sway than other groupings and individuals within a figuration of groupings – *and in their discourses*. These may be organized groups or unintentionally networked groupings, we-groups with a shared and manifest we-image, or groupings that are defined as a collective only by others. In other words, we use these data to answer questions such as: Which groups shape the discourses and interpretations of social or historical reality? Which groups or groupings (have to) submit to these discourses, even if they are not compatible with their own experiences and collective memories? And which groupings have more or less no voice in the public discourses? In addition to showing how

---

16 This formulation does justice to the fact that, in order to extend the historical framework of our studies, we always ask our interviewees to talk about the history of their family, and, following Halbwachs, we assume that biographical self-presentations and narrations are framed by the way the speakers locate themselves in particular we-groups (Halbwachs 1985 [French original: 1925]). Compare Mannheim, who in a similar context used the concept of the "frame group" or (in German) *"Rahmengruppe"* (1980: 245–253, 320: n. 53).

concrete discourses shape individual and collective representations or narrations, e.g., in the cases of family histories or local histories, and how far, and in which ways, individuals are able to evade or resist them. In our own sociological studies these texts also serve to reconstruct the voices of the established and the more subdued voices of outsiders, their we- and they-images, in the interplay of power balances between diverse groups and groupings.[17]

In biographical-narrative interviews, the biographer is first invited to tell his or her story as freely as possible. In the resulting we- and self-presentations of individuals or families, we not only gain insights into dominant contemporary discourses, but also into discourses that were potent in the past, and the way that power balances or inequalities between different groupings have changed over time. In practice this means either that discourses that were dominant in the past continue to be adopted unquestioningly by the speakers[18] in certain sequences of the interview, or that they speak of them critically, or speak against them, try to justify their differing viewpoints or conduct in the past, or distance themselves from past patterns of interpretation or activity, when representing their current perspective. The analysis of biographical self-presentations often shows how discourses that were efficacious in the past may shine through in certain sequences of the interview (especially in the narrative phases), while the speakers remain unaware of the discrepancy between these older patterns of interpretation and their current perspectives which they offer to us more or less emphatically. Thus, they continue to be influenced by older discourses on a non-conscious level. This is especially the case when dominant contemporary discourses contain no explicit discussion of past discourses – due to continuing power inequalities in the figurations between certain groupings. In other words, not only our

---

17 Perhaps it should be noted that Rogers Brubaker does not deny the empirical possibility and existence of either organized groups or we-groups. But he emphasizes that *groupness* is the product of processes of social construction and that it "is a variable, not a constant" – inside as well as outside of groups (Brubaker 2004: 4, 3).

18 We avoid using the term "narrator" because we wish to emphasize that the difference between different text types is important in the analysis, and that we systematically include and interpret all types of presentation. The distinction proposed by Kallmeyer and Schütze (1977) between different kinds of texts and their possible meanings in the context of narrative interviews, is an instrument which helps us to detect the differences between present and past perspectives, between legitimations that guide actions and secondary legitimations, or between standardized elements of hegemonic we-discourses and more individual or specific patterns of interpretation in a person's self-thematization.

apparently individual decisions, but also power relations and contemporary dominant discourses which enable an unconnected co-existence of conflicting patterns of interpretation determine how far we pay attention to, question, disregard or (often unknowingly) reproduce patterns of interpretation or discourses which were dominant in the past. It is thus easily possible that conflicting patterns of interpretation and discourse fragments can be activated in an individual's stock of knowledge, and can lead to inconsistencies such as are often observed in familial and biographical we- and self-representations, without the speakers being aware of them. If the interviewers have been socialized in the same or similar discourses, they often do not notice these inconsistencies and contradictions, or only after a careful analysis of the interview. Alfred Schütz (Schütz 1944) argued that everyday knowledge is essentially more inconsistent, less coherent and more vague than scientific knowledge, and points out that between members of a so-called in-group these characteristics of their knowledge are at first no problem in everyday communication: "The system of knowledge thus acquired – incoherent, inconsistent, and only partially clear, as it is – takes on for the members of the in-group the appearance of a *sufficient* coherence, clarity, and consistency to give anybody a reasonable chance of understanding and of being understood" (Schütz 1944: 501).

Moreover, in biographical narrations and self-presentations in general, it is necessary to distinguish between present perspectives which are more often evident in *argumentative* sequences, and past perspectives which are more often evident in *narrations* of self-experienced events. "The narration's proximity to the past thus increases in the course of the narration, and perspectives entirely different from the present perspective show themselves, which becomes clear in the argumentation parts or also in the narrated anecdotes" (Rosenthal 2006: 3). Besides this actor-centered approach, we believe that a combination of arguments from figurational sociology and discourse analysis can help to explain why biographers are often unaware of these contradictions in the present of the interview, and why, when speaking about an experience in their past, they remain in their past perspective. This means that a reinterpretation of the meaning of this experience is not "imposed" upon them (in the sense proposed by Schütz), and they are able to avoid questioning the meaning of the event. This can be illustrated by an example. In a biographical interview conducted by Gabriele Rosenthal in the context of her research on the biographies of former members of the Hitler Youth movement, one interviewee framed talking about her youth in the "Third Reich" and her

BIOGRAPHIES – DISCOURSES – FIGURATIONS

time in the League of German Girls (*Bund Deutscher Mädel*, BDM), right at the beginning of the interview by the argument that she could say nothing about the persecution of the Jews and the so-called *Reichskristallnacht* (the "Night of Broken Glass"). She said she came from a small town "where people weren't aware of it", because there were hardly any Jews living there. She thus followed the apologetic discourse dominant in Germany in the present of the interview – a discourse still influenced by the unequal power relationship between those who were persecuted by the Nazis and those who were not persecuted – by speaking of her own ignorance of Nazi crimes at the time, and framed her biographical self-presentation as being untouched by this topic. In the context of her account of her schooldays and the BDM, she mentioned the 9 November 1938. She said that on the following morning, as she walked along the main shopping street on her way to school, she saw that many shops had been destroyed. The windows were broken and the shops had been plundered. She evaluates this experience by saying: "After all most of the shops in the main shopping street belonged to wealthy Jews." This evaluation reflects the discourse into which she was socialized in the Nazi period[19] as it was imposed and supported by the established, or the non-persecuted. It is what shaped her perception of the ruined shops at that time. She was thus reproducing a discourse that was utilized in the past by the Nazis, the powerful established grouping, to maintain their power. In a certain way, this discourse lives on in today's apologetic discourse in respect of Nazi crimes, which persists despite the counter discourses that have become established, and even "dominant", in Germany meanwhile. It is what allows the speaker to assume that her argument will be understood by the interviewer, and that it is not necessary to explain the connection between this pogrom and the wealth of the Jewish shop owners. The implicit anti-Semitic discourse in respect of the wealth and resulting influence of the Jews, which she was explicitly taught in her youth, both in school and in the Nazi youth organization, still shapes her view of the past. The failure to critically reflect on the anti-Semitic prejudices she had learned and absorbed in her youth, and the refusal of empathy in relation to the Jewish shop owners who were disenfranchised in the November pogrom – as well as to others who were persecuted in the town where the speaker lived – is partly due, or so we assume, to the fact that the later, and today still current, apologetic discourse in respect of the Nazi period does not require anyone to question what they

---

19 See Rosenthal (1987); for a more detailed interpretation of this inconsistency, see Rosenthal (1994).

experienced, and the figuration of persecuted and non-persecuted people in Germany still gives more voice, or more social weight, to the voices of the non-persecuted, the followers of the regime, and the "free-riders" and perpetrators involved in the persecution of large groupings in society, and in depriving them of their rights.

Our conclusion is that discourses cannot be separated from the social figurations to which they belong and which they *co-constitute*. Figurations and discourses are inseparably bound together.[20] The idea that one determines the other is *not always* wrong, but is basically an inappropriate application of physico-mechanical causality models to the world of human beings, in other words the world of the constant interweaving of discursive and non-discursive practices that ultimately cannot be disbanded.

7.4 Voices of established and outsiders in Palestine and Uganda

Two empirical studies are presented very briefly below which were focused in part on the reconstruction of figurations of established and outsiders, their we-images and their collective memories. Both studies involved collecting and analyzing life stories and family histories of members of very different groupings. The first study was carried out in the context of the Middle East conflict in the Palestinian territories of the West Bank,[21] and the second in the context of the post-conflict process in the West Nile region of Uganda.[22] After comparing the empirical findings of research in these different contexts, both with a history of violent collective conflict in the past, or still going on in the present, one common feature was easy to identify: the people we interviewed regard their individual and their collective past, the

---

20 Organized groups and we-groups always form *interpretation communities*, and the they-groups or "Others" defined by them are always (at least partially) produced and shaped by the discourses of the dominant groups.

21 This project, entitled *Belonging to the Outsider and Established Groupings: Palestinians and Israelis in Various Figurations*, was funded by the DFG (German Research Foundation) from 2010 to 2015. Besides Gabriele Rosenthal, the project leaders were Shifra Sagy (Ben Gurion University of the Negev, Beer Sheva, Israel) and Mohammed S. Dajani Daoudi (Palestinian Territories). See Rosenthal (2016b).

22 We took part in the research project *Conflict regulation and post-conflict processes in Ghana and Uganda* at the University of Bayreuth, which was led by Dieter Neubert and also funded by the DFG (2009–2012) (see Bogner and Neubert 2016; 2013a; 2013b; 2012; Bogner and Rosenthal 2014; 2017a).

past of their families, and that of other we-groups, in ways that are shaped, and sometimes interfered with, by present hegemonic discourses, but also by discourses that prevailed in the past (and to some extent live on in the present). Their individual and collective practices of self-thematization and remembering are generally molded by the (more) established we-group(s) within a web of interdependent groupings, although this varies depending on the regional, local, historical or situative context. The socially dominant grouping usually has a firmly established we-image which is the basis of a strong we-feeling, or feeling of belonging, and is in a position to determine – *not only among its own members* – which we-image and associated collective memory they must support (see Rosenthal 2016a; Elias 2008; Elias and Scotson 1965). The same is true with regard to their standardized they-images of other groupings. Thus, they are (at least to some extent) able to impose rules which regulate: a) what is to be remembered and how, b) which parts of the collective memory must replace memories of self-experienced events or those handed down within the family, c) which framings should be used when interacting with members of other groupings. Like all norms, these (usually unwritten) rules are not always followed, and sometimes they are deliberately violated. In both regions, biographical and ethnographical interviews with outsiders gave us a very good opportunity to learn about components and interpretations of collective history which are sidelined or silenced by the dominant discourses (see Bogner and Rosenthal 2014; Bogner and Rosenthal 2017a; Worm and Hinrichsen 2016).

West Bank

In the West Bank, a team of Palestinian, Israeli-Palestinian and German researchers led by Gabriele Rosenthal set out to investigate the *life stories* of Palestinians, as well as *everyday interactions* between Christians and Muslims, and between other distinguishable sections of society, such as the refugees of 1948 and the long-time residents in a particular town or area, or Palestinians from Israel and from the West Bank. Initially, almost all the interviewees vehemently presented the same we-image with great consistency: 'We Palestinians have no internal conflicts, we only have conflicts with the (Jewish) Israelis', and spoke in terms of a strongly stereotyped collective memory which almost always refers to the same collective data, in particular the *Nakba* ("the catastrophe") in the context of the founding of the state of Israel in 1948, and hardly ever to memories handed down within the family. We interpreted this in the first place as being due to the presence of German researchers, who represent the so-called Western world in the eyes of the Palestinians (see Rosenthal 2016c: 20–21). Conversations in everyday contexts and biographical interviews conducted in this region were very much colored by the Middle East conflict and its complex figurations of Palestinians, Jewish Israelis and representatives of the so-called Western (predominantly Christianized) world. Speaking about the individual's life and the family's history is framed by presentations of the national we-group and its collective fate, and is thus embedded in, and intertwined with, the overpowering figuration with the Jewish Israelis, and the confrontations and power inequalities that are associated with it, and characterized, to a high degree, by violence and coercion. As a result, most interviewees present themselves as representatives of a conflict-free we-group of Palestinians, and family and individual self-presentations are focused on the thematic field of "our suffering under the Israeli occupation". They underline that there are no conflicts between people living in the refugee camps and those who live outside. They insist that "we are one people" and that "we only have conflicts with the Israelis or the Jews". Both the Christian and the Muslim interviewees present a picture of peaceful co-existence between these two groupings within the Palestinian we-group: they argue that the relationship between the two groupings is harmonious, while playing down, or explicitly denying, the serious nature of tensions which are often implied or described.[23] The familial and individual we- and self-presentations are permeated by an argumentative reproduction and defense of this we-image, by the naming of important events in the collective history and collective memory, and by exemplifying stories intended to demonstrate how people have suffered under the Israeli occupation, or foreign domination. Because of this framing, long narrative sequences were rare in the interviews, and getting people to tell us about biographical areas outside this thematic field required consistent initial narrative prompts.

---

23 In the fieldwork phases in autumn 2013 and spring 2014, slightly different views were expressed in interviews with Christians. Before the backdrop of the recent changes of government and political power shifts in the Islamic countries, and especially escalation of the conflicts in Egypt and Syria, they began to speak about their fears concerning developments in the Arab world; some of the interviewees indicated that these days there were less private contacts between Muslims and Christians, and that more significance was being attached to whether someone was Christian or Muslim (Hinrichsen et. al. 2016).

In order to find out to what extent the presentation of this harmonizing we-image and collective memory was evoked by an interactive framing based on the national belongings of the interviewers, we asked the Palestinian researchers in our team to carry out interviews and participant observations with no non-Palestinians present. This resulted in similar findings, especially in respect of the dominance of the collective memory which was restricted or reduced to certain historical dates, with a focus on the suffering of the we-group under Israeli rule, and the harmonizing of relationships between different parts of the we-group. Palestinians defend this image of harmony even in internal discourses, at least in public and semi-public discourses, and also in interactions between Christians and Muslims. It is obviously important to them to maintain it and thus to gain reassurance. Such efforts at collective self-reassurance through the conception of a conflict-free we-group are always particularly vigorous at times of fierce or violent collective conflicts, and must always be seen in the light of the official Israeli policy of creating splits among the non-Jewish part of the population, on the principle of "divide and rule". As a result, Palestinians are anxious to resist any attempt to divide them into different categories or "minorities" which would be even more powerless against the stronger conflict party of the "Jewish" Israelis, who in reality are "culturally" and socio-politically just as heterogeneous. In their meetings with the researchers, they fight against these (more or less intentional) attempts to split them up by repeatedly insisting that they are a community in which no one suffers discrimination because of their religion, their status as a refugee or long-time resident, or because of their legal status.

With time the research team was able to observe that this practiced and unchanging presentation of a harmonizing we-image sometimes dissipated after repeated meetings, or was no longer used at a second interview, and that memory processes were then framed in different terms (for example "my suffering due to the early death of my father"). In some interviews, the dominant discourse on the national we-group played no role at all. Sometimes, first interviews were welcomed as a kind of therapeutic session where the interviewees could talk freely about the discrimination they suffered, for example as homosexual men. Some interviews were determined by a presentation by the interviewees of their own discriminated we-group (e.g. "we homosexual Palestinians") to a "Western" interviewer, in the belief that the interviewer would be more tolerant than the people they had to deal with in their own environment. In the course of the research, it became increasingly clear that for some people the interviews represented an opportunity to talk about their personal problems, or the way their we-group (or the grouping to which they are regarded as belonging) is discriminated against. Most of these interlocutors could be regarded as outsiders in Palestinian society, such as members of binational families or people in a binational marriage relationship, people who have lived abroad for many years, or men who are defined as homosexual.[24] Because of this empirical finding, the research team actively sought such outsiders as interviewees. The result was an empirical confirmation of the assumption that the harmonizing we-image is not used by people who are outsiders in a multiple (and thus relatively pronounced and "individualized") sense in their lifeworld. This applies for instance to those who are outsiders *in more than one* of the following respects: in relation to long-time residents in their local context, in relation to the members of big, established families, in relation to people with citizenship and relatively unrestricted travel rights, above all the Israelis, or who have another ascribed feature which may be used to make them social outsiders (such as being in a confessional, sexual or political minority position, being disabled, or having confessionally mixed parents). These people spend more time *narrating* their "individual" experiences, which do not belong to the thematic field of "suffering under the Israeli occupation"; they embark on longer streams of narration and, more importantly, also thematize conflicts and increasing tensions between the different Palestinian groupings. They thematize how they feel discriminated against as Christians or Muslims, or as inhabitants of the refugee camps, and speak about the local tensions between long-time residents and refugees, or between Christians and Muslims.[25] Unlike those we- and self-representations that are mainly based on the harmonizing we-image and the relevant parts of the collective memory, and are thus dominated by the figuration between the Palestinians and the Jewish Israelis or the state

---

24 There may be considerable differences between self-definition and definition by others (as for instance between the we-image of a grouping and the they-image attributed to it by others), just as the content of this categorization may greatly vary. In our interviews in the West Bank – in contrast to Israel – we have not yet been able to interview a woman who implied, or openly admitted, that she was lesbian.

25 In their analysis of interviews conducted by them, Arne Worm and Hendrik Hinrichsen (2016) have concluded that speaking about such experiences of religious or ethnic discrimination, or about violent episodes of conflicts between Christians and Muslims, can be a way of speaking indirectly about the way the interviewees experience discrimination as homosexuals and their resulting fear of violent attacks.

of Israel, the outsiders narrate more of their own life history and tell stories that reflect more of their personal biographical relevances. Their presentations are dominated by the figuration containing themselves as relatively "individualized" outsiders and the we-group of established Palestinians – although (and this must be stressed here) the figuration between them and the state of Israel is also an important term of reference for their self-interpretation. In certain contexts it has a massive influence on the we- and self-images presented by them, especially in the context of "political" discourses.

West Nile

A study carried out in West Nile (northern Uganda) also showed us the great importance of conducting interviews with outsiders, and of reconstructing power inequalities, or asymmetric power balances, between different groupings (or individuals), and the hegemonic discourses which are connected with these asymmetries and whose rules are followed (or violated) in the interviews. This region is the home province of the former head of state and dictator, Idi Amin. Biographical and ethnographic interviews were conducted with civilians, ex-rebels, members of the politico-administrative system, members of aid or development organizations, and survivors of violence perpetrated by both rebels and government soldiers. The interviews took place in the framework of a study of local peace processes in sub-Saharan Africa. We cannot go into the history of West Nile here (see Mischnick and Bauer 2009: 4–24; Leopold 2005; Rice 2009; Eckert 2010), except to point out that after the end of Amin's rule in 1979 this region became the area of operation of various rebel organizations which at first mainly consisted of former soldiers and functionaries of his regime. All parties involved in the fights during the second phase (1994–2002) of the armed rebellion in West Nile carried out terrorist attacks on the local civilian population – with whom the two main rebel groups then operating in this province nevertheless maintained close relations, and by whom they were at first strongly supported. But this support waned as brutal attacks against the civilian population increased, by the rebels apparently more so than by the army during the course of this period. In 2002 a peace agreement was signed between the government and the last active rebel organization anchored in this region, the "Uganda National Rescue Front II" (UNRF II) (see Bogner and Neubert 2016; 2013a; 2013b; 2012; Bogner and Rosenthal

2014; Mischnick and Bauer 2009; Bauer 2013: 173–180; Bauer 2009; Refugee Law Project 2004).

The figurations between the groupings interviewed for this study show that people who were robbed, kidnapped, raped or maimed by local rebels are now usually pronounced outsiders in this region. Just as in the interviews with outsiders in Palestine, these people gave us much longer accounts of their lives and of their suffering which they usually regarded as something individual. From them, too, we learned about components of the collective history which are not often mentioned in public discourses in this region, but which are occasionally implied, for instance (in rare cases) by interviewees who are respected local leaders or prominent supporters of the central government (or the ruling party), and who feel secure enough to be more forthright (Bogner and Rosenthal 2014; see also Peters 2008). As in Palestine, these outsiders do not fit their individual life history into the we-image and collective memory that is consistently presented in the dominant local discourse, and they are therefore not subject to the rules of this discourse. By contrast, the ex-rebels we interviewed gave us a stereotyped version of the history of West Nile (often at the beginning of the interviews) which has gradually become *institutionalized* in public discourses in and on this region. In this version, West Nile's past is presented as a continuous collective history of victimhood. This can be summed up in the usually unspoken message "We are the true victims of Ugandan history", while it remains unclear, or undecided, whether this "we" is a reference only to the rebels, or to all inhabitants of West Nile, or to a particular sub-grouping among them. The rebels are thus presented as part of a big collective of victims, but an outstanding part that has been hit especially hard by the common suffering and disadvantages (Rice 2009: 256; for an academic version, and an example, of this we-image, see Leopold 2005: esp. 70–73). They belong both to the we-group of the local population as a whole, and to the we-group of the "ex-combatants", to whom not only the ex-rebels but also all ex-soldiers from the region belong. The fact that they call their organizations "ex-combatants' associations" suggests that this name can be understood as the expression of a kind of socio-political coalition – or at least as a sign of willingness to enter into such a coalition. The government has created and sealed a corresponding commonality of interests by paying pensions to soldiers and functionaries from the time of Amin's government, including the ex-rebels of the UNRF II (see the newspaper report by Namutebi and Karugaba [2011] in *New Vision*, 5 Sept. 2011). Members of the predecessor organization of this rebel group,

BIOGRAPHIES – DISCOURSES – FIGURATIONS   249

the first UNRF, who helped to mediate the peace agreement between the later UNRF II and the government, had already become political allies of Yoweri Museveni, today head of the government, in the mid-1980s. In addition, the recent peace agreement supports, at least implicitly, the way the rebels interpret the situation, according to which their struggle has achieved something positive for the inhabitants of West Nile, namely the government's promise to promote the "development" of this region in special ways, after many years of a development blockade. This definition of the situation that was negotiated in the peace agreement between the leaders of UNRF II and the government allows the rebels to present themselves in public discourses as keepers and defenders of the interests of the local population, and especially of their need for "development" and reconstruction. Even if this is a view that is no longer generally shared, it is practically never attacked or criticized, obviously in order to avoid endangering the peace agreement signed in 2002 (see also Bauer 2013: 179–180, 177; Bauer 2009: 39–40; Peters 2008: 44–47, 53–55, 22; Brix n.d. = 2009: 37–39; Weber 2009: 66–67; Mischnick and Bauer 2009: 80–81, 85). In one of our group interviews with victims of collective violence, fear of the ex-rebels and their influence on the government and in the administration of the province was openly mentioned by one participant as a reason why the victims of collective violence were afraid to talk about their problems publicly.

Unlike the rebels, the victims cannot resort to standardized "historical building blocks" in the public discourse in the construction of their stories. Therefore their stories have the character of *individual* constructions; they appear to be narrations of highly specific experiences, for which it is impossible to tell how many other people might have suffered the same fate. The principal reason why these interviews contain detailed narrations of the violence they suffered at the hands of the rebels, is because they experienced these acts of violence only as something that happened to them personally, and they have had no chance to develop a we-image and a collective memory as a separate grouping or we-category. The victims have the problem that the we-concepts available to them for their self-presentation are mainly the same as those used by the perpetrators. This makes it difficult for them to depict their experiences in the interview. But once they have freed themselves from these inhibiting we-concepts, their memories and stories of their experiences of violence are obviously subject to very few restricting rules regarding what may and may not be talked about.

7.5 Conclusion: methodological consequences

From our considerations and our empirical experience, it is possible to draw some relatively simple conclusions regarding principles of methodology and research design; but as simple as these principles may be, they are seldom put into practice. As already mentioned, we adopt as far as possible a long-term perspective and implement this methodologically, for instance by conducting multigenerational studies, by analyzing the findings of historical research, and by examining archival material and other accessible data, including spatial arrangements, architecture and spatial structures. In the analysis of interviews, we track down both past and present discourses, and the rules they imply for the presentation of collective, familial and personal histories. Using a figurational and processual or *diachronic* approach, we always try to see our interviewees in terms of the we-groups they belong to (or are believed to belong to), belongings which change over time, and in terms of their interdependencies with other groupings. Consequently, we do not follow the logic of "comparative groups" (defined using mainly quantitative relations); the development of our sample is guided by what we discover in the course of the research *and during the process of data collection* and analysis, and what this makes us want to find out. This can be related to other groupings with whom the interviewees form social figurations, to their great dependencies, or to the unequal or asymmetric power balances which make certain groupings "outsiders" in the sense proposed by Elias and Scotson. We make a strong plea for inclusion of the voices of outsiders, because as sociologists we need to avoid falling into the trap of uncritically reproducing the prevailing public discourses – which all too often also dominate scientific discourses.

The questions which we believe should be asked in biographical case reconstructions can be summed up as follows:

1. Which forms of we- and self-presentation are shaped by the hegemonic discourses of which grouping(s)?
2. How and at what points do the interviewees or biographers deviate from these discourses, and which persons or groupings deviate from these standardized forms of (individual and collective) self-thematization? The same applies to the standardized forms of their they-images of other people.
3. Which plural and possibly *competing* discourses can be discovered from both a synchronic and a diachronic perspective? This also applies to indi-

viduals who belong to several we-groups and (thus) to multiple discursive contexts.

4. Which framings of the interviews evoke we- and self-presentations which tend to comply with the dominant discourses, and which framings help to free we- and self-presentations from the dominant discourses?
5. To what extent do these framings change during the interview, or in later meetings?
6. To what extent do collective belongings which are *ascribed* to the interviewers influence the framing of the interviews?
7. To what extent can different or similar we- and self-presentations be observed in other, everyday or institutional, formal or informal, settings?

Last but not least, we also need to ask which discourses empower the speakers and which disempower them and require them to de-thematize or deny their familial and individual past. Discourses, in the sense of more or less institutionalized – and by the same token collective or "social" – practices of collective and individual self-interpretation and of interpreting the world and history, including not least the collective histories of relevant we-groups, often strongly influence the self-descriptions in biographical interviews, but, as shown by examples from our research, this strong influence is neither without gaps nor inescapable in every situation. Discourses demand, and promote, the interactive production of framings for presenting we- and they-images and interpretations of the world, but individuals obviously do have varying degrees of freedom of choice in respect of these framings and discourse rules, depending on their social and situative contexts. In this connection it is clear that in most of the aforementioned contexts *diverse*, and often conflicting or competing, belongings and discourses are involved and shape the way people talk about themselves.

Appendix

Transcription symbols

Speaker 1: and so #we went#	
Speaker 2: #hmhm yes#	simultaneous utterances
(says he)	approximate transcription
( )	incomprehensible (space between brackets approximately corresponding to length/duration of passage)
((slowly)) ((coughs))	transcriber's comments, also descriptions of moods & non-verbal utterances or sounds
\... ((slowly))\	\marks beginning and end of phenomenon
((vividly))	general change of mood, probably continuing
,	brief pause
(5)	pause in full seconds
many mo- , more	sudden halt/faltering /(self-) interruption
ye=yes	rapid speech, words closely linked
ye: s	sound lengthened
›yes‹	softly, in a low voice
no	loudly, stressed

Criteria to define the sequences

The three main criteria to define the beginning/end of a textual sequence are:

- conversational turn-taking (changes of speaker)
- thematic shifts and changes
- textual sorts among the textual sorts we distinguish: argumentation, description, and narration.

Textual sorts: Narration/Description/Argumentation

Narration refers to a chain of sequences of events of the past. Sequence of actual or fictitious occurrences that are related to each other through a series of temporal and/or causal links.

Subcategories of narration: report, single story, non-self-experienced stories, exemplifying narrative, retrospective and prospective narration, inserted narrative (providing background information).

Report is a brief narrative with a *low degree* of indexicality. "Narration in which the presentation of events is limited to an unilinear chain of occurrences without elaboration of situations..." (Kallmeyer/Schütze 1977: 187). Telegram style. Reports are frequently given as part of an explanation. As they are sometimes hard to distinguish from argumentation, the mixed category: report/argumentation may serve to label a sequence.

Single stories are salient episodes occurring within a narrative; these have the highest degree of indexicality and detail. They are bound to a specified time, place and person. "A story has a beginning, the situation as it has been before at a certain point of time, then something is happening and changing the situation and finally the story has an end, the situation as it is now (or at the time, when the story ends)" (Hermanns 1987: 45)

Stories of non-self-lived experiences, relating a story experienced by somebody else

Exemplifying narrative adds plausibility to a line of argument.

Evaluation is an argumentation *within a narrative*, expressing some "meaning", making the story more plausible, and with respect to climaxes in the story, taking on the character of judgements of justifications. They can introduce a narrative sequence, such as "then something really extraordinary happened"; they can be embedded in the story or occur at the end of the sequence of events, e.g., "that really was most exciting". The decisive difference between evaluation and argumentation followed by an exemplifying narrative is that here the story serves the purpose of justifying the argument whereas evaluation – esp. initial evaluation – serves more the function of justifying the narrative (why one is telling the story at all).

Description "the decisive feature distinguishing them from narratives is that descriptions present static structures" (Kallmeyer/Schütze 1977: 201)

Description of qualities/features of situations, including representation of actions and events – but with the purpose of demonstrating qualities or as cause or expression of qualities – "The dynamic element of the content being presented is 'frozen'" (ibid.)

Condensed situations events frequently experienced are compressed into one exemplary situation.

Argumentation: Lines of reasoning – accounts: abstract elements occurring both within the story-telling sequence (evaluations) and aside from it. Theorizing, declaration of general ideas, they show the narrator's general orientation and what he/she thinks of himself/herself and of the world.

References

Adler, A. (1937): Significance of early recollections. In: Int. Journal of Individual Psychology. 4, 283–287

Ahrens, E./Strüber, E. Volpers, R. (1989): Lebensgeschichten von Prostituierten. In: Rosenthal, G. (Hrsg.), 62–80

Alber, I. (2016a): Zivilgesellschaftliches Engagement in Polen: Ein biographietheoretischer und diskursanalytischer Zugang, Wiesbaden

Alber, I. (2016b): Doing civil society in post-socialist Poland. Triangulation of biographical analysis and discourse analysis. In: Przeglad Socjologiczny, vol. 65 (4) 91–110. http://cejsh.icm.edu.pl/cejsh/element/bwmeta1.element.desklight-d55c5337-815b-40e0-a17c-629842727fa4

Alheit, P. (1983): Alltagszeit und Lebenszeit in biographischen Thematisierungen. In: ders.: Alltagsleben. Zur Bedeutung eines gesellschaftlichen "Restphänomens". Frankfurt a.M./New York: Campus, 188–197

Alheit, P. (1985): Wirklichkeitsrekonstruktion und Wirklichkeitskonstitution in biographischen Erzählungen. Zur Kritik zweier prominenter Interpretationsansätze. In: Franz, H.W. (Hrsg.) 22. Deutscher Soziologentag 1984. Beiträge der Sektions- und Ad-hoc-Gruppen. Opladen: Westdeutscher Verlag, 92–96

Alheit, P. (1990a): Alltag und Biographie. Studien zur gesellschaftlichen Konstitution biographischer Perspektiven. Erweitere Neuauflage. (Werkstattberichte des Forschungsschwerpunkts Arbeit und Bildung, Bd. 4) Bremen: Universität Bremen

Alheit, P. (1990b): Biographizität als Projekt. (Werkstattberichte des Forschungsschwerpunkts Arbeit und Bildung, Bd. 12) Bremen: Universität Bremen

Alheit, P./Dausien, B. (1990): Biographie. Eine problemgeschichtliche Skizze. (Werkstattberichte des Forschungsschwerpunkts Arbeit und Bildung, Bd. 14) Bremen: Universität Bremen

Alheit, P./Fischer-Rosenthal, W./Hoerning, E. (1990) (Hrsg.): Biographieforschung. Eine Zwischenbilanz in der deutschen Soziologie. (Werkstattberichte des Forschungsschwerpunkts Arbeit und Bildung, Bd. 13): Bremen: Universität Bremen

Alheit, P./Dausien, B. (2000): Die biographische Konstruktion der Wirklichkeit: Überlegungen zur Biographizität des Sozialen, in: Hoerning, E. (Ed.): Biographische Sozialisation, Stuttgart, 257–284

Arnason, J. P. (2003): Civilizations in dispute: Historical questions and theoretical traditions, Leiden/Boston

Allport, G. (1942): The use of personal documents in psychological science. New York: Social Science Research council

Anderson, J.R. (1976): Language, Memory, and Thought. Hillsdale, N.J.: Erlbaum

Apitzsch, U. Siouti, I. (2014): 'Transnational Biographies. In: Zeitschrift für Qualitative Forschung, 15 (1–2): 11–23

Bahl, E. (2017): Precarious Transnational Biographies: Moroccan Juveniles in the Spanish Enclaves Ceuta and Melilla. In: Rosenthal, G. & Bogner, A., 185–208

Bahl, E. (2021): Verflochtene Geschichten im postkolonialen Grenzraum. Biographien, Zugehörigkeiten und Erinnerungspraktiken in Ceuta und Melilla. Göttinger Beiträge zur soziologischen Biographieforschung. Göttingen: Universitätsverlag Göttingen. DOI: 10.17875/gup2021-1600

Bahl, E./Worm, A. (2018): Biographische und ethnographische Zugänge zu Wir-Bildern, Sie-Bildern und Handlungspraktiken in einer Organisation. Die spanische Polizeieinheit Guardia Civil in Ceuta und Melilla. In: Zeitschrift für Qualitative Forschung 19(1+2) 233–253

Bahl, E./Rosenthal, G. (Eds.) (2021): Navigating Through Increasing Social Inequalities in Times of Covid-19: A Research Report on Interviews with Migrants in the Middle East and Europe and Migrants and Indigenous People in South America. Göttingen: Centre for Global Migration Studies. https: //publications.goettingen-research-online.de/bitstream/2/96783/1/cemig-04-bahl-rosenthal.pdf

Bar-On, D. (1989): Legacy of Silence. Encounters with Children of the Third Reich. Cambridge: Harvard University Press

Bar-On, D. (1994): Fear and Hope. Israel: Ghetto Fighters' House. In Hebräisch

Bartlett, F.C. (1932/1967): Rembering. Cambridge

Bastiaans, J. (1988): Vom Menschen im KZ und vom KZ im Menschen. Zur Behandlung des KZ-Syndroms und dessen Spätfolgen. In: Bar-On, D./Beiner, F./Brusten, M. (Hrsg.): Der Holocaust. Familiale und gesellschaftliche Folgen. Wuppertal: Universität Wuppertal, 62–73

Bauer, I. (2009): Nationale und internationale Friedensakteure in Postkonfliktsituationen: Die Friedensdynamik in West Nile/Uganda, Master thesis, Universität Hamburg, unpublished.

Bauer, I. (2013): Lokale und internationale Akteure in der Friedensentwicklung, in: Heinemann-Grüder, A./Bauer, I. (Eds.): Zivile Konfliktbearbeitung: Vom Anspruch zur Wirklichkeit, Opladen, 171–182

Becker, J. (2013): Old men's truth: The "poverty generation" of neighborhood men talk about life in Jerusalem's Old City. In: Middle East Journal of Culture and Communication 6 (3), 264–285

Becker, J. (2016): Commitment to the Old City and ambivalent emplacement. In: Rosenthal, G. (2016b), 125–146

Becker, J. (2017): Verortungen in der Jerusalemer Altstadt: Lebensgeschichten und Alltag in einem engen urbanen Raum. Bielefeld: transcript.

References

Becker, J./Rosenthal, G. (2022): Ethnographie und Biographieforschung. In: Poferl, A./Schröer, N. (Hrsg.): Handbuch soziologische Ethnographie. Wiesbaden: VS Verlag, 367–382

Beneker, H./Driever, U. (1989): Die erzählte Lebensgeschichte von Ordensschwestern. In: Rosenthal, G. (Hrsg.), 81–113

Berger, Peter L./Luckmann, Thomas (1966): The social construction of reality: A treatise in the sociology of knowledge, Garden City, NY.

Bertalanffy, L. v. (1966): Mind and body re-examined. In: Journal of Humanistic Psychology, 113–138

Bertaux, D./Bertaux-Wiame, I. (1991): "Was du ererbt von deinen Vätern …": Transmissionen und soziale Mobilität über fünf Generationen, BIOS, vol. 4, no. 1, 13–40

Binswanger, L. (1931/55): Geschehnis und Erlebnis. In: Ausgewählte Vorträge und Aufsätze, Bd. 2, Berlin: Francke

Birren, J.E./Hedlund, B. (1987): Contributions of Autobiography to Developmental Psychology. In: Eisenberg, N. (Hrsg.): Contemporary Topics in Developmental Psychology. New York: Wiley, 394–415

Blumer, H. (1973): Der methodologische Standort des Symbolischen Interaktionismus. In: Arbeitsgruppe Bielefelder Soziologen (Hrsg.): Alltagswissen, Interaktion und gesellschaftliche Wirklichkeit, Bd. 1, Reinbek bei Hamburg: rowohlt, 80–146

Bogner A. (1986): The structure of social processes: A commentary on the sociology of Norbert Elias. In: Sociology 20(3): 387–411

Bogner, A. (1989): Zivilisation und Rationalisierung. Der Zivilisationstheorien M. Webers, N. Elias' und der Frankfurter Schule. Opladen: Westdeutscher Verlag

Bogner, A. (1992): The theory of the civilizing process: An idiographic theory of modernization? Theory, Culture & Society, vol. 9 (no. 2) 23–53

Bogner, A. (2021): Kollektive Gewalt – ein soziologisch relevantes Forschungsthema? Die "child soldiers" der LRA in Uganda. In: Köttig, Michaela/Witte, Nicole (Hrsg.): Biographie und Kollektivgeschichte. Weinheim: BeltzJuventa, 237–257

Bogner, A./Neubert, D. (2012): Die Komplexität der Akteursfigurationen bei "Konflikttransformation" und "Postkonflikt"-Prozessen: Beobachtungen am Beispiel Nordghanas und Nordugandas, in: Dierk Spreen/Trutz von Trotha (Eds.): Krieg und Zivilgesellschaft, Berlin, 373–406

Bogner, A./Neubert, D. (2013a): Deeskalation (und Eskalation) in gewaltsamen Gruppenkonflikten: Fallstudien aus Uganda und Ghana, in: Heinemann-Grüder, A./Bauer, I. (Eds.): Zivile Konfliktbearbeitung: Vom Anspruch zur Wirklichkeit, Opladen, 153–170

Bogner, A./Neubert, D. (2013b): Negotiated peace, denied justice? The case of West Nile (northern Uganda): Africa Spectrum, vol. 48, no. 3, 55–84

Bogner, A./Neubert, D. (2016): The complexity of actor-figurations in "conflict transformation" and "post-conflict" processes: Observations from northern Ghana and northern Uganda, in: Tonah, S./Anamzoya, A.S. (Eds.): Managing chieftaincy and ethnic conflicts in Ghana, Accra, 255–29

Bogner, A./Rosenthal, G. (2014): The "untold" stories of outsiders and their significance for the analysis of (post-) conflict figurations: Interviews with victims of collective violence in northern Uganda (West Nile): Forum Qualitative Sozialforschung/ Forum: Qualitative Social Research, vol. 15, no. 3, art. 4, http: //www.qualitative-research.net/index.php/fqs/article/view/2138

Bogner, A./Rosenthal G. (2017a): Rebels in northern Uganda after their return to civilian life. Between a strong we-image and experiences of isolation and discrimination. In: Canadian Journal of African Studies, 51 (2), 175–197. http: //dx.doi.org/10.1080/00083968.2017.1306451

Bogner, A./Rosenthal, G. (2017b): Biographies – Discourses – Figurations. Methodological considerations from the perspectives of social constructivism and figurational sociology. In: Rosenthal, G./Bogner, A. (Eds.): Biographies in the Global South. Frankfurt a. M.: Campus, 15–49

Bogner, A./Rosenthal, G. (2020): Child Soldiers in Context. Biographies, Familial and Collective Trajectories in Norther Uganda. Göttingen: University Press, Göttinger Series in Sociological Biographical Research. Free download: https: //doi.org/10.17875/gup2020-1325

Bogner, A./Rosenthal, G. (2022): Social-constructivist and figurational biographical research. In: Current Sociology, art. 001139212211325. Free download: DOI: https: //doi.org/10.1177/00113921221132511

Böhme, G. (1990): Lebensgestalt und Zeitgeschichte. In: Bios, 3 (2), 135–153

Bourdieu, P. (1986/1990): Die biographische Illusion. In: Bios, 1, 75–81

Bower, G.H. (1981): Mood and Memory. In: American Psychology, 36, 129–148

Brandhorst, R. (2015): Migration und transnationale Familien im sozialen Wandel Kubas. Wiesbaden: Springer

Brandhorst, R (2023): The migration motive and transnational engagement nexus. A case study of transnational families between Cuba and Germany, In: Journal of Ethnic and Migration Studies, 49: 7, 1803–1825, DOI: 10.1080/1369183X.2021.1878874

Breckner, R. (2007): Case-oriented comparative approaches: The biographical perspective as opportunity and challenge in migration research, in: Karin Schittenhelm (ed.): Concepts and methods in migration research, Conference Reader, 113–152, http: //sowiserv2.sowi.uni-due.de/cultural-capital/reader/Concepts-and-Methods.pdf

Breckner, R. (2010): Sozialtheorie des Bildes. Zur interpretativen Analyse von Bildern und Fotografien. Bielefeld: transcript. ISBN 978-3-8376-1

Breckner, R. (2021): Iconic mental spaces in social media: A methodological approach to visual biographies. In: Breckner, R./Liebhart, K. & Pohn-Lauggas, M. (Ed.), Visuelle Analysen aus sozialwissenschaftlichen Perspektiven. Oldenbourg: de Gruyter, 3–31

Breckner, R./Massari, M. (2019): Past, present and future of biographical research. A dialogue with Gabriele Rosenthal. IN: Rassegna Italiana Sociologia, 1, 155–184. DOI: 10.1423/93563

Breuer, S. (1988): Über die Peripetien der Zivilisation, in: Helmut König (ed.): Politische Psychologie heute, Leviathan Sonderheft 9, Opladen, 411–432

Breuer, S. (2006a [1986]): Sozialdisziplinierung, in: Stefan Breuer (ed.): Max Webers tragische Soziologie, Tübingen, 326–348

REFERENCES

Breuer, S. (2006b [1996]): Gesellschaft der Individuen, Gesellschaft der Organisationen: Norbert Elias und Max Weber im Vergleich, in: Stefan Breuer (ed.): Max Webers tragische Soziologie, Tübingen, 349–370

Brix, J. (n.d. = 2009): (Re-)Integrationsprozesse ehemaliger Kombattanten in Ugandas Yumbe Distrikt und der Kampf um die Friedensdividende, Master thesis, Universität Bayreuth, unpublished

Dausien, B. (1996): Biographie und Geschlecht: Zur biographischen Konstruktion sozialer Wirklichkeit in Frauenlebensgeschichten, Bremen.

Dausien, B. (2010): "Biographie" als Gegenstand und Perspektive einer interdisziplinären Geschlechterforschung: Rückblickende Gedanken, in: Kreutziger-Herr,A./Noeske, N./Rode-Breymann, S. Unseld, M. (Eds.): Gender Studies in der Musikwissenschaft – Quo Vadis?, Hildesheim, 107–116

Broder, H. (1993): Die Analität des Bösen. In: Hannah Arendt. Besuch in Deutschland. Nördlingen: Rotbuch, 7–22

Brose, H.-G./Hildenbrand, B. (1988a): Biographisierung von Erleben und Handeln. In: dies. (Hrsg.), 11–39

Brose, H.-G./Hildenbrand, B. (Hrsg.) (1988): Vom Ende des Individuums zur Individualität ohne Ende. Opladen: Leske & Budrich

Brubaker, R. (2004): Introduction, in: Rogers Brubaker (ed.): Ethnicity without groups, Cambridge/London, 1–6

Bruner, J. (1987): Life as Narrative. In: Social Research, 54 (19), 11–32

Bude, H. (1985): Der Sozialforscher als Narrationsanimateur. Kritische Anmerkungen zu einer erzähltheoretischen Fundierung der interpretativen Sozialforschung. In: KZfSS (37), 327–336

Bührmann, A. D./Schneider, W. (2008): Vom Diskurs zum Dispositiv: Eine Einführung in die Dispositivanalyse, Bielefeld

Bührmann, A. D./Ernst, S. (Eds.) (2010): Care or control of the self?: Norbert Elias, Michel Foucault, and the subject in the 21st Century, London

Chartier, R. (1989): Gesellschaftliche Figuration und Habitus: Norbert Elias und "Die höfische Gesellschaft", in: Roger Chartier (ed.): Die unvollendete Vergangenheit: Geschichte und die Macht der Weltauslegung, Berlin, 37–57

Chassein, B. Hippler, H.J. (1987): Reliabilität und Validität retrospektiver Daten. Befunde aus der kognitiven Psychologie. In: Friedrichs, J. (Hrsg.): Technik und sozialer Wandel. 23. Deutscher Soziologentag 1986, Beiträge der Sektions- und Ad-Hoc-Gruppen. Opladen: Westdeutscher Verlag, 453–456

Chodoff, P. (1963). Late Effects of the Concentration Camp Syndrome. Arch. General Psychiatry 8, 323–333

Chodoff, P. (1975): Psychiatric Aspects of the Nazi Persecution. In: American Handbook of Psychiatry. Vol. 6, New York: Basic Books, 932–946

Cohler, B.J. (1982): Personal Narrative and Life Course. In: Baltes, P.B. (Ed.): Life-Span Development and Behavior. New York: Academic Press, 205–241

Collins, A.M./Quillian, M.R. (1969): Retrieval time from semantic memory. In: Journal of Verbal Learning and Verbal Behavior, 8, 240–247

Cremerius, J. (1981): Die Konstruktion der biographischen Wirklichkeit im analytischen Prozeß. In: ders. (Hrsg.): Freiburger literaturpsychologische Gespräche, 1. Folge, Frankfurt a. M.: Lang, 15–38

Dieckhöner, R. (1989): Lebensgeschichten von Frauen nach der Invitro-Fertilisation. In: Rosenthal, G. (Hrsg.), 114–129

Doering, H./Müller, A. (1989): Lebensgeschichten von Lesben. In. Rosenthal, G. (Hrsg.), 234–257

Doyle, A.C. (1889/1975): The Sign of the Four. New York: Ballantine Books

Eckert, F. (2010): Kontinuität trotz Brüchen: Kriegerische Identität am Rande Ugandas im langen 20. Jahrhundert, Master thesis, Universität Bayreuth, unpublished

Ehrenfels, Chr. v. (1890): Über Gestaltqualitäten. In: Vierteljahrsschrift für wissenschaftliche Philosophie, XIV, 3, 249–292

Eissler, K. R. (1968): Weitere Bemerkungen zum Problem der KZ-Psychologie. In: Psyche 22, 452–463

Eissler, K.R. (1963/1984): Die Ermordung von wievielen seinen Kinder muß ein Mensch symptomfrei ertagen können, um eine normale Konstitution zu haben? In: Lohmann, H. M. (Hrsg.): Psychoanalyse und Nationalsozialismus. Frankfurt a.M.: Fischer, 159–209

Elias, N. (2002 [1969]): Die höfische Gesellschaft: Untersuchungen zur Soziologie des Königtums und der höfischen Aristokratie. (= Gesammelte Schriften, Band 2): Frankfurt a.M.

Elias, N. (2006): The court society (The collected works of Norbert Elias, vol. 2): Stephen Mennell (ed.): Dublin.

Elias, N. (2007): Involvement and detachment (The collected works of Norbert Elias, vol. 8): Stephen Quilley (ed.): Dublin

Elias, N. (2008): Towards a theory of established-outsider relations, in: Norbert Elias/John L. Scotson, The established and the outsiders (The collected works of Norbert Elias, vol. 4): Cas Wouters (ed.): Dublin, 1–36

Elias, N. (2009a): Figuration, in: Elias, N., Essays III (The collected works of Norbert Elias, vol. 16): Richard Kilminster/Stephen Mennell (Eds.): Dublin, 1–3

Elias, N. (2009b): The retreat of sociologists into the present. In: Elias, N., Essays III (The collected works of Norbert Elias, vol. 16): Richard Kilminster/Stephen Mennell (Eds.): Dublin, 107–126

Elias, N. (2010a): The society of individuals (The collected works of Norbert Elias, vol. 10): Robert van Krieken (Ed.): Dublin

Elias, N. (2010b): Mozart: The sociology of a Genius, in: Mozart and other essays on courtly art (The collected works of Norbert Elias, vol. 12): Eric Baker/Stephen Mennell (Eds.): Dublin, 56–179

Elias, N. (2011): The symbol theory (The collected works of Norbert Elias, vol. 13): Richard Kilminster (Ed.): Dublin

Elias, N. (2012a): What is sociology? (The collected works of Norbert Elias, vol. 5): G. Bogner/Katie Liston/Stephen Mennell (Eds.): Dublin

Elias, N. (2012b): On the process of civilisation: Sociogenetic and psychogenetic investigations (The collected works of Norbert Elias, vol. 3): Stephen Mennell/Eric Dunning/ Johan Goudsblom/Richard Kilminster (Eds.): Dublin

Elias, N. (2013): Studies on the Germans (The collected works of Norbert Elias, vol. 11): Stephen Mennell/Eric Dunning (Eds.): Dublin

Elias, N./Dunning, E. (1986): Quest for excitement: Sport and leisure in the civilizing process, Oxford

Elias, N./Scotson, J. L. (1965): The established and the outsiders, London

Elias, N./Scotson, J. L. (2008): The established and the outsiders (The collected works of Norbert Elias, vol. 4): Cas Wouters (ed.): Dublin

Embree, L. (1979): Theorien sozialer Relevanz: Aron Gurwitsch und Alfred Schütz. In: Sprondel, W./Grathoff, R. (Hrsg.): Alfred Schütz und die Idee des Alltags in den Sozialwissenschaften. Stuttgart: Enke, 65–77

Erikson, E.H. (1959/1973): Identität und Lebenszyklus, Frankfurt a.M.: Suhrkamp

Eulering, N./Milbradt, J. (1989): Lebensgeschichten von Homosexuellen. In: Rosenthal, G. (Hrsg.), 130–158

Fann, K.T. (1970): Peirce's Theory of Abduction. The Hague: Nijhoff

Fischer, W. (1978): Struktur und Funktion erzählter Lebensgeschichten. In: Kohli, M. (Hrsg.): Soziologie des Lebenslaufs. Darmstadt/Neuwied: Luchterhand, 311–336

Fischer, W. (1982): Time and Chronic Illness. A Study on Social Constitution of Temporality. Berkeley (Habilitationsschrift)

Fischer, W. (1982b): Alltagszeit und Lebenszeit in Lebensgeschichten von chronisch Kranken. In: Zeitschrift für Sozialisationsforschung und Erziehungssoziologie, 2, 5–19

Fischer, W. (1985): Prekäre Leiblichkeit und Alltagszeit. Kontingenz und Rekurrenz in der Zeiterfahrung chronisch Kranker. In: Fürstenberg, F./Mörth, J. (Hrsg.): Zeit als Strukturelement von Lebenswelt und Gesellschaft. Linz: Trauner, 237–257

Fischer, W. (1987): Affirmative und transformative Erfahrungsverarbeitung. In: Friedrichs, J. (Hrsg.): Technik und sozialer Wandel. 23. Deutscher Soziologentag 1986. Beiträge der Sektions- und Ad-Hoc-Gruppen. Opladen: Westdeutscher Verlag, 465–469

Fischer, W. (1989): Perspektiven der Lebenslaufforschung. In: Herlth, A./Strohmeier, K.P. (Hrsg.): Lebenslauf und Familienentwicklung. Opladen: Leske & Budrich, 279–294

Fischer, W./Kohli, M. (1987): Biographieforschung. In: Voges, W. (Hrsg.): Methoden der Biographie- und Lebenslaufforschung. Opladen: Leske & Budrich, 25–50

Fischer-Rosenthal, W. (1990a): Von der "biographischen Methode" zur Biographieforschung: Versuch einer Standortbestimmung. In: Alheit, P. u.a. (Hrsg.), 11–25

Fischer-Rosenthal, W. (1990b): Diesseits von Mikro und Makro. Phänomenologische Soziologie im Vorfeld einer forschungspolitischen Differenz, In: Österreichische Zeitschrift für Soziologie 15 (3), 21–34

Fischer-Rosenthal, W. (1991a): Zum Konzept der subjektiven Aneignung von Gesellschaft. In: Flick, U. u.a. (Hrsg.), 78–89

Fischer-Rosenthal, W. (1991b): Biographische Methoden in der Soziologie. In: Flick, U. u.a. (Hrsg.), 253–256

Fischer-Rosenthal, W. (1992): Überlebensgeschichte. Von Daniel, der doch kein Priester wurde, und von Micki, der kein Jude war, und von der Qual des Lebens. In: Psychosozial, 15 (1,2), 17–26

Fischer-Rosenthal, W. (1995). From "Identity" to "Biography". On the social construction of Biography and the question of social order in modern times. In: Kashti, Y. and F. Eros (Eds.) A Quest for Identity: Post war Jewish biographies.

Flick, U./Kardorff, E. v./Keupp, H./Rosenstiel, L.v./Wolff, St. (Hrsg.) (1991): Handbuch Qualitative Sozialforschung. München: Psychologie Verlags Union

Foucault, M. (1969): L'archéologie du savoir, Paris

Foucault, M. (1971): L'ordre du discours, Paris

Foucault, M. (1972): The archaeology of knowledge and the discourse on language, New York

Foucault, M. (1976): Mikrophysik der Macht: Über Strafjustiz, Psychiatrie und Medizin, Berlin

Foucault, M. (1977): Discipline and punish, transl. by A. Sheridan, New York

Foucault, M. (1978a): Dispositive der Macht: Über Sexualität, Wissen und Wahrheit, Berlin

Foucault, M. (1978b): The will to knowledge: The history of sexuality: An introduction, vol. 1, transl. by R. Hurley, New York

Foucault, M. (1980): Truth and power, in: M. Foucault, Power/Knowledge: Selected interviews and other writings, 1972–1977, Colin Gordon (ed. and transl.): New York, 109–133

Foucault, M. (2003): Das Spiel des Michel Foucault (Gespräch): in: Michel Foucault, Schriften in vier Bänden: Band III: 1976–1979, Daniel Defert/François Ewald (Eds.): Frankfurt a.M., 391–429

Freud, A. (1971): The infantile neurosis: Genetic and dynamic considerations. In: Psychoanalytic Study of the Child, 26, 79–90

Freud, S. (1899/1960): Über Deckerinnerungen. Gesammelte Werke, Frankfurt a.M.: Fischer, Bd. 1, 465 ff

Freud, S. (1901/1960): Zur Psychopathologie des Alltagslebens. Gesammelte Werke, Bd. 4

Freud, S. (1905/1960): Drei Abhandlungen zur Sexualtheorie. Gesammelte Werke, Bd. 5

Freud, S. (1910): Eine Kindheitserinnerung des Leonardo da Vinci, Gesammelte Werke, Bd. 8, 127 ff.

Freud, S. (1926/1960): Hemmung, Symptom und Angst. Gesammelte Werke, Bd. 14

Frisch, M. (1968): Das Lesen und der Bücherfreund. In: Ausgewählte Prosa. Frankfurt a.M., 9–11

Fuchs, W. (1983): Jugendliche Statuspassage oder individualisierte Jugendbiographie? In: Soziale Welt, 34, 341–371

Fuchs, W. (1984): Biographische Forschung. Opladen: Westdeutscher Verlag

Funkenstein, A. (1993): The Incomprehnsible Catastrophe. Memory and Narrative. In: The Narrative Studies of Lives, Vol. 1, Josselson, R./Lieblich, A. (Eds.), Newbury Park, Sage, 21–29

Glaser, B./Strauss, A. (1967): The Discovery of Grounded Theory. Chicago: Aldine

Goudsblom, J. (1979): Soziologie auf der Waagschale. Frankfurt a.M: Suhrkamp

Goffman, E. (1961): Asylums, New York: Anchor

REFERENCES

Goffman, E. (1967): Stigma. Frankfurt a.M.: Suhrkamp

Gordon, Th. (1977): Lehrer-Schüler-Konferenz. Hamburg: Hoffmann und Campe

Grathoff, R. (1985) (Hrsg.): Alfred Schütz – Aron Gurwitsch. Briefwechsel 1939–1959. München: Fink

Greenspan, H. (1992): Lives as Texts: Symptoms as Modes of Recounting in the Life Histories of Holocaust Survivors. In: Rosenwald, G./Ochberg, R., 145–164

Greenwald, H. (1958): The Call Girl. New York: Ballantine Books

Grote, Ch. (1987): Chronische Krankheit als biographisch relevante Krise? Fallstudie einer MS-Kranken. (Diplomarbeit) Universität Bielefeld, Fakultät für Soziologie.

Grote, Ch./Rosenthal, G. (1992): Frausein als Entlastungsargument. In: Tel Aviver Jahrbuch für Deutsche Geschichte, 289–318

Grubrich-Simitis, I. (1979): Extremtraumatisierung als kumulatives Trauma. In: Psyche, 33, 991–1023

Gurwitsch, A. (1966): Studies in Phenomenology and Psychology. Evanston IL: Northwestern University Press

Gurwitsch, A. (1929/1966): Phenomenology of Thematics and the Pure Ego. In: id., 175–286

Gurwitsch, A. (1943a/1966): Contribution to the phenomenological Theory of Perception. In: id, 332–349

Gurwitsch, A. (1943b/1966): William James' theory of the "transitive parts" of the stream of consciousness. In: id, 301–331

Gurwitsch, A. (1964/2010): The Field of Consciousness. The Collected works of Aron Gurwitsch. Vol. III. Heidelberg, London, New York: Springer

Habermas, J. (1988): Der philosophische Diskurs der Moderne: Zwölf Vorlesungen, Frankfurt a.m.

Halbwachs, M. (1985 [French: 1925]): Das Gedächtnis und seine sozialen Rahmenbedingungen, Frankfurt a.M.

Hahn, A. (1982): Zur Soziologie der Beichte und anderer Formen institutionalisierter Bekenntnisse: Selbstthematisierung und Zivilisationsprozeß. In: KZfSS, 34, 407–434

Hahn, A. (1988): Biographie und Lebenslauf. In: Brose, H-G./Hildenbrand, B. (Hrsg.), 91–106

Halbwachs, M. (1925/1985): Das Gedächtnis. Frankfurt a.M. : Suhrkamp

Hateley, B.J. (1985): Telling Your Story, Exploring Your Faith. St. Louis, Md.: CBP Press

Heinemeier, S. u.a. (1981): Arbeitslosigkeit und Biographie-Konstruktion: Bericht über ein laufendes Forschungsprojekt. In: Matthes, J. u.a. (Hrsg.), 169–189

Heinritz, Ch. (1988): BIOLIT. Literaturüberblick aus der Biographieforschung und der Oral History 1978–1988. Bios 1, Heft 1: 121–167; Heft 2: 103–138

Henningsen, J. (1971): "Jeder Mensch erfindet sich eine Geschichte". Max Frisch und die Autobiographie. In: Literatur in Wissenschaft und Unterricht, 4, 167–176

Hermanns, H. (1987): Narrative interviews. A new tool for sociological field research. In: Acta Universitatis Lodziensis, Folia Sociolgica 13, Approaches to the study of face-to-face interaction. University of Lodz, 43–56.

Hermanns, H. (1985): Methodologische Zugänge in der Biographieforschung. In: Franz, H-W. (Hrsg.): 22. Deutscher Soziologentag 1984. Opladen: Westdeutscher Verlag, 87–88

Hermanns, H. (1991): Narratives Interview. In: Flick, U. u.a. (Hrsg.), 182–185

Hermanns, H./Tkocz, C./Winkler, H. (1984): Berufsverlauf von Ingenieuren. Biographie-analytische Auswertungen narrativer Interviews. Frankfurt a.M./New York: Campus

Hildenbrand, B. (1999): Fallrekonstruktive Familienforschung, Wiesbaden: Springer

Hildenbrand, B./Jahn, W. (1988): "Gemeinsames Erzählen" und Prozesse der Wirklich-keitskonstruktion in familiengeschichtlichen Gesprächen. In: Zeitschrift für Soziolo-gie, 15, 203–217

Hinrichsen, H. (2020): Die Generation Oslo im Westjordanland. Historische Generatio-nen in prozesssoziologischer Perspektive. Göttinger Beiträge zur soziologischen Bio-graphieforschung. Göttingen: Universitätsverlag Göttingen. DOI: 10.17875/gup2020-1328

Hinrichsen, H. (2021): Generational Figuration and We-Group Formation in the Pales-tinian West Bank since the 1970s. In: Delmotte, F./Gornicka, B. (Ed.), Elias in Troubled Times. Basingstoke: Palgrave Macmillan, 277–293

Hinrichsen, H./Becker, J./Rosenthal, G. (2016): On the brittleness of the homogenizing we-discourse: Christians in Bethlehem and Ramallah, in: G. Rosenthal (2016b): 31–44

Hinrichsen, H./Becker, J. (2022). Changes in a transnational migrant society: Social figu-rations and everyday life in Jordan. In: Rosenthal, G., 239–281. https://univerlag.uni-goettingen.de/handle/3/isbn-978-3-86395-571-7

Hoffmann-Riem, Ch. (1980): Die Sozialforschung einer interpretativen Soziologie. In: KZfSS, 32 (2), 339–371

Hohn, H.-W./Windolf, P. (1988): Lebensstile als Selektionskriterien – Zur Funktion "bio-graphischer Signale" in der Rekrutierungspolitik von Arbeitsorganisationen. In: Bro-se, H.G./Hildenbrand, B. (Hrsg.), 179–209

Hopf, Ch. (1978): Die Pseudo-Exploration – Überlegungen zur Technik qualitativer Inter-views in der Sozialforschung. In: Zeitschrift für Soziologie, 7, 97–115

Hopf, Ch. (1991): Qualitative Interviews in der Sozialforschung. Ein Überblick. In: Flick, U. u.a. (Hrsg.), 177–181

Hoppe, K. (1971): The Aftermath of Nazi Persecution Reflected in Recent Psychiatric Liter-ature. In: Krystal, H./Niederland, W.D. (Eds.): Psychic Traumatization. Boston: Little, Brown and Company, 169–204

Husserl, E. (= CM): Cartesian Mediations. The Hague: Nijhoff, 1982

Husserl, E. (= EJ.): Experience and Judgement. Evanston, Illinois, Northwestern Univer-sity Press, 1997

Husserl, (= Ideas I): General Introduction to pure Phenomenology. The Hague: Nijhoff, 1982, (Collected Works I)

Husserl, E. (= LI II): The Shorter Logical Investigations. Second German edition of Lo-gische Untersuchungen. London: Routledge, 2001, https://antilogicalism.files.word-press.com/2017/07/logical-investigations.pdf

REFERENCES 267

Husserl, E. (= Time): The phenomenology of the conscious of internal time. Dordbrecht/ Boston/London: Kluwer Academic Publishers. 1991. https: //phil180s15.files.wordpress.com/2015/05/husserl-phenomenology-of-time-consciousness.pdf

Inhelder, B./Piaget, J. (1958): The growth of logical thinking from childhood to adolescence. An essay on the construction of formal operational structures. New York: Basic Book

Inowlocki, L. (1988): Ein schlagendes Argument. Geschichtliche Rechtfertigungen und biographische Konstruktionen von Jugendlichen in rechtsextremistischen Gruppen. In: Bios, 1 (2), 49–58

Inowlocki, L. (1992): Zum Mitgliedschaftsprozeß Jugendlicher in rechtsextremistischen Gruppen. In: Psychosozial, 15 (3), 54–65

Inowlocki, L. (2000): Sich in die Geschichte hineinreden. Zur Entstehung der Gruppenmitgliedschaft rechtsextremer Jugendlicher. Weinheim: Deutscher Studienverlag

James, W. (1905): The Principles of Psychology. New York.

Jaspers, K. (1923/1973): Allgemeine Psychopathologie. Berlin: Springer

Kallmeyer, W./Schütze, F. (1977): Zur Konstitution von Kommunikationsschemata. In: Wegner, D. (Hrsg.): Gesprächsanalyse. Hamburg: Buske, 159–274

Keller, R. (2005): Analysing discourse. An approach from the sociology of knowledge. In: Forum Qualitative Sozialforschung/Forum: Qualitative Social Research, 6(3), art. 32, http: //nbn-resolving.de/urn: nbn: de: 0114-fqs0503327

Keller, R. (2008): Michel Foucault. Konstanz: UVK

Keller, R. (2011): The sociology of knowledge approach to discourse (SKAD). In: Human Studies, 34(1), 43–65

Keller, R. (2012): Entering discourses. A new agenda for qualitative research and sociology of knowledge. In: Qualitative Sociology Review, 8 (2), 46–75

Keller, R. (2013): Doing discourse research. An introduction for social scientists. London: Sage

Kerz-Rühling, I. (1989): Die psychoanalytische Erzählung. Zum Problem der Objektivitität. In: Psyche, 4, 307–330

Kestenberg, J./Kestenberg, M. (1987): Child Killing and Child Rescuing. In: Neumann, G.G. (Ed.): Origins of Human Aggression. New York: Human Sciences Press, 139–154

Kestenberg, J. (1991): Kinder von Überlebenden und überlebende Kinder. In: Stoffels, H. (Hrsg.): Schicksale der Verfolgten. Berlin: Springer, 110–126

Kilminster, R. (2007): Norbert Elias: Post-philosophical sociology, London/New York

Klein, H. (1968): Problems in the psychotherapeutic treatment of Israeli survivors of the Holocaust. In: Krystal, H. (Ed.): Massive psychic trauma. New York: Int. Univ. Press

Klüger, R. (1992): weiter leben. Eine Jugend. Göttingen. Wallstein

Knaurs moderne Psychologie (1972): Hrsg. von Legewie, H./Ehlers, W. München/Zürich: Droemer Knaur

Knoblauch, H. (2007): Kultur, die soziale Konstruktion, das Fremde und das Andere, in: Jochen Dreher/Peter Stegmaier (Eds.): Zur Unüberwindbarkeit kultureller Differenz: Grundlagentheoretische Reflexionen, Bielefeld, 21–42

Köttig, M. (2004) Lebensgeschichten rechtsextrem orientierter Mädchen und junger Frauen – Biographische Verläufe im Kontext der Familien- und Gruppendynamik; Gießen: Psychosozial-Verlag

Köttig, M. (2005): Triangulation von Fallrekonstruktionen; In: Dausien, B./Lutz, H./Rosenthal, G./Völter, Bettina (Hrsg.): Biographieforschung im Diskurs. Theoretische und methodische Verknüpfungen: Opladen: VS Verlag, 65–83

Koffka, K. (1915): Zur Grundlegung der Wahrnehmungspsychologie. Eine Auseinandersetzung mit V. Benussi. In: Zeitschrift für Psychologie, LXXIII, 11–91

Koffka, K. (1922): Perception: An Introduction of the Gestalt Theory. In: The Psychological Bulletin. Vol. 19, 10, 531–585

Koffka, K. (1925): Psychologie. In: Dessoir, M. (Hrsg.): Lehrbuch der Psychologie. Berlin: Ullstein, 497–609

Koffka, K. (1935/1963): Principles of Gestalt Psychology. New York: Harbinger

Kohlberg, L. (1974): Zur kognitiven Entwicklung des Kindes. Frankfurt a.M.: Suhrkamp

Köhler, W. (1918): Nachweis einfacher Strukturfunktionen beim Schimpansen und beim Haushuhn. Berliner Abhandlungen

Köhler, W. (1947): Gestalt Psychology. New York

Köhler, W. (1969): The Task of Gestalt Psychology. Princeton: Princeton University Press

Kohli, M. (1981): Zur Theorie der biographischen Selbst- und Fremdwahrnehmung. In: Matthes, J. (Hrsg.): Lebenswelt und soziale Probleme. Verhandlungen des 20. Soziologentages. Frankfurt a.M.: Campus, 502–520

Kohli, M. (1983): Biographieforschung im deutschen Sprachbereich. ASI-News 6, Beiheft "Qualitative Ansätze in der Forschungspraxis", 5–32

Kohli, M. (1985): Die Institutionalisierung des Lebenslaufs. In: KZfSS, 37, 1–27

Kohli, M. (1988): Normalbiographie und Individualität. Zur institutionellen Dynamik des gegenwärtigen Lebenslaufsregimes. In: Brose, H.G./Hildenbrand, B. (Hrsg.), 33–53

Kohli, M./Robert, G. (Hrsg.) (1984): Biographie und soziale Wirklichkeit. Stuttgart: Metzler

Kraimer, K. (1983): Anmerkungen zu einem "erzählgenerierenden" Instrument der kommunikativen Sozialforschung. In: Garz, D./Kraimer, K. (Hrsg.): Brauchen wir andere Forschungsmethoden? Frankfurt, 86–111

Kris, E. (1956): The Recovery of Childhood Memories in Psychoanalysis. In: The Psychoanalytical Study of the Child, 11, 54–88

Labov, William/Waletzky, Joshua (1967): Narrative analysis. Oral versions of personal experiences. In: Helms, June (ed.): Essays on the verbal and visual arts. Seattle, WA: University of Washington Press, 12–44

Landweer, H. (1997): Mikrophysik der Scham? Elias und Foucault im Vergleich, in: G. Klein/Katharina Liebsch (Eds.): Zivilisierung des weiblichen Ich, Frankfurt a.M., 365–399

Leary, K. R./Arbor, A. (1989): Psychoanalytical process and narrative process: A crititcal consideration of Schafer's "narrational project". In: Int. Rev. Psycho-Anal., 16, 179, 179–190

Leitner, H. (o.J.) Text oder Leben? In: Biographie oder Lebenslauf? Studienbrief der Universität Hagen, Kurseinheit 2, Fachbereich Erziehungs- und Sozialwissenschaften

REFERENCES 269

Lemke, T. (2001): Max Weber, Norbert Elias und Michel Foucault über Macht und Subjektivierung, Berliner Journal für Soziologie, vol. 11, (1), 77–95

Leopold, M. (2005): Inside West Nile: Violence, history and representation on an African frontier, Oxford

Lewin, K. (1922): Das Problem der Willensmessung und das Grundgesetz der Assoziation. In: Psychologische Forschung. Berlin: Springer

Lewin, K. (1927/1992): Law and experiment in psychology. In: Science in Context, Vol. 5 (2), 385–416

Lewin, K. (1930/1931). The conflict between Aristotelian and Galileian modes of thoughts in contemporary psychology. In: Journal of General Psychology, 141–177. https://philarchive.org/archive/KURTCB-4

Linton, M. (1979): I remember it well. In: Psychology Today, 13, 81–86

Lisch, R./Kriz, J. (1978): Grundlagen und Modelle der Inhaltsanalyse. Reinbeck: rororo

Lorenzer, A. (1979): Die Analyse der subjektiven Struktur von Lebensläufen und das gesellschaftlich Objektive. In: Baacke, D./Schulze, Th. (Hrsg.): Aus Geschichten lernen. München: Juventa, 129–145

Mader, W. (1989): Autobiographie und Bildung – Zur Theorie und Praxis der "Guided Autobiography". In: Hoerning, E.M./Tietgens, H. (Hrsg.): Erwachsenenbildung: Interaktion mit der Wirklichkeit. Bad Heilbrunn, 145–154

Mannheim, K. (1952a [1928]): The problem of generations, in: Karl Mannheim, Essays on the sociology of knowledge, Paul Kecskemeti (ed.): London, 276–322

Mannheim, K. (1952b [1929]): "Competition" as a cultural phenomenon, in: Karl Mannheim, Essays on the sociology of knowledge, Paul Kecskemeti (ed.): London, 191–229

Mannheim, K: (1980): Eine soziologische Theorie der Kultur und ihrer Erkennbarkeit (Konjunktives und kommunikatives Denken): in: Karl Mannheim, Strukturen des Denkens, David Kettler/Volker Meja/Nico Stehr (Eds.): Frankfurt, 155–322

Matthes, J. (1985): Zur transkulturellen Relativität erzählanalytischer Verfahren in der empirischen Sozialforschung. In: KZfSS, 37, 310–326

Matthes, J./Pfeifenberger, A./Stosberg, M. (1981) (Hrsg.): Biographie in handlungswissenschaftlicher Perspektive. Nürnberg: Sozialwissenschaftliches Forschungszentrum

Mayering, Ph. (1983): Qualitative Inhaltsanalyse. Weinheim/Basel: Beltz

McAdams, D./Ochberg, R. (1983): Psychobiography and Life Narratives. Duke University Press.

Mead, G. H. (1934): Mind, Self and Society. Chicago: University Press

Merleau-Ponty, M. (1942/1976): Die Struktur des Verhaltens. Berlin

Merleau-Ponty, M. (1969): Signes. Paris

Michel, S./Schiebel, M. (1989): Lebensgeschichten von rechtsextremen Jugendlichen. In: Rosenthal, G. (Hrsg.), 212–233

Mischnick, R./Bauer, I. (2009): Yumbe peace process: 2009 Report, Kampala

Mitscherlich, M. (1987): Erinnerungsarbeit. Frankfurt a.M.: Fischer

Moore, Y. (1994): Narrative Biographical Analysis. Life stories of second generation to Holocaust survivors past and present. Unv. Magister Arbeit, Ben Gurion University, Beer Sheva, Israel (in Englisch)

Morgenthaler, F. (1978): Technik. Zur Dialektik der psychoanalytischen Praxis. Frankfurt a.M.

Müller, G.E. (1917): Zur Analyse der Gedächtnisfähigkeit und des Vorstellungsverlaufs. In: Deutsche Zeitschrift für Psychologie, II Erg. Bd. 9.

Neugarten, B. (1973): Personality change in late life: A developmental perspective. In: Eisdorfer, C./Lawton, M.P. (Eds.): The psychology of adult development and aging. Washington, D.C.: American Psychological Association

Neugarten, B. (1979): Time, age and the life-cycle. In: American Journal of Psychiatry, 136, 887–894

Niederland, W.G. (1980): Folgen der Verfolgung: Das Überlebenden-Syndrom. Frankfurt a.M.: Edition Suhrkamp

Niethammer, L. (1990): Kommentar zu Pierre Bourdieu: Die biographische Illusion. In: Bios, 1, 91–93

Nittel, D. (1991): Report: Biographieforschung. Hrsg. von der Pädagogischen Arbeitsstelle des Deutschen Volkshochschul-Verbandes e.V., Reinheim: Lokay

Ochberg, R. (1994): Life Stories and Storied Lives. In: The Narrative Studies of Lives, Vol. 2, Josselson, R./Lieblich, A. (Eds.), Newbury Park, Sage, 113–144

Oevermann, U. (1983): Zur Sache: Die Bedeutung von Adornos methodologischem Selbstverständnis für die Begruendung einer materialen soziologischen Strukturanalyse. In: Friedeburg, L.v./Habermas, J. (Hrsg.): Adorno-Konferenz 1983. Frankfurt a.M.: Suhrkamp, 234–289

Oevermann, U. (1988): Eine exemplarische Fallrekonstruktion zum Typus versozialwissenschaftlichter Identitätsformation. In: Brose, H.G./Hildenbrand, B. (Hrsg.), 243–286

Oevermann, U. u.a. (1979): Die Methodologie einer "objektiven Hermeneutik" und ihre allgemeine forschungslogische Bedeutung in den Sozialwissenschaften. In: Soeffner, H.G. (Hrsg.): Interpretative Verfahren in den Sozial- und Textwissenschaften. Stuttgart: Metzler, 352–434

Oevermann, U. u.a. (1980): Zur Logik der Interpretation von Interviewtexten. In: Heinze, Th./Klusemann, H.W./Soeffner, H.-G. (Hrsg.) Interpretationen einer Bildungsgeschichte. Bensheim: Päd extra, 15–69

Oevermann, U./Schuster, L./Simm, A. (1985): Zum Problem der Perseveranz in Delikttyp und modus operandi. Wiesbaden: BKA-Forschungsreihe

Oevermann, U. et al. (1987): Structures of meaning and objective hermeneutics. In: Meja, Volker/Misgeld, Dieter/Stehr, Nico (eds.): Modern German sociology. New York: Columbia University Press, 436–447.

Ohly, H.P./Legnaro, A. (1987): Analyse von Lebensverläufen. Biographieforschung. Kohortenanalyse, Life-Event-Daten. Bibliographie 1984–1986. Bonn: Informationszentrum Sozialwissenschaften

Ohly, H.P: (1984): Analyse von Lebensverläufen. Biographieforschung. Kohortenanalyse, Life-Event-Daten. Bibliographie 1981–1983. Bonn: Informationszentrum Sozialwissenschaften.

Ornstein, A. (1985): Survival and recovery. In: Psychoanalytical Inquiry, 14, Vol. 5, 99–130

REFERENCES   271

Osterland, M. (1983): Die Mythologisierung des Lebenslaufs. Zur Problematik des Erinnerns. In: Baethge, M./Essbach, W. (Hrsg.): Soziologie: Entdeckung im Alltäglichen. Frankfurt a.m./New York: Campus

Paris, S./Lindauer, B. (1977): Constructive aspects of children's comprehension and memory. In: Kail, R.V./Hagen, J.W. (Eds.): Perspectives on the development of memory and cognition. Hillsdale, N.J.: Erlbaum, 35–60

Paul, I.H. (1967): The Concept of Schema in Memory Theory. In: Holt, R. (Ed.): Motives and Thought. Psychological Issues, V (2–3), 218–258

Paul, S. (1987): Die Entwicklung der biographischen Methode in der Soziologie. In: Jüttemann, G./Thomae, H. (Hrsg.): Biographie und Psychologie. Berlin: Springer, 26–36

Peirce, Ch.S. (1933/1980): Collected Papers of Charles Sanders Peirce. Edited by Charles Hartsphorne and Paul Weiss. Cambridge: Belknap press.

Peters, F. (2008): Das Labor oder der bittere Geschmack des Friedens: Grundlegend verschiedene Referenzrahmen zum Frieden in West Nil – Uganda, Master thesis, Universität Bayreuth, unpublished

Piaget, J. (1955/1974): Die Bildung des Zeitbegriffs beim Kinde. Frankfurt a.M.: Suhrkamp

Piaget, J. (1968/1973): Der Strukturalismus. Olten: Walter

Piaget, J. (1973): Das Erwachen der Intelligenz beim Kinde. Klett: Stuttgart

Piaget, J. (1977): The development of thought: Equilibration of cognitive structures. New York: Viking Press.

Piaget, J./Inhelder, B. (1973): Memory and Intelligence. New York: Basic Books

Piaget. J. (1933/1954): The Construction of Reality in the Child. New York: Basic Books

Plügge, H. (1967): Der Mensch und sein Leib. Tübingen: Niemeyer

Pohn-Weidinger, M. ((2014): Heroisierte Opfer: Bearbeitungs- und Handlungsstrukturen von "Trümmerfrauen" in Wien, Wiesbaden.

Pohn-Lauggas, M. (2016): In Worten erinnern, mit Bildern sprechen. Zum Unterschied zwischen visuellen und mündlichen Erinnerungspraktiken. In: Sonderheft Materiale Visuelle Soziologie, hrsg. v. Breckner, R. und Raab, J., Zeitschrift für Qualitative Forschung (ZQF), Jg. 17 (1+2), 59–80

Pohn-Lauggas, M. (2017): Biography and Discourse: A biography and discourse analysis combining case study on women's involvement in National Socialism. In: Current Sociology, Vol. 65 (7), 1094–1111. http://dx.doi.org/10.1177/0011392116660856.

Pohn-Lauggas, M. (2021): Memory in the shadow of a family history of resistance: A case study of the significance of collective memories for intergenerational memory in Austrian families, in: Memory Studies Vol. 14(2), 180–196, https://doi.org/10.1177/1750698019849698.

Refugee Law Project (2004): Negotiating peace: Resolution of conflicts in Uganda's West Nile region, Refugee Law Project Working Paper No. 12, Kampala, www.refugeelawproject.org/working_papers/RLP.WP12.pdf (4 May 2011)

Reiff, R./Scheerer, M. (1959): Memory and Hypnotic Age Regression. New York: International University Press

Resnick, S. (1975): Neue Formen der Psycho-Therapie: Gestalt-Therapie. In: Psychologie heute. 2 (2), 66–73

Rice, Andrew (2009): The teeth may smile but the heart does not forget: Murder and memory in Uganda, New York.

Riegel, K. (1977): The dialectics of time. In: Datan, N./Reese, H. (Eds.): Life-span developmental psychology: Dialectic perspectives on experimental research. New York: Academic Press.

Riemann, G. (1984): "Na wenigstens bereitete sich da wieder was in meiner Krankheit vor". Zum Umgang psychiatrischer Patienten mit übermächtigen Theorien, die ihr eigenes Selbst betreffen. In: Kohli, M./Robert, G. (Hrsg.), 118–141

Riemann, G. (1985): Zu einigen auffälligen und argumentativen Sequenzen in biographisch-narrativen Interviews. In: Franz, H.-W. (Hrsg.): 22. Deutscher Soziologentag 1984. Beiträge der Sektions- und Ad-hoc-Gruppen. Opladen: Westdeutscher Verlag, 381–383

Riemann, G. (1986): Einige Anmerkungen dazu, wie und unter welchen Bedingungen das Argumentationsschema in biographisch-narrativen Interviews dominant werden kann. In: Soeffner, H.G. (Hrsg.) (1986): Sozialstruktur und soziale Typik. Frankfurt a.M.: Campus, 112–157

Riemann, G. (1987): Das Fremdwerden der eigenen Biographie. München: Fink

Ruoff, M. (2009): Foucault-Lexikon: Entwicklung – Kernbegriffe – Zusammenhänge, 2nd edition, Paderborn

Rießbeck, K. (1988): Extracorporale Befruchtung – Die Rettung eines weiblichen Lebensentwurfes? Eine Fallrekonstruktion. Diplomarbeit im Fach Psychologie. Friedrich-Alexander-Universität Erlangen-Nürnberg

Rogers, C. R. (1951): Client-centered Therapy. Boston

Rosenfield, I. (1988): The Invention of Memory. New York: Basic Books

Rosenthal, G. (Hrsg.) (1986): Die Hitlerjugend-Generation. Essen: Blaue Eule

Rosenthal, G. (1987): "Wenn alles in Scherben fällt..." Von Leben und Sinnwelt der Kriegsgeneration. Opladen: Leske & Budrich

Rosenthal, G. (1988): Leben mit der soldatischen Vergangenheit in zwei Weltkriegen. Ein Mann blendet seine Kriegserlebnisse aus. In: Bios, 1 (2), 27–38

Rosenthal, G. (Hrsg.) (1989): Wie erzählen Menschen ihre Lebensgeschichte? Forschungsbericht des Lehrprojekts: "Biographie". Universität Bielefeld, Fakultät für Soziologie

Rosenthal, G. (1989a): Leben mit der NS-Vergangenheit heute. Zur Reparatur einer fragwürdigen Vergangenheit im bundesrepublikanischen Alltag. In: Vorgänge, (3), 87–101

Rosenthal, G. (Hrsg.) (1990): "Als der Krieg kam, hatte ich mit Hitler nichts mehr zu tun". Zur Gegenwärtigkeit des "Dritten Reiches" in erzählten Lebensgeschichten. Opladen: Leske & Budrich

Rosenthal, G. (1990a): Die Auswertung. Hermeneutische Rekonstruktion erzählter Lebensgeschichten. In: dies. (Hrsg.), 246–251

Rosenthal, G. (1990b): Oskar Vogel: Teilnehmer des Ersten und Zweiten Weltkrieges. In: dies. (Hrsg.), 142–163

Rosenthal, G. (1990c): Zweiter Weltkrieg und Nationalsozialismus: Zwei Themen ohne Zusammenhang? In: dies. (Hrsg.), 223–240

REFERENCES 273

Rosenthal, G. (1991/2019): German War Memories. Narrability and the Biographical and Social Functions of Remembering. In: Oral History, 19 (2), 34–41, New edition 2019. In: Oral History Journal @50. The voice of history 1969 – 2019. https://www.jstor.org/stable/40179226

Rosenthal, G. (1992): Antisemitismus im lebensgeschichtlichen Kontext. Soziale Prozesse der Dehumanisierung und Schuldzuweisung. In: ÖZG, Österreichische Zeitung für Geschichtswissenschaften, 3 (4) 449–479

Rosenthal, G. (1993): Erzählbarkeit, biographische Notwendigkeit und soziale Funktion von Kriegserzählungen. Zur Frage: Was wird gerne und leicht erzählt. In: Hartewig, K. (Hrsg.): Der lange Schatten. Widerspruchsvolle Erinnerungen an den Zweiten Weltkrieg und die Nachkriegszeit aus der Mitte Europas. Bios, Sonderheft, 5–24

Rosenthal, G. (1993a): Die erzählte Lebensgeschichte: eine zuverlässige historische Quelle?. In: Weber, W. (Hrsg.): Spurensuche. Neue Methoden in der Geschichtswissenschaft. Regensburg: Roderer, 8–17

Rosenthal, G. (1993b): Reconstruction of life stories: Principles of selection in generating stories for narrative biographical interviews, The Narrative Study of Lives, vol. 1, no. 1, 59–91.

Rosenthal, G. (1994): Die erzählte Lebensgeschichte als historisch-soziale Realität. Methodologische Implikationen für die Analyse biographischer Texte. In: Berliner Geschichtswerkstatt. Alltagskultur, Subjektivität und Geschichte. Münster: Westfälisches Dampfboot, 125–138

Rosenthal, G. (1995): Erlebte und erzählte Lebensgeschichte: Gestalt und Struktur biographischer Selbstbeschreibungen, Frankfurt a.M.

Rosenthal, G. (1995a): Zerstörtes Leben – Fragmentierte Lebensgeschichten von Überlebenden der Shoah. In: Fischer-Rosenthal, W./Alheit, P. Hoerning, E. (Ed.): Biographien in Deutschland. Opladen: Westdeutscher Verlag

Rosenthal, G. (Ed.) (1998/2010): The Holocaust in Three Generations. Families of Victims and Perpetrators of the Nazi-Regime. London: Cassell. New edition 2010: Opladen: Barbara Budrich

Rosenthal, G. (1998/2010a): Traumatic family past. In: Rosenthal, chapter 4.

Rosenthal, G. (1999): Sexuelle Gewalt in Kriegs- und Verfolgungszeiten. In: Medica mondiale/Fröse, M./Volpp-Teuscher, I. (Hrsg.): Krieg, Geschlecht und Traumatisierung. Frankfurt: Iko-Verlag, 25–56

Rosenthal, G. (2001): Transgenerationale Folgen von Verfolgung und Täterschaft. In: Streeck-Fischer, A./Sachsse, U./Özkan, I. (Hrsg.): Körper Seele Trauma. Biologie, Klinik und Praxis. Göttingen: Vandenhoeck & Ruprecht, 174–206

Rosenthal, G. (2002): Veiling and Denying the Past. The Dialogue in Families of Holocaust Survivors and Families of Nazi Perpetrators. In: History of the Family. An International Quarterly. Special Issue: Family History – Life Story, 7, 225–238

Rosenthal, G. (2003): The Healing Effects of Storytelling. On the Conditions of Curative Storytelling in the Context of Research and Counseling. In: Qualitative Inquiry, 9 (6), 915–933

Rosenthal, G. (2004): Biographical research, in: Seale, C./Gobo,G./Gubrium, J.F./Silverman, D. (Eds.): Qualitative research practice, London, 48–64

Rosenthal, G. (2006): The narrated life story: On the interrelation between experience, memory and narration, in: Kate Milnes/Christine Horrocks/Nancy Kelly/Brian Roberts/David Robinson (Eds.): Narrative, memory and knowledge: Representations, aesthetics and contexts, Huddersfield, 1–16

Rosenthal, G. (2012): A plea for a more interpretative, more empirical and more historical sociology, in: Devorah Kalekin-Fishman/Ann B. Denis (Eds.): Tradition and renewal: The shape of sociology for the twenty-first century, London, 202–217

Rosenthal, G. (2016a): The social construction of individual and collective memory, In: Sebald, G./Wagle. J. (Eds.): Theorizing social memories: Concepts, temporality, functions, London, 32–55

Rosenthal, G. (Ed.) (2016b): Established and Outsiders at the Same Time. Self-Images and We-Images of Palestinians in the West Bank and in Israel. Göttingen: Göttingen University Press, Göttingen Series in Social and Cultural Anthropology. Free download: https://univerlag.uni-goettingen.de/handle/3/isbn-978-3-86395-286-0.

Rosenthal, G. (2016c): We-images and collective memories in the West-Bank. In: Rosenthal, G. (2016b), 17–30

Rosenthal, G. (2017): História de vida narrada e história de vida vivenciada: Forma e estrutura de descrições autobiográficas. (Erlebte und erzählte Lebensgeschichte: Gestalt und Struktur biographischer Selbstbeschreibungen). Porto Alegre: ediPUCRS

Rosenthal, G. (2018): Interpretative Social Research. Göttingen: Göttingen University Press. (in German 2015). Free download: https://doi.org/10.17875/gup2018-1103

Rosenthal, G. (Ed.) (2022): Transnational biographies: Changing we-images, belongings and power balances of migrants and refugees. Göttingen: Göttingen University Press, Göttingen Series in Sociological Biographical Research. Free download: DOI: 10.17875/gup2022-2187

Rosenthal, G./Bar-On, D. (1992): A biographical case study of a victimizer's daughter. In: Journal of Narrative and Life History, 2 (2) 105–127

Rosenthal, G./Dasberg, M./Moore, Y. (1998/2010): The collective trauma of the Lodz Ghetto: the Goldstern family. In: Rosenthal, G., chapter 6

Rosenthal, G./Völter, B./Gilad, N. (1998/2010): A love-hate relationship with Germany: The Arad family. In: Rosenthal, G., chapter 11.

Rosenthal, G./Bogner, A. (Eds.) (2009): Ethnicity, belonging and biography: Ethnographical and biographical perspectives, Münster.

Rosenthal, G./Bogner, A. (Eds.) (2017): Biographies in the Global South. Life Stories Embedded in Figurations and Discourses. Frankfurt a. M.: Campus.

Rosenthal, G., Bahl, E., & Worm, A. (2017). Illegalized migration courses from the perspective of biographical research and figurational sociology: The land border between Spain and Morocco. In Rosenthal, G./Bogner, A., 103–159

Rosenthal, G. /Albaba, A./Sangalli Cé, L. (2022): Migrants from Mauritania: On the existence of slavery today and the unequal power changes of the Bidhan, the Soudan and the Haratin. In: Rosenthal, G. (Ed.): Transnational Biographies. Göttingen Series of Biographical Research. Göttingen: Göttingen University Press, 81–114

Rosenwald, G./Ochberg, R. (1992) (Eds.): Storied Lives. New Haven, London: Yale University Press

Röttgers, K. (1988): Die Erzählbarkeit des Lebens. In: Bios, 1 (1), 5–19

Rubin, E. (1921): Visuell wahrgenommene Figuren. Kobenhavn: Gyldendalske Boghandel

Rubinstein, B.B. (1965): Psychoanalytical Theory and the Mind-Body Problem. In: Greenfield, N.S./Lewis, W.C. (Eds.): Psychoanalysis and Current Biological Thought. Madison: University of Wisconsin Press, 35–56

Ruoff, M. (2009): Foucault-Lexikon: Entwicklung – Kernbegriffe – Zusammenhänge, 2nd edition, Paderborn.

Ruokonen-Engler, M.-K./Siouti, I. (2016): Biographical Entanglements, Self-reflexivity and Transnational Knowledge Production. In: Qualitative Inquiry, 22 (7) 745–752

Rush, G. (1987): Erkenntnis, Wissenschaft, Geschichte. Von einem konstruktivistischen Standpunkt. Frankfurt a.M.

Sangalli Cé, L. (in press): Sudanese Migrants in Germany and Jordan: Changing of Belongings in the Context of Family and Life History. Göttingen: Göttingen University Press, Göttingen Series in Sociological Biographical Research

Sarasin, Philipp (2010): Michel Foucault zur Einführung, 4th edition, Hamburg

Schäfer, M. (2021): Polizist*in werden – Polizist*in sein. Strukturen und Widersprüche polizeilicher Arbeit. Göttinger Beitrag zur soziologischen Biographieforschung. Göttingen: Universitätsverlag Göttingen. DOI: 10.17875/gup2021-1579

Schäfer, T./Völter, B. (2005): Subjekt-Positionen: Michel Foucault und die Biographieforschung, in: Bettina Völter/Bettina Dausien/Helma Lutz/G. Rosenthal (Eds.): Biographieforschung im Diskurs, Wiesbaden: VS-Verlag, 161–188

Schafer, R. (1983): The Analytic Attitude. New York: Basic Books

Schibilsky, M. (1989a): Trauerwege. Beratung für helfende Berufe. Düsseldorf: Patmos

Schibilsky, M. (1989b): Biographische Homiletik. In: Bibel und Liturgie. Themenheft 3

Schiebel, M. (1991): Rechtsextreme Deutungsmuster: Genese und Wandlung in Biographiekonstruktionen. Fallstudie eines ehemals rechtsextremen Jugendlichen. Diplomarbeit. Universität Bielefeld, Fakultät für Soziologie

Schiebel, M. (1992): Biographische Selbstdarstellungen rechtsextremer und ehemals rechtsextremer Jugendlicher. In: Psychosozial, 15 (3), 66–77

Schmidt, S. J. (1991): Gedächtnis – Erzählen – Identität. In: Assmann, A./Harth, D. (Hrsg.): Mnemosyne. Formen und Funktionen der kulturellen Erinnerung. Frankfurt a.M.: Fischer, 378–397

Schütz, A. (1932/1974): Der sinnhafte Aufbau der sozialen Welt. Frankfurt a.M.: Suhrkamp; published in English 1967: "The Phenomenology of the Social World". Evanston, IL: Northwestern University Press.

Schütz, Alfred (1944): The stranger: An essay in social psychology, American Journal of Sociology, vol. 49, no. 6, 499–507

Schütz, A. (1945/1962): Collected Papers I. The Problem of Social Reality. The Hague: Nijhoff

Schütz A. (1966): Collected Papers III: Studies in Phenomenological Philosophy. The Hague: Nijhoff

Schütz, A. (1970): Reflections on the Problem of Relevance. New Haven: Yale University Press

Schütz, A./Luckmann, Th. (1979): Strukturen der Lebenswelt. Frankfurt a.M. : Suhrkamp; published in English 1973: The structures of the live-world. Evanston IL: Northwestern University Press

Schütze, F. (1976a): Zur Hervorlockung und Analyse von Erzählungen thematisch relevanter Geschichten im Rahmen soziologischer Feldforschung. In: Arbeitsgruppe Bielefelder Soziologen (Hrsg.): Kommunikative Sozialforschung. München: Fink, 159–260

Schütze, F. (1976b): Zur linguistischen und soziologischen Analyse von Erzählungen. In: Internationales Jahrbuch für Wissens- und Religionssoziologie, Bd. 10. Opladen: Westdeutscher Verlag, 7–41

Schütze, F. (1977): Die Technik des narrativen Interviews in Interaktionsfeldstudien. Arbeitsberichte und Forschungsmaterialien Nr. 1 der Universität Bielefeld, Fakultät für Soziologie

Schütze, F. (1981): Prozeßstrukturen des Lebenslaufs. In: Matthes, J. u.a. (Hrsg.), 67–156

Schütze, F. (1982): Narrative Repräsentation kollektiver Schicksalsbetroffenheit. In: Lämmert, E. (Hrsg.): Erzählforschung. Ein Symposion. Stuttgart: Metzler, 568–590

Schütze, F. (1983): Biographieforschung und narratives Interview. In: Neue Praxis, 3, 283–294

Schütze, F. (1984): Kognitive Figuren des autobiographischen Stegreiferzählens. In: Kohli, M. Robert, G. (Hrsg.), 78–117

Schütze, F. (1987): Das narrative Interview in Interaktionsfeldstudien I. Studienbrief der FernUniversität Hagen. Kurseinheit 1. Fachbereich Erziehungs-, Sozial- und Geisteswissenschaften

Schütze, F. (1987b): Symbolischer Interaktionismus. In: Sociolinguistics. 1, Berlin/New York: de Gruyter

Schütze, F. (1989): Kollektive Verlaufskurve oder kollektiver Wandlungsprozeß. In: Bios, 2 (1), 31–110

Schütze, F. (1992): Pressure and Guilt. The Experience of a Young German Soldier in World War II and its Biographical Implications. In: International Sociology, 7, (2 u. 3), 187–208; 347–367

Schütze, Fritz (2007a): Biography analysis on the empirical base of autobiographical narratives: How to analyse autobiographical narrative interviews, Part I, in: INVITE – Biographical counselling in rehabilitative vocational training: Further education curriculum 1, Module B.2.1., http: //www.uni-magdeburg.de/zsm/projekt/biographical/1/B2.1.pdf (19 January 2017).

Schütze, Fritz (2007b): Biography analysis on the empirical base of autobiographical narratives: How to analyse autobiographical narrative interviews, Part II, in: INVITE-Biographical counselling in rehabilitative vocational training: Further education curriculum, Module B.2.2., http://www.uni-magdeburg.de/zsm/projekt/biographical/1/B2.2.pdf (1 February 2017).

REFERENCES

Schelling, W. A. (1985): Lebensgeschichte und Dialog in der Psychotherapie. Göttingen: Vandenhoeck & Ruprecht

Schuler, H./Stehle, W. (Hrsg.) (1986): Biographische Fragebogen als Methode der Personalauswahl. Stuttgart

Schwäbisch, L./Siems, M. (1974): Anleitung zum sozialen Lernen für Paare, Gruppen und Erzieher. Hamburg: rororo

Sebok, Th./Umiker-Sebeok, J. (1983): "You Know My Method": A Juxtaposition of Charles S. Peirce and Sherlock Holmes. In: Evo, U./Sebeok, Th. (Ed.): The Sign of Three: Dupin, Holmes, Peirce. Bloomington: Indiana University Press, 11–54

Smith, D. (2001): Norbert Elias and modern social theory. London.

Snyder, M./White, Ph. (1982): Moods and Memories: Elation, Depression, and the Rembering of the Events of one's Life. In: Journal of Personality, 50, 149–167

Soeffner, H.-G. (1982): Statt einer Einleitung: Prämissen einer sozialwissenschaftlichen Hermeneutik. In: ders. (Hrsg.): Beiträge zu einer empirischen Sprachsoziologie. Tübingen: Narr, 9–48

Spence, D. P. (1982): Narrative Truth and Historical Truth. Ney York: Norton

Spies, T. (2009): Diskurs, Subjekt und Handlungsmacht: Zur Verknüpfung von Diskurs und Biografieforschung mithilfe des Konzepts der Artikulation, Forum Qualitative Sozialforschung/Forum: Qualitative Social Research, vol. 10, no. 2, Art. 36, http://nbn resolving. de/urn: nbn: de: 0114-fqs0902369 (11

Steinbach, L. (1980/1985): Lebenslauf, Sozialisation und "erinnerte Geschichte". In: Niethammer, L. (Hrsg.): Lebenserfahrung und kollektives Gedächtnis. Frankfurt a.M.: Suhrkamp, 393–435

Straub, J. (1991): Identitätstheorie im Übergang? In: Sozialwissenschaftliche Literatur Rundschau.

Straus, E. (1930/1978): Geschehnis und Erlebnis. Berlin/Heidelberg/New York: Springer

Strube, G./Weinert, F.E. (1987): Autobiographisches Gedächtnis: Mentale Repräsentation der individuellen Biographie. In: Jüttemann, G./Thomae, H. (Hrsg.): Biographie und Psychologie. Berlin: Springer, 151–167

Taboda Gómez, V. (2021): Interviews with Women from Indigenous Communities in Paraguay. In: Bahl, E./Rosenthal, G. (Ed.), 89–120. https://publications.goettingen-research-online.de/bitstream/2/96783/1/cemig-04-bahl-rosenthal.pdf

Thomas, W./Znaniecki (1918–1920/1965): Methodologische Vorbemerkung. In: Volkart, E. (Hrsg.): William I. Thomas. Person und Sozialverhalten. Berlin: Luchterhand, 63–85

Thomas, William Isaac/Znaniecki, Florian (1958 [1918–1922]): The Polish peasant in Europe and America, vol. 2, New York

Thrasher, F. M. (1928): The Gang: A Study of 1,313 Gangs in Chicago. Chicago

Trautman, E.C. (1961): Psychiatrische Untersuchungen an Überlebenden der nationalsozialistischen Vernichtungslager 15 Jahre nach der Befreiung. In: Der Nervenarzt 32, (12), 545–551

Tyrangiel, S. (1989): Emigrantenkinder – die zweite Generation. In: Herzka, H. S./Schuhmacher von, A./Tyrangiel, S. (Hrsg.): Die Kinder der Verfolgten. Göttingen: Vandenhoeck & Ruprecht, 23–80

Tuider, E. (2007): Diskursanalyse und Biographieforschung: Zum Wie und Warum von Subjektpositionierungen, Forum Qualitative Sozialforschung/Forum: Qualitative Social Research, vol. 8, no. 2, Art. 6, http: //nbn-resolving.de/urn: nbn: de: 0114-fqs070268 (8 October 2014).

Van Krieken, R. (1990): The organisation of the soul: Elias and Foucault on discipline and the self, Archives Européen de Sociologie, vol. 31 (2), 353–371

Völter, B. (2000): Intergenerational Dialog in Families of Jewish Communists in East Germany. A Process-Orientated Analysis. In: Breckner, R./Kalekin-Fishman, D./Miethe, I.: Biographies and the Division of Europe. Opladen: Leske & Budrich, 139–157

Völter, B. (2003): Judentum und Kommunismus. Deutsche Familiengeschichte in drei Generationen. Opladen: Leske + Budrich

Waldenfels, B. (1980): Der Spielraum des Verhaltens. Frankfurt a.M.: Suhrkamp

Waldenfels, B. (1983): Das umstrittene Ich. Ichloses und ichhaftes Bewußtsein bei A. Gurwitsch und A. Schütz. In: Grathoff, R./Waldenfels, B. (Hrsg.): Sozialität und Intersubjektivität. München: Fink, 15–30

Weber, N. (2009): Der Frieden ist da – wo bleibt die Entwicklung?: Erwartungen nach dem Friedensabkommen in Yumbe, master thesis, unpublished.

Wikipedia, International Sociological Association, http://de.wikipedia.org/wiki/International_Sociological_Association (28 September 2014)

Wikipedia, Louis Wirth, 28.09.2014, http://de.wikipedia.org/wiki/Louis_Wirth

Worm, A. (2017): Civil War and the Figurations of Illegalized Migration: Biographies of Syrian migrants coming to the European Union. In: Rosenthal, G./Bogner, A. (Ed.): Biographies in the Global South. Life Stories Embedded in Figurations and Discourses. Frankfurt a. M.: Campus, 160–184

Worm, A. (2019): Fluchtmigration aus Syrien. Eine biographietheoretische und figurationssoziologische Studie. Göttinger Beiträge zur soziologischen Biographieforschung (1), Göttingen: Universitätsverlag. 10.17875/gup2019-1228

Worm, A./Hinrichsen, H. (2016): The way outsiders speak: Counter discourses, self- and we-images of stigmatized gay men in the West Bank, in: G. Rosenthal (2016b): 67–86

Worm, A./Hinrichsen, H./Albaba, A. (2016): The homogenizing we-discourse and the social positioning of the refugee camps. In: Rosenthal, G. (2016b), 45–65

Wundrak, R. (2009): Emerging transnational migrant networks in Eastern Europe: The Chinese community in Bucharest post-1989. In: Rosenthal, G./Bogner, A. (Ed.): Ethnicity, Belonging and Biography. Hamburg/London: LIT, 203–225

Wundrak, R. (2010): Die chinesische Community in Bukarest: Eine rekonstruktive, diskursanalytische Fallstudie über Immigration und Transnationalismus. Wiesbaden: VS-Verlag

Wundrak, R. (2018): Biographie als Praxis-Diskurs-Formation. Eine praxeologische Perspektive auf lebensgeschichtliche Interviews. In: Alber, I./Griese, B./Schiebel, M. (Hrsg.): Biographieforschung als Praxis der Triangulation. Wiesbaden: VS-Verlag, 83–104

Wertheimer, M. (1922): Untersuchungen zur Lehre von der Gestalt. In: Psychologische Forschung, 1, Berlin: Springer, 47–58

References 279

Wertheimer, M. (1923): Untersuchungen zur Lehre von der Gestalt II. In: Psychologische Forschung, 2, 301–350

Wertheimer, M. (1928): Gestaltpsychologische Forschung. In: Saupe, E. (Hrsg.): Einführung in die neuere Psychologie. Osterwieck im Harz: Zwickfeldt Verlag, 47–54

Wertheimer, M. (1933): Zum Problem der Unterscheidung von Einzelinhalt und Teil. In: Zeitschrift für Psychologie, 129, 353–357

Wetzel, J. (1988): Auswanderung aus Deutschland. In: Wolfgang Benz (Hrsg.): Die Juden in Deutschland 1933–1945. München: Beck, 413–498

Widdershoven: G. (1993): The Story of Life. Hermeneutic Perspectives on the Relationship Between Narrative and Life History. In: The Narrative Studies of Lives, Vol. 1, Josselson, R./Lieblich, A. (Eds.), Newbury Park, Sage, 1–20

Wirth, L. (1928): The Ghetto. Chicago

Zeigarnik, B. (1927): Über das Behalten von erledigten und unerledigten Handlungen. In: Psychologische Forschung, 9, 1–85

Zorbaugh, H.W. (1929): The Gold Coast and the Slum: A Sociological Study of Chicago's Near North Side. Chicago